Software Best Practice 2

ESSI Practitioners' Reports

Springer

Berlin
Heidelberg
New York
Barcelona
Hong Kong
London
Milan
Paris
Tokyo

Michael Haug   Eric W. Olsen
Gonzalo Cuevas   Santiago Rementeria (Eds.)

Managing the Change: Software Configuration and Change Management

Software Best Practice 2

With 40 Figures and 14 Tables

 Springer

Editors:

Michael Haug
Eric W. Olsen
HIGHWARE GmbH
Winzererstraße 46
80797 München, Germany

Michael@Haug.com
ewo@home.com

Gonzalo Cuevas
Santiago Rementeria
SOCINTEC S.A.
Mayor 10
48930 Las Arenas, Spain

gcuevas@fi.upm.es
srementeria@socintec.es

ISBN 3-540-41785-0 Springer-Verlag Berlin Heidelberg New York

Library of Congress Cataloging-in-Publication Data
Software best practice.
    p. cm.
    Includes bibliographical references and index.
    1. Software quality approaches : testing, verification, and validation / M. Haug,
E. W. Olsen, L. Consolini, eds. -- 2. Managing the change : software configuration and
change management / M. Haug ... [et al.], eds. -- 3. Software management approaches :
project management, estimation, and life cycle support / M. Haug ... [et al.], eds. --
4. Software process improvement : metrics, measurement, and process modelling /
M. Haug, E. W. Olsen, L. Bergman, eds.
    ISBN 3540417842 (v. 1) -- ISBN 3540417850 (v. 2) -- ISBN 3540417869 (v. 3) --
ISBN 3540417877 (v. 4)
    1. Software engineering. I. Haug, Michael, 1951-

QA76.758 .S6445 2001
005.1--dc21   2001041181

Springer-Verlag Berlin Heidelberg New York,
a member of BertelsmannSpringer Science + Business Media GmbH

http://www.springer.de

© Springer-Verlag Berlin Heidelberg 2001
Printed in Germany

Cover design: design & production GmbH, Heidelberg
Typesetting: Camera-ready by editors
Printed on acid-free paper   SPIN: 10832679   45/3142 ud – 543210

Foreword

C. Amting

Directorate General Information Society, European Commission, Brussels

Under the 4th Framework of European Research, the European Systems and Software Initiative (ESSI) was part of the ESPRIT Programme. This initiative funded more than 470 projects in the area of software and system process improvements. The majority of these projects were process improvement experiments carrying out and taking up new development processes, methods and technology within the software development process of a company. In addition, nodes (centres of expertise), European networks (organisations managing local activities), training and dissemination actions complemented the process improvement experiments.

ESSI aimed at improving the software development capabilities of European enterprises. It focused on best practice and helped European companies to develop world class skills and associated technologies to build the increasingly complex and varied systems needed to compete in the marketplace.

The dissemination activities were designed to build a forum, at European level, to exchange information and knowledge gained within process improvement experiments. Their major objective was to spread the message and the results of experiments to a wider audience, through a variety of different channels.

The European Experience Exchange (EUREX) project has been one of these dissemination activities within the European Systems and Software Initiative. EUREX has collected the results of practitioner reports from numerous workshops in Europe and presents, in this series of books, the results of Best Practice achievements in European Companies over the last few years.

EUREX assessed, classified and categorised the outcome of process improvement experiments. The theme based books will present the results of the particular problem areas. These reports are designed to help other companies facing software process improvement problems.

The results of the various projects collected in these books should encourage many companies facing similar problems to start some improvements on their own. Within the Information Society Technology (IST) programme under the 5th Framework of European Research, new take up and best practices activities will be launched in various Key Actions to encourage the companies in improving their business areas.

Preface

M. Haug
HIGHWARE, Munich

In 1993, I was invited by Rainer Zimmermann and David Talbot to participate in the industrial consultation group for the then-new ESSI initiative. Coming from a Software Engineering background and having been responsible for industrial software production for more than 20 years, I was fascinated by the idea of tackling the ubiquitous software quality problem in a fresh new way, in helping not only a particular organisation to improve their software process, but to create the framework for an exchange of the experience gained among those organisations and beyond, to spread this experience throughout the European Software Industry.

While serving as an evaluator and reviewer to the Commission within the ESSI initiative, I had the opportunity to have a more or less superficial look at more than 100 Process Improvement Experiments (PIEs) at workshops, conferences and reviews. Consequently, the desire to collect and consolidate information about and experience from *all* of the more than 300 PIEs in a more organised way became immanent. In short, the idea for EUREX was born.

EUREX is an ESSI dissemination project. The budget limitations applicable to such projects did not allow us to conduct reviews or interviews of all of the more than 300 projects. Therefore, a distributed and staged approach was taken: a set of regional workshops became the platform to collect the information. The results of these 18 workshops held in Europe over a period of two years, together with contributions from representative PIEs and with expert articles rounding out the experience reports, is now in your hands: a series of books focussing on the central problem domains of Software Process Improvement.

Each of the books concentrates on a technical problem domain within the software engineering process, e.g. software testing, verification and quality management in Vol. 1. All of the books have a common structure:

Part I SPI, ESSI, EUREX describes the context of the European Software and Systems Initiative and the EUREX project. While Part I is similar in all books, the problem domains are differentiated for the reader. It consists of the chapters:

1 Software Process Improvement
2 The EUREX project
3 The EUREX taxonomy.

In Part II we present the collected findings and experiences of the process improvement experiments that dealt with issues related to the problem domain addressed by the book. Part II consists of the chapters:

4 Perspectives

5 Resources for Practitioners

6 Experience Reports

7 Lessons from the EUREX Workshops

8 Significant Results

Part III offers summary information for all the experiments that fall into the
problem domain. These summaries, collected from publicly available sources,
provide the reader with a wealth of information about each of the large number of
projects undertaken. Part III includes the chapters:

9 Table of PIEs

10 Summaries of Process Improvement Experiment Reports

A book editor managed each of the books, compiling the contributions and
writing the connecting chapters and paragraphs. Much of the material originates in
papers written by the PIE organisations for presentation at EUREX workshops or
for public documentation like the Final Reports. Whenever an author could be
identified, we attribute the contributions to him or her. If it was not possible to
identify a specific author, the source of the information is provided. If a chapter is
without explicit reference to an author or a source, the book editor wrote it.

Many people contributed to EUREX[PI], more than I can express my appreciation
to in such a short notice. Representative for all of them, my special thanks go to
the following teams: David Talbot and Rainer Zimmermann (CEC) who made the
ESSI initiative happen; Mechthild Rohen, Brian Holmes, Corinna Amting and
Knud Lonsted, our Project Officers within the CEC, who accompanied the project
patiently and gave valuable advice; Luisa Consolini and Elisabetta Papini, the
Italian EUREX team, Manu de Uriarte, Jon Gómez and Iñaki Gómez, the Spanish
EUREX team, Gilles Vallet and Olivier Bécart, the French EUREX team, Lars
Bergman and Terttu Orci, the Nordic EUREX team and Wilhelm Braunschober,
Bernhard Kölmel and Jörn Eisenbiegler, the German EUREX team; Eric W. Olsen
has patiently reviewed numerous versions of all contributions; Carola, Sebastian
and Julian have spent several hundred hours on shaping the various contributions
into a consistent presentation. Last but certainly not least, Ingeborg Mayer and
Hans Wössner continuously supported our efforts with their professional publishing know-how; Gabriele Fischer and Ulrike Drechsler patiently reviewed the
many versions of the typoscripts.

The biggest reward for all of us will be, if you – the reader – find something in
these pages useful to you and your organisation, or, even better, if we motivate
you to implement Software Process Improvement within your organisation.

[PI] Opinions in these books are expressed solely on the behalf of the authors. The European
Commission accepts no responsibility or liability whatsoever for the content.

Table of Contents

List of Contributors

Antonio de Amescua
Universidad Carlos III de Madrid
amescua@inf.uc3m.es

Gonzalo Cuevas
SOCINTEC
gcuevas@fi.upm.es

Tomás San Feliu
Universidad Politécnica de Madrid
tsanfe@fi.upm.es

Michael Haug
HIGHWARE
Michael_Haug@compuserve.com

Ulf Nyman
Contextor AB
ulfnyman@swipnet.se

Santiago Rementeria
SOCINTEC
srementeria@socintec.es

Jose A. Calvo-Manzano
Universidad Politécnica de Madrid
jacalvo@fi.upm.es

Jörn Eisenbiegler
Forschungszentrum Informatik FZI
eisen@fzi.de

Miguel García
Universidad Politécnica de Madrid
mgcordero@fi.upm.es

Bernhard Kölmel
Forschungszentrum Informatik FZI
koelmel@fzi.de

Eric W. Olsen
HIGHWARE
ewo@home.com

Walter Tichy
University of Karlsruhe
tichy@ira.uka.de

Part I

SPI, ESSI, EUREX

1 Software Process Improvement
A European View

1.1 Introduction[1]

Enterprises in all developed sectors of the economy – not just the IT sector – are increasingly dependent on quality software-based IT systems. Such systems support management, production, and service functions in diverse organisations. Furthermore, the products and services now offered by the non-IT sectors, e.g., the automotive industry or the consumer electronics industry, increasingly contain a component of sophisticated software. For example, televisions require in excess of half a Megabyte of software code to provide the wide variety of functions we have come to expect from a domestic appliance. Similarly, the planning and execution of a cutting pattern in the garment industry is accomplished under software control, as are many safety-critical functions in the control of, e.g., aeroplanes, elevators, trains, and electricity generating plants. Today, approximately 70% of all software developed in Europe is developed in the non-IT sectors of the economy. This makes software a technological topic of considerable significance. As the information age develops, software will become even more pervasive and transparent. Consequently, the ability to produce software efficiently, effectively, and with consistently high quality will become increasingly important for all industries across Europe if they are to maintain and enhance their competitiveness.

1.2 Objectives – Scope of the Initiative

The goal of the European Systems and Software Initiative (ESSI) was to promote improvements in the software development process in industry, through the take-up of well-founded and established – but insufficiently deployed – methods and technologies, so as to achieve greater efficiency, higher quality, and greater economy. In short, the adoption of Software Best Practice.

---

[1] All material presented in Chapter 1 was taken from publicly available information issued by the European Commission in the course of the European Systems and Software Initiative (ESSI). It was compiled by the main editor to provide an overview of this programme.

The aim of the initiative was to ensure that European software developers in both user and vendor organisations continue to have the world class skills, the associated technology, and the improved practices necessary to build the increasingly complex and varied systems demanded by the market place. The full impact of the initiative for Europe will be achieved through a multiplier effect, with the dissemination of results across national borders and across industrial sectors.

1.3   Strategy

To achieve the above objectives, actions have been supported to:

- Raise awareness of the importance of the software development process to the competitiveness of all European industry.
- Demonstrate what can be done to improve software development practices through experimentation.
- Create communities of interest in Europe working to a common goal of improving software development practices.
- Raise the skill levels of software development professionals in Europe.

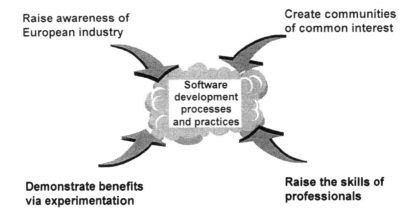

Fig. 1.1 A focused strategy for achieving Best Practice

1.4   Target Audience
(Who can participate, Who will benefit)

Any organisation in any sector of the economy, which regards generation of software to be part of its operation, may benefit from the adoption of Software Best Practice. Such a user organisation is often not necessarily classified as being in the software industry, but may well be an engineering or commercial organisation in which the generation of software has emerged as a significant component of its operation. Indeed as the majority of software is produced by organisations in the non-IT sector and by small and medium sized enterprises (SMEs), it is these two groups who are likely to benefit the most from this initiative.

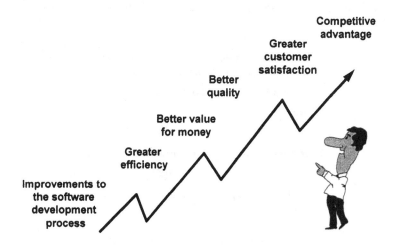

Fig. 1.2 The benefits of Software Best Practice

In addition to the user organisations participating directly in the initiative, software vendors and service providers also stand to benefit, as demand for their methodologies, tools and services is stimulated and valuable feedback is given on the strengths and weaknesses of their offerings.

1.5   Dimensions of Software Best Practice

Software Best Practice activities focus on the continuous and stepwise improvement of software development processes and practices. Software process improvement should not be seen as a goal in itself but must be clearly linked to the business goals of an organisation. Software process improvement starts with addressing the organisational issues. Experiences in the past have shown that before any investments are made in true technology upgrades (through products like tools and infrastructure computer support) some critical process issues need to be addressed and solved. They concern how software is actually developed: the methodology and methods, and, especially, the organisation of the process of development and maintenance of software.

Organisational issues are more important than methods and improving methods is, in turn, more important than introducing the techniques and tools to support them.

Finding the right organisational framework, the right process model, the right methodology, the right supporting methods and techniques and the right mix of skills for a development team is a difficult matter and a long-term goal of any process improvement activity. Nevertheless, it is a fundamental requirement for the establishment of a well-defined and controlled software development process.

1. **Business:** *market, customers, competition, ...*
   & People issues: *skills, culture, teamwork, ...*

   ### Business & People ⬇ driven

2. **Process**

   ⬇

3. **Technical approach:** *methods, procedures, ...*

   ⬇

4. **Technical support:** *tools, computers, ...*

Fig. 1.3 Anatomy of a successful SPI programme

Software development is a people process and due consideration should be given to all the players involved. Process improvement and implementation concerns people and needs to take into account all people related aspects (human factors). These are orthogonal to the technology and methodology driven approaches and are crucial to the success of adopting best practice.

Successful management of change includes staff motivation, skilling and promotion of the positive contributions that staff can make.

The people aspects cover all the different groups which have an input to the software development process including Management, and Software Engineers.

In order to ensure an appropriate environment for the successful adherence to a total quality approach it is imperative that Senior Management are fully aware of all the issues. Their commitment and involvement are crucial to the successful implementation of the improvement process and it might be necessary to raise their awareness regarding this issue.

It is important to identify clear milestones that will enable the software developer to measure progress along the road of software improvement. Certification through schemes such as ISO 9000, while not an end in itself, can play a valuable role in marking and recognising this progress.

1.6   European Dimension

The objectives of Software Best Practice can be accomplished by understanding and applying the state-of-the-art in software engineering, in a wide range of industries and other sectors of the economy, taking into account moving targets and changing cultures in this rapidly evolving area. The full impact for Europe will then be achieved by a multiplier effect, with the dissemination of results across national borders and across industrial sectors.

The definition of best practice at the European level has three main advantages. Firstly, there is the matter of scale. Operating on a European-wide basis offers the possibility to harness the full range of software development experience that has been built up across the full spectrum of industry sectors in addition to offering exposure to the widest selection of specialist method and tool vendors. In the second place, it maximises the possibility to reduce duplication of effort. Finally, it offers the best possibility to reduce the present fragmentation of approaches and, at the same time, to provide a more coherent and homogeneous market for well-founded methods and tools.

Moreover, as we move towards the Information Society, we need to develop and build the technologies necessary to create the Information Infrastructure (such as is envisaged in the Commission White Paper on "Growth, Competitiveness and Employment"); a dynamic infrastructure of underlying technologies and services to facilitate fast and efficient access to information, according to continually changing requirements. Within this context, software is seen as a major enabling technology and the way in which we develop software is becoming a key factor for industrial competitiveness and prosperity.

All of the above factors can be enhanced through the creation and use of standards, including de-facto standards for "best practice" and, indeed, standards are vital in the long term. However, the proposed actions should not, at this stage of evolving standards, be restricted to one particular standard. Furthermore, the actions cannot wait for a full and accepted set to be established before being able to implement improvement. Nevertheless, a close look at the ISO-SPICE initiative and active contribution to it is suggested.

1.7 Types of Projects

The European Commission issued three Calls for Proposals for Software Best Practice in the Fourth Framework Programme in the years 1993, 1995 and 1996. The first call was referred to as the "ESSI Pilot Phase". The aim was to test the perceived relevance of the programme to its intended audience and the effectiveness of the implementation mechanisms. Before the second call in 1995 a major review and redirection took place. Following the revision of the ESPRIT Work programme in 1997, a further call was issued of which the results are not been reviewed in this book. The four calls varied slightly in their focus. In the following, all types of projects supported by the ESSI initiative will be presented.

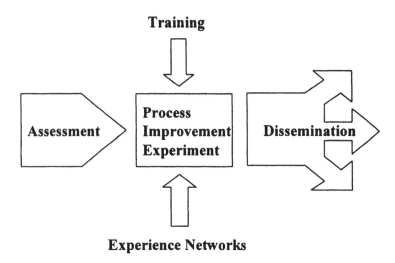

Fig. 1.4 Lines of complementary action

1.7.1 Stand Alone Assessments[2]

The main objective of the Stand Alone Assessments action was to raise the awareness of user organisations to the possibilities for improvement in their software development process, as well as give the momentum for initiating the improve-

---

[2] Stand Alone Assessments have been called only in the year 1995.

ment process. Assessments were targeted particularly at organisations at the lower levels of software development maturity.

It was expected that assessments will stimulate the pursuit of quality through continuous improvement of the software development process.

An underlying methodology was needed to carry out an assessment. This methodology had to recognise that software development is governed by the processes which an organisation uses to capitalise upon the potential talent of its employees (people) in order to produce competitive, top quality, software systems and services (products).

Most assessment methods are based on questionnaires and personnel interviews. An assessment resulted in the identification of an organisation's strengths and weaknesses, provides a comparison with the rest of the industry, and was accompanied by a series of recommendations on how to address the weak aspects of the software development process, from a technological and organisational point of view.

No single standard methodology was advocated; however, the adopted approach had to be a recognised assessment methodology, such as BOOTSTRAP, TickIT, etc.

The following types of assessment have been envisaged:

Self-assessments, which were conducted if the organisation had the required resource capacity to allow it to absorb the load of conducting the assessment. In this case, it was expected that an internal assessment team was set up, trained in the selected methodology, and that it carried out the assessment according to an agreed schedule. This type of assessment may have conducted with the support of the methodology provider or under the guidance of external assessors.

Assessments carried out by external assessors. The organisation was expected to select an external assessor who conducted the assessment. Again, an internal assessment team was expected to be set up to collaborate with the assessors.

Both types of assessment had to cater for measuring the organisation's existing situation, positioning the organisation relatively to the rest of the industry in terms of software development process and allowing the organisation to plan and prioritise for future improvements.

1.7.2 Process Improvement Experiments (PIEs)[3]

PIEs are aimed at demonstrating software process improvement. These followed a generic model and demonstrated the effectiveness of software process improve-

---

[3] Process Improvement Experiments have been called in the years 1995, 1996 and 1997. As the project type "Application Experiment" can be considered the predecessor of PIEs, it is legitimate to say that PIEs have been subject to all ESSI calls and have formed not only the bulk of projects but also the "heart" of the initiative.

ment experiments on an underlying baseline project that is tackling a real development need for the proposing organisation.

Process Improvement Experiments (PIEs) formed the bulk of the Software Best Practice initiative. Their aim was to demonstrate the benefits of software process improvement through user experimentation. The results had to be disseminated both internally within the user organisations to improve software production and externally to the wider community to stimulate adoption of process improvement at a European level.

The emphasis was on continuous improvement through small, stepped actions. During a PIE, a user organisation undertook a controlled, limited experiment in process improvement, based on an underlying baseline project. The baseline project was a typical software project undertaken by the user organisation as part of its normal business and the results of the experiment should therefore be replicable.

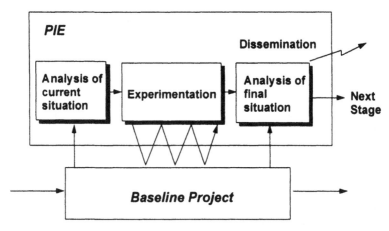

Fig. 1.5 A PIE in relation to an underlying baseline project

The introduction of a Configuration Management System, improvements to the design documentation system, the use of a Computer Aided Design (CAD) tool, the application of Object Oriented Programming techniques, the development of a library for software re-use and the introduction of metrics, are some examples of possible improvement steps for Software Best Practice and the focus of a PIE.

It was expected that a PIE was carried out as part of a larger movement within the user organisation towards process improvement. Participants were expected to have considered their strengths and weaknesses, and to have at least an idea of the general actions required. They also needed to demonstrate that they were aware of quality issues and were considering the people aspects of their actions.

Dissemination of the results of the experiment, from a software engineering and business point of view, to the wider community, was an essential aspect of a PIE and was undertaken with the support of the Software Best Practice Dissemination Actions.

1.7.3 Application Experiments[4]

These experiments were targeted at building up a comprehensive set of examples to show that the adoption of improved software development practices were both possible and had clear industrial benefits. The experiments involved the introduction of state-of-the-art software engineering (e.g. management practices, methodologies, tools) into real production environments that address specific applications, and then evaluating the resulting impact.

Within the context of this book (and the project EUREX) these Application Experiments have been treated like PIEs, i.e. their specific results have been included.

1.7.4 Dissemination Actions[5, 6]

Dissemination Actions aimed at raising awareness and promoting the adoption of software best practice by Industry at large. Actions provided software producing organisations with information concerning the practical introduction of software best practice, how it can contribute to meeting business needs and how those organisations can benefit: particularly, by showing the real life business benefits – and costs – in a way which could be of interest to companies intending to address related problems.

The Dissemination Actions widely disseminated Software Best Practice information by making it available and packaging it in a form suitable for "focused target audiences":

- The experience gained by the participants in PIEs (Process Improvement Experiments): experiences and lessons learned which could be of interest to industry at large.
- Software Best Practice material and experiences available world-wide. For example, valuable and generally useful software engineering material which is representative of a class of processes, methodologies, assessment methods, tools, etc. Relevant world-wide experiences.

---

4 Application Experiments have only been called in 1993. See also the footnote to Process Improvement Experiments.
5 Dissemination Actions have been called in 1993, 1995 and 1996.
6 The ESSI project EUREX which resulted in this book was such a Dissemination Action.

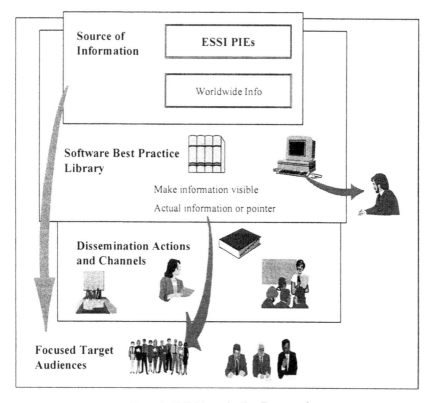

Fig. 1.6 ESSI Dissemination Framework

1.7.5 Experience/User Networks[7]

There was opportunity for networks of users, with a common interest, to pursue a specific problem affecting the development or use of software. Experience/User Networks mobilised groups of users at a European level and provided them with the critical mass necessary to influence their suppliers and the future of the software industry through the formulation of clear requirements. A network had to be trans-national with users from more than one Member or Associated State.

By participating in an Experience/User Network, a user organisation helped to ensure that a particular problem – with which it is closely involved – is addressed and that it is able to influence the choice of proposed solution.

Software suppliers (methodologies, tools, services, etc.) and the software industry as a whole took benefit from Experience/User Networks by receiving valuable

---

[7] Experience/User Networks have only been called in 1995.

feedback on the strengths and weaknesses of their current offerings, together with information on what is additionally required in the marketplace.

1.7.6 Training Actions[8]

Training actions have been broad in scope and covered training, skilling and education for all groups of people involved – directly or indirectly – in the development of software. In particular, training actions aimed at:

- increasing the awareness of senior managers as to the benefits of software process improvement and software quality
- providing software development professionals with the necessary skills to develop software using best practice

Emphasis had been placed on actions which served as a catalyst for further training and education through, for example, the training of trainers. In addition, the application of current material – where available and appropriate – in a new or wider context was preferred to the recreation of existing material.

1.7.7 ESSI PIE Nodes (ESPINODEs)[9]

The primary objective of an ESPINODE was to provide support and assistance, on a regional basis, to a set of PIEs in order to stimulate, support, and co-ordinate activities. ESPINODEs acted closely with local industry and were particularly aimed at helping to facilitate exchange of practical information and experience between PIEs, to provide project assistance, technical and administrative support, and to exploit synergies.

On a regional level, an ESPINODE provided a useful interface between the PIEs themselves, and between the PIEs and local industry. This included improving and facilitating access to information on ESSI/PIE results, and raising interest and awareness of local companies (notably SMEs) to the technical and business benefits resulting from software process improvement conducted in the PIEs.

At the European level, an ESPINODE exchanged information and experience with other ESPINODEs, in order to benefit from the transfer of technology, skills and know-how; from economies of scale and from synergies in general – thus creating a European network of PIE communities.

---

[8] Training Actions have been called in 1993 and 1996. Whereas the projects resulting from the call in 1996 were organised as separate projects building the ESSI Training Cluster ESSItrain, the result of the call in 1993 was one major project ESPITI which is described in chapter 2.3.2.

[9] ESSI PIE Nodes have only been called in 1997.

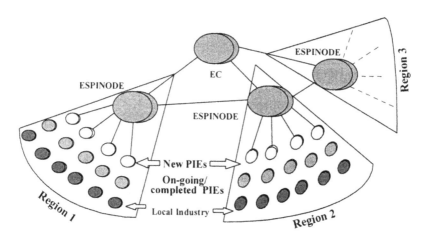

Fig. 1.7 ESPINODE collaboration model

1.7.8   Software Best Practice Networks (ESBNETs)[10]

The objective of an ESBNET was to implement small scale software best practice related activities on a regional basis, but within the context of a European network. A network in this context was simply a group of organisations, based in different countries, operating together to implement an ESBNET project, according to an established plan of action, using appropriate methods, technologies and other appropriate support. By operating on a regional level, it was expected that the specific needs of a targeted audience will be better addressed. The regional level was complemented by actions at European level, to exploit synergies and bring cross-fertilisation between participants and their target audiences. A network had a well defined focus, rather than being just a framework for conducting a set of unrelated, regional software best practice activities.

The two ESSI tasks newly introduced in the Call for Proposals in 1997 – ESPI-NODEs and ESBNETs – aimed to continue and build upon the achievements of the initiative so far, but on a more regional basis. ESPINODEs aim with first priority to provide additional support to PIEs, whilst ESBNETs aim to integrate small-scale software best practice actions of different type implemented on a regional basis – with an emphasis on the non-PIE community.

By operating on a regional level, it was expected that ESPINODEs and ESB-NETs will be able to tailor their actions to the local culture, delivering the message and operating in the most appropriate way for the region. Further, it was expected that such regional actions will be able to penetrate much more into the very corners of Europe, reaching a target audience which is much broader and

---

10

Software Best Practice Networks have only been called in 1997.

probably less experienced in dealing with European initiatives. Such an approach should be of particular interest to SMEs and other organisations not in the traditional IT sector, for which it is perhaps difficult to deal directly with an organisation based in a different country, due to – for example – a lack of resources, cultural and language reasons.

Regional Support within European Networks

• **Disseminate the results beyond those directly involved in ESSI**

• **Ensure that projects act as a 'catalyst' for further action**

• **Increase the participation in ESSI**

• **Reach organisations never involved before**

Fig. 1.8 ESPINODEs and ESBNETs

2 The EUREX Project

M. Haug, E.W. Olsen
HIGHWARE, Munich

The European Experience Exchange project (EUREX) was conceived, proposed, and carried out as an ESSI Dissemination Action (see Chapter 1). The overall objective of EUREX was to evaluate the experiences of several hundred ESSI Process Improvement Experiments (PIEs) and to make this experience accessible to a broad European audience in a convenient form. In particular, the goal was to collect and make available to interested practitioners information about Software Best Practice and its introduction in specific problem domains.

In the following sections, we briefly review the history of the EUREX project.

2.1 Target Audience and Motivation

Over 70% of the organisations that participated in events organised during the course of the ESPITI project (see section 1.3.2 below) were Small or Medium Enterprises (SMEs), and many of which had substantially fewer than 250 employees. This response rate demonstrated a significant interest on the part of SMEs in finding out more about Software Process Improvement (SPI). Therefore, the primary target audience for EUREX was those European SMEs, and small teams in the non-IT organisations, engaged in the activity of developing software. Within these organisations, the focus was on management and technical personnel in a position to make decisions to undertake process improvement activities.

The ESPITI User Survey presents a clear picture of the needs and requirements of SMEs concerning software process improvement. For example, 25% of those who responded requested participation in working groups for experience exchange. However, SMEs are faced with many difficulties when it comes to trying to implement improvement programmes.

For example, SMEs are generally less aware than larger companies of the benefits of business-driven software process improvement. It is perceived as being an expensive task and the standard examples that are quoted in an attempt to convince them otherwise are invariably drawn from larger U.S. organisations and therefore bear little relevance for European SMEs. ESSIgram No 11 also reported that "peer review of experiment work in progress and results would be helpful."

Thus, SMEs need to see success among their peers, using moderate resources, before they are prepared to change their views and consider embarking upon SPI actions.

For those SMEs that are aware of the benefits of SPI, there are frequently other inhibitors that prevent anything useful being accomplished. Many SMEs realise that they should implement software process improvement actions but do not know how to do this. They do not have the necessary skills and knowledge to do it themselves and in many cases they do not have the financial resources to engage external experts to help them. Consequently, SPI actions get deferred or cancelled because other business priorities assume greater importance. Even those SMEs that do successfully initiate SPI programmes can find that these activities are not seen through to their natural completion stage because of operational or financial constraints.

Many of the concerns about the relevance of SPI for SMEs were addressed by EUREX in a series of workshops in which speakers from similarly characterised companies spoke about their experiences with SPI. The workshops were in integral part of the EUREX process and provided much of the data presented in this volume.

The Commission funded EUREX in large measure because the evaluation of approximately 300 PIEs was too costly for an independent endeavour. Even if some resource-rich organisation had undertaken this task, it is likely that the results would not have been disseminated, but would rather have been used to further competitive advantage. Commission support has insured that the results are widely and publicly distributed.

Many ESSI dissemination actions have been organised as conferences or workshops. PIE Users register in order to discharge their obligations to the Commission; however, the selection and qualification of contributions is often less than rigorous. In addition, many public conferences have added PIE presentation tracks with little organisation of their content. Small audiences are a consequence of the competition of that track with others in the conference. The common thread in these experiences is that organisation of the actions had been lacking or passive.

EUREX turned this model on its end. PIE Users were approached proactively to involve them in the process. In addition, the information exchange process was actively managed. The EUREX workshops were organised around several distinct problem domains and workshop attendees were supported with expert assistance to evaluate their situations and provide commentary on solutions from a broadly experienced perspective. (See chapter 3 for a detailed discussion of the domain selection process.) Participants were invited through press publications, the local chambers of commerce, the Regional Organisations of EUREX and through co-operation with other dissemination actions.

This approach provided a richer experience for attendees. Since the workshops were domain-oriented, the participants heard different approaches to the same issues and were presented with alternative experiences and solutions. This was a more informative experience than simply hearing a talk about experiences in a vacuum, with no background and no possibility for comparison or evaluation. The opportunity to exchange views with one's peers and to hear advice from respected experts provides substantial benefit not found using a passive approach to dissemination.

Our approach also offered a better experience for European Industry as a whole. Since we have categorised and evaluated approximately 300 different improvement experiments, we present a broad practical view of the selected problem domains. This is distinctly different from purely academic approaches that offer little practical experience. EUREX is an opportunity to derive additional benefit from the PIEs, beyond that of obligatory presentations. We hope to lend an authoritative voice to the overall discussion of Software Process Improvement.

2.2   Objectives and Approach

As mentioned above, the objective of EUREX was to assess, classify, categorise, and exploit the experience of the ESSI PIE Prime Users and Associated Partners (collectively referred to here simply as Users or PIE Users) and then to make this experience accessible. In particular, we sought to provide a broad European audience with data about Software Best Practice and its introduction in selected problem domains.

The approach is broken down into two phases. The first phase required the classification and collection of data and the second phase involves the analysis, distribution and dissemination of the resulting information. The phases were implemented in three steps:

1. Classify and categorise the base of PIE Users and the Problem Domains addressed by them. All of the available material from over 300 PIEs was assessed, the categorisation was designed such that over 90% of the material under consideration fell into one of the selected Problem Domains (see chapter 3).
2. Plan and conduct a series of Regional Workshops in order to collect information from PIE projects as well as for disseminating the PIE's experiences at a regional level. 18 workshops in 8 European countries were undertaken. (Refer to chapter 7 for the best of the workshop material.)
3. Publish the first four of the Software Best Practice Reports and Executive Reports to detail the experiences. In addition, a Web-site provides access to the background material used by EUREX.

Steps 1 and 2 fall within phase one and steps 2 and 3 are within phase two. Notice that, because multiple benefits are derived from the same activity, the two phases overlapped somewhat. This approach is intended to convey to the largest possible audience the experiences of the Commission's Process Improvement Experiment program.

The EUREX Software Best Practice Reports (of which this volume is one) and Executive Reports are directed at two distinct audiences. The first is the technically oriented IT manager or developer interested in the full reports and technology background. The second is senior management, for whom the Executive Reports a summary of benefits and risks of real cases are appropriate.

2.3 Partners

The EUREX project was carried out by the following partners:

- HIGHWARE GmbH, Germany (Coordinator)
- Editions HIGHWARE sarl, France
- GEMINI Soc. Cons. A, Italy
- SOCINTEC, Spain
- SISU, Sweden
- MARI Northern Ireland Ltd., United Kingdom.

The fact that MARI has left the consortium (as they did with other projects as well) caused some disruption and delay for the project. The partners were able to compensate largely, e.g. the number of workshops held and the countries covered. Even the book about the domain assigned to MARI, Object Orientation, was prepared with the help of FZI Forschungszentrum Informatik, Karlsruhe, Germany.

2.4 Related Dissemination and Training Actions

Other ESSI Dissemination Actions that have also generated significant results that may be of interest to the reader. These actions include SISSI and ESPITI, both described briefly below.

2.4.1 Software Improvement Case Studies Initiative (SISSI)

European companies must face the challenge of translating software engineering into a competitive advantage in the market place, by taking full advantage of the existing experiences and results. The process of overcoming existing barriers is not an easy one, particularly if individual companies must face them on their own. It is a major issue to put at the disposal of companies a set of written case studies providing a practical view of software process improvement (SPI) impact and best practices. Successful experiences can demonstrate that existing barriers can be dismantled. This learning process, which takes time and requires continuity in the long term, is being fostered by the SISSI project.

2.4.1.1 Overview

The target audience for the SISSI case studies is senior executives, i.e. decision-makers, in software producing organisations through Europe. This includes both software vendors and companies developing software for in-house use. The material has been selected in such a way that it is relevant for both small and large organisations.

SISSI produced a set of 33 case studies, of about 4 pages each, and distributed 50 case studies overall, together with cases from previous projects. Cases are not exclusively technical; rather, they have a clear business orientation and are focused on action. Cases are a selected compendium of finished Process Improvement Experiments (PIEs) funded by the ESSI program of the EC. They are classified according to parameters and keywords so tailored and selective extractions can be made by potential users or readers. The main selection criteria are the business sector, the software process affected by the improvement project and its business goals.

The dissemination mechanisms of SISSI were the following: a selective telephone-led campaign addressed to 500 appropriate organisations together with follow up actions; an extensive mailing campaign targeting 5000 additional organisations which have selected the relevant cases from an introductory document; joint action with the European Network of SPI Nodes – ESPINODEs – to distribute the SISSI material and provide continuity to the SISSI project; WWW pages with the full contents of the case studies; synergic actions with other Dissemination Actions of the ESSI initiative, like EUREX, SPIRE, RAPID; co-operation with other agents like European publications, SPI institutions, or graduate studies acting as secondary distribution channels.

SISSI developed an SPI Marketing Plan to systematically identify and access this target market in any European country and distributed its contents through the European Network of SPI Nodes both for a secondary distribution of SISSI Case Studies, and for a suitable rendering of the ESPINODEs services. The plan was implemented for the dissemination of the SISSI Case Studies in several European countries, proving its validity.

2.4.1.2 Objectives

The main goals of the approach taken in the SISSI project have been as follows:

- The material produced has been formed by a wide variety of practical real cases selected by the consultants of the consortium, and documented in a friendly and didactic way to capture interest between companies.
- The cases have clearly emphasised the key aspects of the improvement projects in terms of competitive advantage and tangible benefits (cost, time to market, quality).

- Most of the cases have been successful cases, but also not successful ones have been sought in order to analyse causes of failure, i.e. inadequate analysis of the plan before starting the project.
- The project has not been specially focused on particular techniques or application areas, but it has been a selected compendium of the current and finished Process Improvement Experiments – PIEs –. They have been classified according to different parameters and keywords so tailored and selective extractions can be made by potential users or readers. The main selection criteria have been: business sector (finance, electronics, manufacturing, software houses, engineering, etc.), the software process, the business goals and some technological aspects of the experiment.
- The Dissemination action should open new markets promoting the SPI benefits in companies not already contacted by traditional ESSI actions.
- The SISSI Marketing Plan should provide the methodology and the information not only to disseminate the SISSI material, but has to be generic enough to direct the marketing of other ESSI services and SPI activities in general.

The SISSI material should be used in the future by organisations and other dissemination actions and best practices networks as a reference material to guide lines of software improvement and practical approaches to face them. In particular, SISSI has to provide continuity of the action beyond the project itself supporting the marketing of SPI in any other ESSI action.

2.4.2   ESPITI

The European Software Process Improvement Training Initiative (ESPITI) was officially launched on 22 November 1994 in Belfast, Northern Ireland. The final event was held in Berlin, Germany in Spring 1996. The Initiative aimed to maximise the benefits gained from European activities in the improvement and subsequent ISO 9000 certification of the software development process through training. A sum of 8.5 million ECU was allocated to the Initiative for a period of 18 months, to support actions intended to:

- Identify the true needs of European industry for training in software process improvement (SPI).
- Increase the level of awareness of the benefits of software process improvement and ISO 9001.
- Provide training for trainers, managers and software engineers.
- Support the development of networks between organisations at regional and European levels to share knowledge and experience and form links of mutual benefit.
- Liase with similar initiatives world-wide and transfer their experiences to Europe.

2.4.2.1 Organisational Structure

The Initiative was implemented through a network of 14 Regional Organisations addressing the local needs of 17 EU and EFTA countries. Regional Organisations (ROs) have been existing commercial organisations that were contracted to carry out a specific range of activities in support of the ESPITI goals. The ROs were divided into 2 sets, each set supported by a Partner. The two Partner organisations, Forschungszentrum Karlsruhe GmbH from Germany and MARI (Northern Ireland) Ltd from the United Kingdom, have been co-ordinating and supporting co-operation at European level through the provision of services to the ROs. These services included provision of:

- Preparation of a user survey in all countries involved to determine the local SPI needs.
- An electronic communication network for exchanging SPI information of mutual interest.
- Guidelines on event organisation, e.g. seminars, training courses and working groups.
- Awareness material for project launches, software process improvement and ISO 9001.
- Assistance in evaluating performance at project and event levels.
- Guidance in programme planning and control.
- Assistance in PR activities.
- Assistance in experience exchange and co-operation between the ROs.

The European Software Institute ESI was also involved in ESPITI, providing the Partners with valuable assistance, including the merging of the European user survey results, liaison with other initiatives and contributions to RO meetings.

2.4.2.2 The ESPITI Approach

The ESPITI project adopted a multi-pronged strategy for improving the competitiveness of the European software industry.

- Survey of European needs was carried out to ascertain the needs and the best approach to adopt to satisfy these needs within each region.
- Seminars for raising awareness of the benefits and approaches to quality management and process improvement.
- Training courses for improving know-how in initiating, assessing, planning and implementing quality management and process improvement programmes.
- Workshops, which aim to teach participants about a subject and direct them in implementing the subject in their Organisations.
- Working groups for enabling dissemination of experience in a subject, and to allow participants to discuss and learn about those experiences.
- Case studies for demonstrating the successes and difficulties in software process improvement.

- Liaisons with similar, related initiatives world-wide to understand their approaches and successes and to transfer the lessons learned there to Europe.
- Public relations activities to promote the aims and objectives of ESPITI and to ensure participation in ESPITI events.
- Evaluation of the ESPITI project to assess the effectiveness of the initiative, and to determine how the initiative could progress from there.

2.4.2.3   The Partners and Regional Organisations

The Partners

- MARI (Northern Ireland) Ltd, United Kingdom
- Forschungszentrum Karlsruhe GmbH, Germany

The Regional Organisations

- Austrian Research Centre, Austria
- Flemish Quality Management Centre, Belgium
- Delta Software Engineering, Denmark
- CCC Software Professionals Oy, Finland
- AFNOR, France
- Forschungszentrum Karlsruhe GmbH, Germany
- INTRASOFT SA, Greece
- University of Iceland, Iceland
- Centre for Software Engineering, Ireland
- ETNOTEAM, Italy
- Centre de Recherche Public Henri Tudor, Luxembourg
- SERC, The Netherlands
- Norsk Regnesentral, Norway
- Instituto Portugues da Qualidade, Portugal
- Sip Consultoría y formación, Spain
- SISU, Sweden
- MARI (Northern Ireland) Ltd., United Kingdom

3 The EUREX Taxonomy

M. Haug, E.W. Olsen
HIGHWARE, Munich

One of the most significant tasks performed during the EUREX project was the creation of the taxonomy needed to drive the Regional Workshops and, ultimately, the content of these Software Best Practice Reports. In this chapter, we examine in detail the process that led to the EUREX taxonomy and discuss how the taxonomy led to the selection of PIEs for the specific subject domain.

3.1 Analysis and Assessment of PIEs

Over 300 Process Improvement Experiments (PIEs) funded by the Commission in the calls of 1993, 1995 and 1996 were analysed using an iterative approach as described below. The technical domain of each of the PIEs was assessed by EUREX and each PIE was attributed to certain technological areas.

Early discussions proved what others (including the Commission) had already experienced in the attempt to classify PIEs: there is no canonical, "right" classification. The type, scope and detail of a classification depends almost entirely on the intended use for the classification. The EUREX taxonomy was required to serve the EUREX project. In particular, it was used to drive the selection of suitable subject areas for the books and, consequently, the selection of regional workshop topics to insure that good coverage would be achieved both by the number of PIEs and by the partners in their respective regions.

3.2 Classification into Problem Domains

A set of more than 150 attributes was refined in several iterations to arrive at a coarse grain classification into technological problem domains. These domains were defined such that the vast majority of PIEs fall into at least one of these domains. There were seven steps used in the process of discovering the domains, as described in the following paragraphs.

In part because of the distributed nature of the work and in part because of the necessity for several iterations, the classification required 6 calendar months to complete.

3.2.1   First Regional Classification

Each partner examined the PIEs conducted within its region and assigned attributes from the list given above that described the work done within the PIE (more than one attribute per PIE was allowed). The regions were assigned as shown in Table 3.1.

Table 3.1 Regional responsibilities of consortium partners

Partner	Region
SISU	Denmark, Finland, Norway, Sweden
MARI	United Kingdom, Ireland
GEMINI	Italy
SOCINTEC	Spain, Portugal, Greece
HIGHWARE Germany	Germany, Austria, The Netherlands, Israel and all other regions not explicitly assigned
HIGHWARE France	Benelux, France

3.2.2   Result of First Regional Classification

HIGHWARE Germany (the consortium co-ordinator) began with a classification of the German PIEs according to the above procedure. This first attempt was distributed among the partners as a working example.

Using the example, each partner constructed a spreadsheet with a first local classification and returned this to HIGHWARE Germany.

3.2.3   Consolidation and Iteration

HIGHWARE Germany prepared a consolidated spreadsheet using the partners' input, and developed from that a first classification and clustering proposal. This was sent to the other partners for review and cross-checking.

3.2.4   Update of Regional Classification

All partners reviewed their classification, in particular the assignment of attributes to PIEs. Corrections were made as necessary.

3.2.5   Mapping of Attributes.

HIGHWARE Germany mapped all key words used by the partners into a new set of attributes, normalising the names of attributes. No attribute was deleted, but the overall number of different attributes decreased from 164 to 127. These attributes were further mapped into classes and subclasses that differentiate members of classes. This second mapping lead to a set of 24 classes each containing 0 to 13 subclasses. The resulting classes are shown in table 3.2.

Table 3.2 Attributes of the Classification

Assessment	Case Tools	Change Management
Configuration Management	Decision Support	Documentation
Estimation	Formal Methods	Life Cycle: Analysis & Design
Life Cycle: Dynamic System Modelling	Life Cycle: Installation & Maintenance	Life Cycle: Requirements & Specification
Life Cycle: Product Management.	Metrics	Modelling & Simulation
Object Orientation	Process Model: Definition	Process Model: Distributed
Process Model: Iterative	Process Model: Support	Project Management
Prototyping	Quality Management	Reengineering
Reuse & Components	Reverse Engineering	Target Environment
Testing, Verification & Validation	User Interface	

3.2.6   Review of Classification and Mapping into Subject Domains

The classification achieved by the above mentioned process was reviewed by the partners and accepted with minor adjustments. It is important to note that up to this point, the classification was independent of the structure of the planned publications. It simply described the technical work done by PIEs in the consolidated view of the project partners.

In the next step this view was discussed and grouped into subject domains suitable for publications planned by the consortium.

3.2.7   Subject Domains Chosen

Out of the original 24 classes, 7 were discarded from the further consideration, either because the number of PIEs in the class was not significant or because the domain was already addressed by other ESSI Dissemination Actions (e.g. formal methods, reengineering, and so on). The 17 final classes were grouped into the subject domains shown in table 3.3 such that each of the resulting 5 domains forms a suitable working title for one of the EUREX books.

Table 3.3 Final Allocation of Domains

Partner	Domain
SISU	Metrics, Measurement and Process Modelling
MARI	Object Orientation, Reuse and Components
GEMINI	Testing, Verification, Validation, Quality Management
SOCINTEC	Configuration & Change Management, Requirements Engineering
HIGHWARE France	Project Management, Estimation, Life Cycle Support

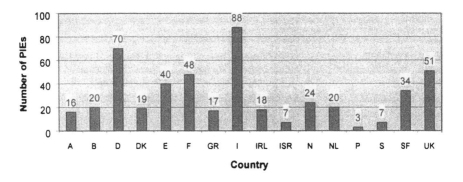

Fig. 3.1 All PIEs by Country

The breakdown of all (unclassified) PIEs on a per-country basis is shown in Fig. 3.1. The distribution of PIEs is somewhat related to population, but there are notable exceptions (e.g. Italy and France).

The classification breakdown of PIEs Europe-wide is worth examining. Referring to Fig. 3.2, notice first that the classification has resulted in a relatively even distribution of projects, only the Project Management classification dips noticeably below the average. The number of PIEs without any classification was held below 10% of the total. (Further discussion of the "No Classification" category appears below.)

3.2.8 Unclassified PIEs

There were 33 PIEs that were not classified by EUREX. There were generally two reasons for lack of classification.

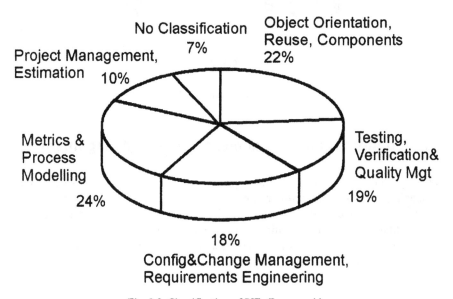

Fig. 3.2 Classification of PIEs Europe-wide

1. Neither the EUREX reviewer alone nor the consortium as a whole was able to reach a conclusion for classification based on the PIE description as published.
2. The PIE addressed a very specific subject that did not correspond to a class defined by EUREX and/or the PIE was dealt with by other known ESSI projects, e.g. formal methods. The consortium tried to avoid too much overlap with other projects.

When one of these rules was applied, the corresponding PIE was given no classification and was not considered further by the EUREX analysis. Fig. 3.3 shows the breakdown of unclassified PIEs by country.

As can be seen in Fig. 3.3, there were 33 PIEs that remained unclassified once the EUREX analysis was complete.

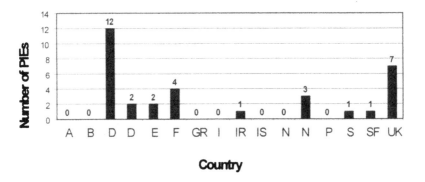

Fig.3.3 Unclassified PIEs.

3.3   Configuration Management, Change Management

Part II presents the results of EUREX project with respect to the classification: "Managing the Change, Configuration Management, Change Management". The attributes associated with this classification were Configuration Management, Change Management and Requirements Management. Within this classification there were a total of 88 PIEs that were assigned one or more of these attributes. The distribution of these PIEs throughout Europe is shown in figure 3.4.

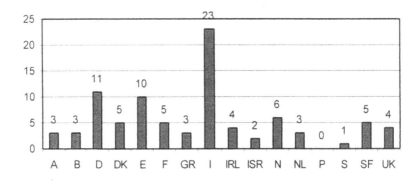

Fig. 3.4 Distribution of PIEs over European Countries

Part II

Managing the Change:
Configuration Management,
Change Management

4 Perspectives

G. Cuevas
SOCINTEC, Bilbao

This chapter presents an overview of Configuration Management, as well as some ideas about process management and planning for configuration management. In addition, four presentations from experts are included, each of them providing a different perspective on this topic. The intent is to provide a functional, clear-cut vision of this aspect of software best practice.

4.1 Domain Overview

Machineware-oriented Configuration Management (CM) has been defined as the means always to know which components and versions of a product are the appropriate ones. It deals with the identification, control and registration of components and other relevant elements in a system, including hardware, software and related documents and support components.

A software configuration can be defined as a selected set of components that are required to specify, design, build and maintain a software product. It may include various software components, such as source files or executables files, as well as related components, such as specification documents, instructions or test sets. Moreover, a configuration can comprise both software lifecycle work products and those elements that are used to create the final deliverable, such as compilers, linkers and other software support tools used in the software process.

Software Configuration Management (SCM) means defining and controlling the products in a software configuration, managing changes to them and monitoring their integrity and traceability during development and maintenance activities. The notion of configuration management extends to the maintenance of the software product; it is not limited to its design and development. This might include, for example, the management of bugs reported and corrected after delivery, as well as change requests. SCM can be seen from a product (configuration) and a process (activities) perspective, and tools often support both.

4.1.1   Risks and Benefits

From a development standpoint, the lack of a sound approach to SCM may result in several obvious problems. These include the loss of files, missing information about versions and releases, different developers updating the same modules, corrected errors reappearing in the code, and the inability to recreate individual executable programs or libraries. The causes of such problems are inherent to:

- The nature of software products, which have many different components in multiple versions and varied physical platforms with complex interrelations, all of which are easy to modify.
- The characteristics of software projects, with diverging versions implemented at different sites that do not necessarily supersede previous (or subsequent) versions.
- Development teams, whose members – possibly in more than one location – manipulate a number of components, often concurrently with other team members and having to recover from staff turnover.

All this in turn results in time wasted on bug fixes and product changes. Ultimately, this translates into a lack of timeliness, poor product quality, and increased development costs.

From a process perspective, especially in environments where software may be developed at different sites or externally supplied, the lack of SCM often results in problems that include one or more of the following:

- Expensive integration of third-party software.
- Expensive integration of commercial off-the-shelf (COTS) software components.
- Inconsistent validation of suppliers' capabilities.
- Expensive integration of departmental and corporate development.
- Expensive maintenance and, on the whole, lack of process control.

On the contrary, the presence of a solid approach to SCM usually produces development benefits that include:

- Easier handling of software complexity, as all components are unambiguously identified.
- Increased level of security against potential losses, unauthorised versions and personnel turnover.
- Enhanced visibility: past (project history), present (progress tracking) and future (planned versions).
- Higher degree of software reuse, both for future versions and in other projects, as components are better classified and more easily retrievable.
- Productivity gains, as developers have more time to develop software as opposed to looking for missing items and co-ordinating their work.

- Reduced time-to-market, as stable and documented software is available sooner.
- Quality gains, as things are done right the first time.

And again, from a process point of view, good SCM means:

- Easier integration of departmental and corporate development, as software components, interfaces, and changes are managed consistently.
- Easier integration of COTS software, as executables are clearly identified and dependencies are well defined.
- Easier integration of third-party software, as files are clearly identified and build procedures well defined.
- Easier validation of suppliers' capabilities, as both customers' requirements and suppliers' deliverables are clearly defined and managed.
- Freer choice between internal and externally contracted maintenance as configuration and change control procedures can be clearly specified.
- Improved process maturity, as the process benefits from a higher level of control over the software configuration.

Proper configuration management ensures that the right working material is used and the right product build is done, i.e. that the expected versions of individual components are in the product to be tested or delivered.

4.1.2 Process Input, Output and Activities

According to the ISO 8402:1994 definition, a process is a set of interrelated resources and activities, which transforms inputs into outputs. SCM is one of the Key Process Areas covered in level 2 of the Capability Maturity Model, and a support process explicitly considered in the coming ISO 15504 (SPICE) standard for software process assessment. As such, there is a set of inputs to it:

- Approved user requirements document.
- Relevant clauses of the contractual document.
- In case of embedded software, system-related plans.

There are other elements feeding the process during the project:

- Configuration items.
- Problem reports and change requests.
- Release strategy and plan.
- Tracking information.

The main outputs of SCM are the following:

- Software configuration management plan, which is started during the requirements specification phase and completed during the high-level design phase.
- Build lists.

- Change history.
- Version and release information.
- Configuration reports.

The SCM system defined (including procedures, standards and tools) must implement an SCM strategy by ensuring the fulfilment of the following activities:

- Configuration identification defines and organises the configuration system, uniquely identifying configuration items. Not all documents and software components need be subjected to CM.
- Configuration control manages configurations, items, libraries, versions and release. Problems and changes are also managed.
- Report on the state of the configuration, maintaining the description, responsible person, status and history of configuration items.

These principal activities, accomplished by procedures within the SCM process, are the essential steps to be achieved.

A system configuration is the set of configuration items that is under control, correctly identified, as well as its interrelations and dependencies. The configuration identification implies the definition and parameters' specification of the configuration items that will be controlled. This means deciding which level of components is going to comprise the minimum configuration item, how they can be grouped together, how different versions of individual components items are related to a group of components, and, finally, how the entire configuration or subportions of it are to be identified.

Also, configuration management deals with dependencies. This means identifying how different component items relate to one another, what are the dependencies between software components items, and, also important, what are the dependencies on non-software configuration items. These dependencies together with the configuration items description will define the object model. The instantiation of this model will be placed in the libraries of the configuration system. Configuration work products are kept and controlled in a repository called a baseline.

The activity of configuration control deals with impact analysis. This is based on the relationship between components and relates to both assessing the effect of modifying one item with respect to other items, and deciding whether modifications are worth making and how long it is likely to take.

Modern configuration management deals with control and management of objects as opposed to files. This relates to the possibility to manage non-software items in the same manner as software items, to describe objects on the basis of a set of attributes, and to define the behaviour of individual objects or groups of objects based on their types and attributes.

The final main activity is focused on the degree of visibility and status of the different items, libraries, versions and changes.

4.1.3 Process Management

This aspect of CM is primarily concerned with the definition and control of configuration management activities during the entire software development and maintenance processes. First of all, roles and responsibilities should be defined for such activities. These not only involve SCM managers and affect the work of developers, but also that of testers, quality assurance staff, and project managers. One process task is therefore to define who does what, how, and when.

A life cycle should be defined in order to line up the configuration items, or its elements, with the output products of each phase. This allows SCM activities to be integrated within the general framework of the development process and to comply with the requirements of the quality system, if there is one in place. The evolution of a component is therefore tracked with respect to the expected phases of development.

Process management also relates to documentation support. This implies defining procedures and methods to ensure the traceability from requirements to specifications, to code, and back to requirements. The relationship between documentation and code must also be defined. Finally, process management relates explicitly to the way testing support is provided, i.e. how traceability from requirements to tests is maintained, and how tests are handled with respect to code.

Software configuration management systems comprise a set of procedures and tools that help implement the criteria for both configuration and product management processes.

4.1.4 Software Configuration Management Plan

The first step in establishing a SCM system is to develop a software configuration management plan. This includes objectives, responsibilities, and the approach and methods to be used.

A plan determines what software work products generated in the project are placed under configuration management, that is, the items to be identified, controlled, and made available throughout the entire lifecycle. Configuration work products are kept in a repository called a baseline. A configuration management library system is established as a repository for software baselines.

A SCM plan should be developed for each project, following a documented procedure. The plan, reviewed and used by all affected groups, is started early on and is materialised at the same time as project planning.

The identification of work products involves an identification scheme and a unique identifier for each configuration item. The items controlled may include any document or piece of software, including support tools. The identification activity also specifies at which point in its lifetime each item is placed under configuration control.

Products from the software baseline library are created and their release is controlled via a documented procedure. The procedure typically involves a Software Configuration Control Board (SCCB). This group reviews change requests, authorises changes to configuration items and baselines, and authorises product builds. Large companies will usually have an organisational equivalent of the SCCB, small companies will often have its functional equivalent, perhaps, the project leader and the SQA leader.

The status of configuration items is recorded according to a documented procedure. The record includes the content and status for all items, current and all past versions and the complete change history of all items, so that all previous versions are recoverable.

The content of the baseline and the facilities and structure of the library system are to be assessed along with the integrity of the baseline and, to ensure integrity, deviations are tracked to closure.

The SCM group periodically audits software baselines to verify that they conform to the documentation that defines them.

The change requests and problem reports for all configuration items are initiated, recorded, reviewed, approved, and tracked according to a documented procedure.

Change requests – from problem reports, requirements changes, corrective actions, and elsewhere – will lead to baseline changes. The proper authority (SCCB) will make these changes, check-in and checkout of items from the baseline must preserve baseline integrity, and regression tests will be performed.

Regression tests ensure that changes to a baseline do not cause unintended effects. The procedure requires that changes undergo a review and regression test step, and that changes have a candidate status until final approval or rejection.

It is important to make available to affected groups standard reports documenting, SCM activities and baseline contents. The kinds of reports envisioned are SCCB minutes, summary of change request and trouble reports, revision histories, as well as audit results. This information helps to provide a view of the whole SCM process for the organisation.

To support a full range of software engineering activities, a fairly sophisticated set of SCM functions is required. While the following functions may be used in varying degrees during requirements, design, implementation, test, and maintenance, they are all required to provide adequate support and effective control:

- A protected baseline for the operational concept, specifications, design, implementations, test, and tools.
- A protected file with a description of all changes and revisions.
- Means for each software engineer to read any unlocked element in the baseline.
- A private workspace where checked-out designs or implementations can be modified.
- Templates that assist in the preparation of new design, implementation, or test descriptions.

- A procedure for approving checkout that permits software engineers to obtain any available baseline element for their private workspace and lock out the SCM copy function to prevent any one else from making simultaneous changes.
- A procedure for approving deletion of defunct elements.
- A way to collect, format, and produce consolidated system documents containing the key element description for any given baseline.
- A way to check that all elements and relevant descriptions have been carried over between baselines.
- A centralised data dictionary containing the official records of all named items and their formats.
- A where-used record of every use of every interface and data item in the system.

One important SCM function that is often overlooked is the need to maintain baseline control over the complete set of tools used to specify, design, implement, test and maintain the software. When a compiler, for example, is modified, it may produce slightly different object code from an identical source program. If this results in a system problem, it may be difficult to find, particularly if the compiler level used is either not known or not available.

SCM control over requirements and specifications is needed to ensure that the product being built and tested is what is wanted. SCM control must also be maintained over the design throughout system life to ensure its integrity and maintainability. To do this, requirements baselines, specification baselines, design baselines, unit baselines, integration baselines, and operational baselines are established and maintained at appropriate points throughout the development cycle.

Project naming conventions are established in the plan and a family of forms and procedures is provided to ensure that every change is recorded, reviewed, and tracked. The specification is used as a basis for the development work and as a reference for developing the functional, system, and acceptance tests.

During the design phase, SCM maintains control over the design and the rationale for establishing it. As changes are made, the appropriate design documentation is correspondingly updated. Additional SCM facilities are needed to record all code changes. Finally, for projects during the maintenance phase, procedures are needed to handle the development of simultaneous versions of the same program. The tools used to design, implement, test, and maintain the software must also be maintained under configuration control.

The purpose of software configuration status accounting is to maintain a continuous record of the status of all baseline items. A software configuration audit is periodically performed to ensure that the SCM practices and procedures are rigorously followed

In the development of software, the use of adequate CM processes and CM tools can dramatically change the way of working. The choice of CM Tools should be done as carefully as the choice of technical platform, data base manager, operating system, etc. A common tool helps to bridge conflicts of interest and to avoid sub-optimisations between different areas of responsibility, for instance between departments of development and of maintenance.

SCM should not be assumed to be a burdensome activity with little value added. The right attitude should consist of finding the level of discipline in an organisation providing appropriate value for the effort, then document that level of discipline in the form of procedures, and finally follow them consistently introducing formal adjustments when required.

4.2   SCM in the View of Different Experts

Below, four perspectives from different experts are presented.

The first contribution, written by Prof. Walter Tichy, from the University of Karlsruhe, starts with some basic definitions and explains the main SCM functions that have been automated, including configuration item identification, version control, configuration selection and building, and change management. The author insists on the need for process support in large teams and in distributed SCM.

The second contribution, provided by Mr. Ulf Nyman, from Contextor AB, is a brief tutorial on SCM. It explains the main concepts involved and provides details about CM activities: configuration identification, control, status accounting and auditing.

In the third contribution, furnished by Dr. Kölmel and Dr. Eisenbiegler of FZI, summarises possible reasons to institutionalise a SCM process, as well as its adoption phases and some results and lessons learned from actual implementations. They also explain the role and limitations of SCM tools and, in particular, the necessity to match tool requirements and sophistication to the actual process needs.

The final contribution, prepared by Professors Calvo-Manzano, García-Cordero (Politechnic University of Madrid), San Feliú and Amescua (Carlos III University of Madrid), describes a detailed model of Configuration and Change Control Boards (CCCB) targeted at large organisations or projects. The paper provides details on the objectives, functions and composition of such Boards, and also about the role of its members and the way to co-ordinate their work. Success factors for CCCB are listed as well.

4.2.1 Software Configuration Management State of the Art

W. F. Tichy
University of Karlsruhe, Karlsruhe

4.2.1.1 Introduction

Configuration management (CM) is the discipline of controlling changes in large and complex systems. Its goal is to prevent the chaos caused by the numerous corrections, extensions, and adaptations that are applied to any large system over its lifetime. The goal of CM is to ensure a systematic and traceable development process, such that a system is in a well-defined state with accurate specifications and verified quality attributes at all times.

CM was first developed in the aerospace industry in the 1950s, when production of spacecraft experienced difficulties caused by inadequately documented engineering changes. Software Configuration Management (SCM) is CM tailored to systems, or portions of systems, that consist predominantly of software [Bersoff80]. A major difference between SCM and traditional CM is that software changes faster than hardware, and therefore needs automatic support. Fortunately, software is on-line and hence can be placed under automatic, programmed control easily.

4.2.1.2 Basic Definitions

The primary objects of interest in SCM are software configuration items, configurations, baselines, and derived items. A *software configuration item*, or simply *item*, is any separately identifiable, machine-readable information unit produced during the course of a software project. It consists purely of information. Examples include requirements documents, design documents, class diagrams, specifications, interface descriptions, source program modules, machine code modules, data base files, test programs, test data, test output, user profiles, user manuals, VLSI designs, icons, images, digitised drawings, sound recordings, etc. A configuration item is the smallest unit of individual change: there are no practicable, smaller units contained in the item that vary independently.

By contrast, a *configuration* is an aggregate of several components, where the components are configuration items or other configurations. Replacing, adding, or deleting components changes a configuration. An example is the configuration of hardware, software, and documentation making up an entire computer system. Each of the three main components is again a large configuration, ultimately composed of individual integrated circuits, code modules, or manual sections, for example.

A *baseline* is the description of a configuration. A baseline is a hierarchically structured parts-list, stating precisely and unambiguously which components make up a given configuration. Since baselines are information units and may change, they are configuration items in their own right. Baselines serve as important reference points in the development of a system: Once a baseline is established, subsequent changes are described relative to it, until the next baseline is recorded.

A *derived item* is generated fully automatically from other items. Examples include compiled code, linked systems, formatted text, and test output. Derived items are special in that they can be deleted, since they can be regenerated when needed (provided the inputs are available and the generator is operational). The space/time trade-off between storage and regeneration is handled by the system building function (see below) of SCM.

4.2.1.3   SCM Functions

The main functions of SCM that have been automated are identification, version control, configuration selection, configuration building, and change management. Additionally, process support tools help teams carry out updating steps involving many items. In software development organisations that are spread over multiple sites, all these functions must be network-enabled, i.e., operate in a distributed environment.

4.2.1.4   Identification

Identification assigns a unique identifier to every configuration item. Reliable identification is crucial for effective CM. A great deal of confusion results if the same identifier is assigned to two different items, for example two different versions of a file. To avoid misidentification, a new and unique identifier is issued whenever an item is changed. A unique identifier typically consists of a descriptive name and several fields with version designators, serial numbers, or dates.

4.2.1.5   Version Control

Issuing a new identifier for every change may obscure relations between items. One may want to record, for instance, that a given configuration item is a revision of another, correcting certain errors. The version control function of SCM records this information. It collects related configuration items into sets called *version groups* and manages the evolution of these sets. The items in a version group are linked by a number of relations. For instance, the relation *revision-of* records historical development lines; the relation *variant-of* connects items that differ in some aspect of function, design, or implementation, but are interchangeable in other respects. Figure 4.1 illustrates a version group with two diverging lines of development; one is a corrective branch the other a parallel branch. The corrective branch is applied to an old version and merged into the main line at a later point.

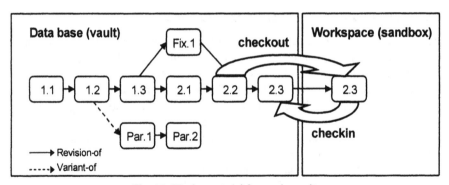

Fig. 4.1 The base model for version units

For practical reasons, version control also incorporates the identification function by simply incrementing a version number for every new item added to the group. Team members update version groups by following the *checking/checkout protocol*. Before commencing work on a configuration item, a developer performs a checkout. The checkout operation copies a selected version from its version group into the developer's workspace, as illustrated in Fig. 4.1. In a workspace, a developer can carry out modifications undisturbed from the activities of other workers. The checkout also places a reservation into the version group. This reservation gives the developer the right to deposit a new version of the item and attach in a straight line of descent to the one that was checked out. Other users wishing to modify the same original version can only create branches emanating from this version. Thus, the reservation grants the right to extend the development history in a straight descent line and prevents additional developers from depositing other changes "in between" the original and the new version. Once the holder of the reservation performs a checking, the current version is copied from the workspace into the version group and linked into the history. Old versions are typically not deleted until it is certain that they are not used anywhere. Version groups with a hundred or more elements are not uncommon.

Version control also maintains a logbook recording the reasons for changes. The log entries typically record time of change and the identity of the developer, plus a short commentary describing the nature of the change. The log is convenient for surveying the changes a system underwent over time. Version control also compresses the space occupied by version groups using *delta storage*. This technique saves only the differences between versions rather than complete copies. With modern delta generators, space consumption is reduced to less than 2-10 percent of full storage [Hunt98]. Whenever a version is needed, a decoder program first reconstructs the data from the differences. SCCS and RCS [Rochkind75, Tichy85] are early version control systems implemented with delta mechanisms.

4.2.1.6   *Configuration Selection and Building*

Configuration selection deals with the problem of which changes to include in a new configuration. For instance, developers would typically select their own changes plus those of others that have been tested, relative to the latest baseline. Another selection criterion is to choose all changes current and tested at a given point in the development history. Another approach is automatic selection, where a configuration program is given a few key software modules, say the main program and a few others, and then searches the version groups for missing modules, using interface information to select the right ones.

Once selection is complete, the configuration is handed over to configuration building or system building. This function produces the desired set of derived items. It performs such tasks as compiling, linking, loading, pre- and post-processing, document formatting, etc. Efficiency is important, so building should avoid redundant processing steps. For example, a program module should not be compiled more than once. The MAKE system [Feldman79] is a classic system building tool. It is driven by a description of the desired configuration (albeit without version numbers), runs specified building processes automatically, and can even trigger tests. ClearCase [Leblang94] offers flexible selection rules based on various version attributes, such as version numbers, branch names, development state, and ownership, and then runs building steps. Important for building tools is the ability to repeat the selection and building steps reliable and exactly at any time, so older configurations can be reconstructed for maintenance.

An important step after configuration building is *regression testing*. It consists of re-running test suites after changes, and comparing the results with expected outputs. Once a test suite is defined, it is run against all future releases of a software system to avoid that old problems reappear.[11] Regression testing is a mechanical task and can be triggered automatically.

4.2.1.7   *Change Management*

Change management is built on top of versions control and configuration handling. It requires that every modification starts with a formal change request; the individual developer can no longer carry out changes without being assigned a change request first. A change request has a unique identifier and a short description of the change order. Change requests are stored in a database. The database tracks them through a series of states. After initial submission, a change request enters one of the states "approved", "rejected", or "delayed". If approved, it is assigned to a developer or team, and then passes through states such as "in progress", "tested", "accepted", and "released". Change requests are also linked to both the faulty configuration items and the corrected versions. This information

---

[11] The term derives from the fact that one wants to prevent a system from *regressing* to a worse state.

can then be used by configuration selection for composing a system that implements a certain set of changes.

The change request database is an important management tool, because it can answer the following questions:

- *"Which changes are complete, which in progress?"*
- *"Which change requests have been/will be implemented in a given release?"*
- *"Which changes are delayed, and which subsystems cause the delays?"*

Without change management, progress tracking and planning remains informal and imprecise, because it requires asking individual workers to determine the change status of a system.

4.2.1.8   Process Support

Once change management is in place, large teams may need process support. Process support for SCM helps manage the SCM database with its numerous versions, branches, and change requests. Process support is needed partly because of the sheer number of items that need to be handled, and partly because large teams work in parallel and the branching in the version groups can become unwieldy. Process support organises branching and merging, tracks change sets (the items that were modified for a given change request), helps with updating workspaces with released changes by others, and organises merging of the work of multiple teams.

A simple models for process support the following. Each team automatically works on its own development branch in each version group it touches. Versions are moved from these branches to a designated release branch only after all conflicting changes have been resolved and tested. Teams work on their branches and in their workspaces in relative isolation. Periodically, say once a week, they synchronise their work with others. During the synchronisation, process support delivers the appropriate configuration items from the release branch to the synchronising workspace and helps resolve conflicts by staging merge runs. When completed, an integrator picks up the changes from a team's branches, tests one more time for conflicts, runs regression tests, and then places the changes onto the release branch. Process support thus simplifies dealing with large numbers of items, branches, and conflicting changes.

4.2.1.9   Distributed SCM

Distributed SCM co-ordinates the work of geographically distributed teams. Distribution requires that the main SCM functions introduced above are all networks enabled. In local area networks, client-server implementations of these functions will do, but in wide-area networks bandwidth between sites may not be sufficient. In this case, each site needs to replicate the relevant parts of the database and a periodic update process must synchronise them. Updates that travel over public networks should be encrypted to foil industrial espionage.

Distributed development places a strong emphasis on process support. If team members rarely meet, telephone calls are difficult because of time-zone differences, and e-mail round-trip becomes a day, informal arrangements on who works on what for how long break down. In this situation, a lot more emphasis will be placed on automated support for scheduling, tracking work, and preventing information loss.

4.2.1.10 Summary

Software configuration management helps control evolving software systems and co-ordinate teams. It is an established sub-field of software engineering, and one that provides recognised benefits for software developers and managers. As the demand for quality software increases, SCM will be crucial for developing and maintaining large, long-lived systems on time and within budget.

4.2.1.11 Bibliography

[Bersoff80]
  Bersoff, Edward H., Henderson, Vilas D., and Siegel, Stanley G. *Software Configuration Management*, Prentice-Hall, Englewood-Cliffs, NJ, 1980.
[Feldman79]
  Feldman, Stuart I., Make a program for maintaining computer programs. *Software – Practice and Experience*, 9(3):255-265, March 1979.
[Hunt98]
  Hunt, James J., Vo, Kiem-Phong, and Tichy, Walter F., Delta Algorithms: An Empirical Analysis *Transactions on Software Engineering and Methodology* 7(2):192-214, April 1998.
[Leblang94]
  Leblang, David. B., The {CM} Challenge: Configuration Management that Works. *Configuration Management*, Tichy, Walter F. (ed), John Wiley & Sons, 1994, 1-37.
[Rochkind75]
  Rochkind, Marc J., The source code control system, *IEEE Transactions on Software Engineering*, SE-1(4):364-370, December 1975.
[Tichy85]
  Tichy, Walter F., RCS – a system for version control, *Software – Practice and Experience*, 15(7):637-654, July 1985.

4.2.2 How Do We Implement the Theory of CM in Practice

U. Nyman
Contextor AB

4.2.2.1 Introduction

Configuration management has the word on it to be hard to understand and unnecessary bureaucratic. If you know its goals and main principles relatively simple processes can be implemented and used. Simplicity justifies the subject and makes it understandable.

When you work with product development you sometimes meet processes with unclear purpose and with badly motivated existence. Things should be "reviewed and approved". Reviewed according to what criteria and against what norms? Be accepted for what?

The goal of configuration management is to document the composition and status of a defined product and its constituent parts, and to publish this so that the right working material is used and the right product is built, during the whole life cycle of the product.

Configuration management is about "the management" of a "configuration". What is then a configuration? The word configuration means "composition" and is used in this context to describe how a product is composed of different parts. Every part can exist in several different versions. Several different products can contain partly similar parts from a standard assortment.

Example – You use a word-processor, with the version 2.1, and discover an error which you duly report according to the instruction in the user manual. This error is expected to be correct in later releases, for instance in versions 2.2 or 2.3.

With a configuration is meant a composition, that is the content of an existing or future product.

A product consist of a number of different parts (components) in which each part uniquely can be identified and exist in several versions. Each separately version controlled part is called a Configuration Item.

As a model of mind you can describe a configuration as a box in which a version of the product is delivered. Compare this with the box in which consumer software packages are delivered. This box contains more, requirement specification, production processes, etc. In the beginning of a product development the box is empty. During the development phase the parts which describes and forms the final product are put into it as the development proceed. The parts are in the form of drawings, documents, machine components, software etc. When needed the parts in the box are replaced with better versions.

When the product is developed the box is closed and the product can be sent to a user or to a production department for duplication. In the box there is all the necessary information for making a change and to create a new modified product. In practice the box correspond to an index of all constituent parts.

You can compare named baselines to internal "lids" in the box. Those lids are locked and usually the customer or the product management has the key. If you want to change anything in a baseline you have to take off the lids and contents above until you get down to the level which is to be changed. After this you put the contents back at the same time as you check that it is consistent with the changes made.

Configuration Management is about how activities should be technically administered. CM is to a large extent "book-keeping and accounting" during product development, and about how decisions are made for changes in product (the content of the "box"). This comprises all that influences the content of the box, also development environment, development model, instructions and plans.

A CM-system consists of CM-procedures and of CM-tools. These co-operate in a CM-process. The procedures cover things like change management, decision forum, etc. The tools cover things like archive storage, product structure, report database, status report, content index, etc.

4.2.2.2 Basic Concepts

In Configuration Management theory there are four central basic concepts. In order better to understand these they should be related to product development and to product content. Figure 4.2 illustrates the connection between CM, product structure and development phases.

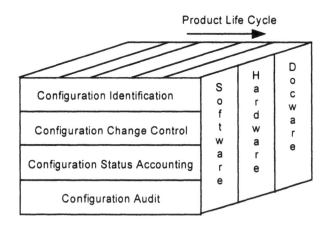

Fig. 4.2 Connection between CM, product structure and development

Configuration Identification
How are the different parts identified and structured?
Treats how the product is structured and how the parts are identified.
Includes product and archive structure and how the parts are version managed.

Configuration Control

How are changes and additions managed?

Treats how changes in the product are controlled and managed.

Includes how changes are proposed, implemented, controlled and accepted.

Configuration Status Accounting

How does the actual configuration is made?

Treats the current status, established baselines and valid configuration.

Includes what is the base for further development and what changes that are part of the valid configuration.

Configuration Audit

Is the real product in accordance with the specified product?

Treats how well the real product corresponds to the decided.

Includes how well the built product contains what it is said to contain, and if the content has known and expected status.

Every basic concept is described in the following section.

4.2.2.3   Configuration Identification

Product Structure

In all product development it is necessary to have a suitable structure for the product. A good product model is a prerequisite for a good CM. In software development it is important to have a clear picture (a goal) for what the final result should look as.

In technical software development sometimes structure and terminology from a military standard called DoD-2167A are used. This standard contains the base for a hierarchical product structure. It is suitable to use in relation with customers with defence connections in order that they "feel at home". This standard has been replaced with others, which are good standards for a development model, but does not contain the same clear product model.

A system consists of independent configurations of software (CSCI – Computer Software Configuration Item) and hardware (HWCI – Hardware Configuration Item). The software parts are called components (CSC – Computer Software Component). A product is composed by an hierarchy of components. One or several software units (CSU – Computer Software Units), implement each component.

As a system is being developed, it may be suitable to have different depths for different branches. Such a view is suited for software oriented systems. In hardware oriented systems a fixed number of levels are more common.

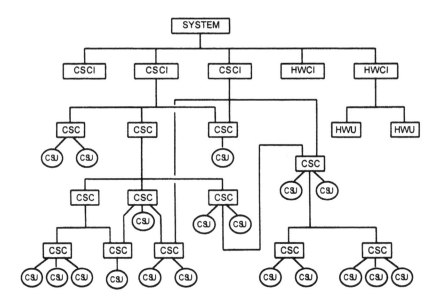

Fig. 4.3 Product structure according to DoD-2167

In Celsius Tech Systems they make each software component an independent configuration item (CI), consisting of 4 documents (requirements specification, design description, testing description, test report) and a number of software units (external interface, internal functionality, accompanying test environment). The size of a software component varies, but 20–100 pages per document and 30–80 software files can be used as a norm.

In the Ericsson Group a model is used describing a product by three complementary structures (projections):

- Functional structure   - relations between functions.
- Implementation structure   - a layer with standard components.
- Delivery structure   - configuration per product.

Functional structure is oriented to logical functions and to user cases. Implementation structure is the common warehouse of physical components (source system) from which several different products are composed. It is oriented to physical separate components consisting of software and/or hardware. The physical structure, which is traditionally hardware oriented, is divided into a fixed number of levels (subsystem, function block, and implementation unit). Delivery structure is product oriented and describes per product its content, structure and number. It works as a table of contents and a building description.

Archive Structure

Beside the product structure you have as a model when developing a product (logic top-down), there is the archive structure in which the physical components are stored and out of which products are integrated together (physical bottom-up). Those structures are often similar but basically differences exists.

An archive structure can for instance be divided in the following objects:

- Configuration
- Configuration Item (CI)
- Storage file

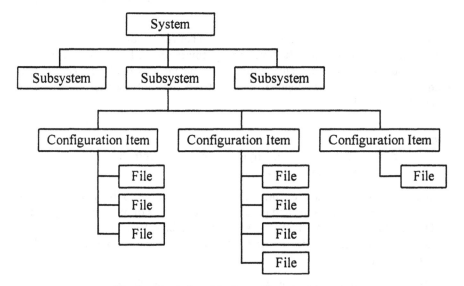

Fig. 4.4 Physical model of a configuration hierarchy

A configuration is a hierarchy of configuration items. A configuration item can for instance be a software component, an instruction manual or a development tool.

A configuration item consists of one or several storage files and/or subordinated configuration items.

- A document physically consists of at least one storage file. One document can for instance consist of a main document and a number of separate subdocuments. One document can have separate storage files for pictures.
- A software module physically consists of at least one storage file with software, usually source code. Several storage file are identified and managed together as one unit.

The relation between archive structure and product model is described in table 4.1.

Table 4.1 Archive structure to product model relationships

Archive structure	Product model
Configuration	Product
Configuration Item	Software Component
Configuration Item	Software Module / Document
Storage file	Source file / Text file

A complete configuration should, besides the hardware of the product, software and documentation also include development environment, for instance compiler, archive tool and text editor, and during development also work procedures like plans, instructions and development model. Used test tools and testing software should be archived.

Identity

There are two parallel ways of identifying components. Both those ways should be considered and correspond during all management.

- One physical way based on principles in used archive tools. This comprises filename, generation name, and groupings, and releases of different groupings.
- One logical way based on attributes used by humans. This comprises abbreviations for components, identity and titles for document, unique item number, version name, etc.

Depending on development environment and tradition the exact rules varies in physical and logical name giving. These rules are described in a CM-plan.

Each software component is registered as a configuration item (CI) and consists of software modules and documents, and import and/or export relations to other software components.

One or several documents usually belong to a software component. A document can be divided into several sub-documents in order to ease maintenance, reviews and releases. The source information of a document consists of one or several files. A document is generated via formatting to a printed paper document.

A number of program modules usually belong to one software component. On program module consists of one or several storage files. Individual files are physically identified by a file name. The code of a software component often is convenient to divide in separate configuration items possible to be released separately. This facilitates parallel development. For instance a division can be done in external interfaces, internal functionality and testing environment.

The source information of a program module consists of one or several storage files with source code. The generation of one software unit consists result in binary files, for instance object code or executable programs.

Version

Name of versions is used for separating different revised releases. For logical version name the following principles exist, numerical combinations (2.4, 4.0.1), character series (A, B) and date (1994-11-23). For storage files it also exists a physical version name supplied by the library tool, for instance filename and sequence (generation) number.

A version name can consist of two or three sequential numbers, separated by a dot (2.4). These numbers are called version number and revision number. When needed, a preliminary character (2.4A) may be added.

Version number is characterised by being stepped from 1, reflect functionality and interface, i.e. say for software it indicates new not backwards compatible interface, and for documents it reflects new or changed facts which influences the product.

Revision number is characterised by being stepped from 0, reflect a revision (improvement), i.e. for software a change is indicated for comprised modules, and for document minor changes.

Preliminary character is characterised by being stepped from A, reflect distributed, but not released, test version not maintained by product responsibility.

Different version names for a unit are illustrated in figure 4.5.

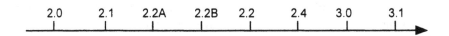

Fig. 4.5 The base model for version units

Branches are different parallel developments of the same configuration item. Branches can for instance occur when maintaining earlier versions, when a new version is already in development. Branches should be considered as temporary dead ends.

A branch name consists of an addition to an original version name in the form of one further revision number separated with a dot (2.4.1). Branches can be made on branches (2.4.1.2). Preliminary versions of branches are named by a preliminary character (2.4.1.A).

A branch number are characterised by being stepped from 1 normally, reflects an alternative development line, and corresponds to addition of an extra revision number.

Different branch names for a unit are illustrated in figure 4.6.

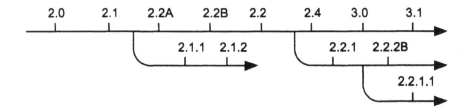

Fig. 4.6 Names for branches

Sometimes a third number is used to indicate error corrections. In this theoretical example a third number is used to indicate branching, but another common use of the numbers with three-position code (x.y.z) is:

X – Big not backward compatible change (new revised product).

Y – Additions that are backwards compatible (major change).

Z – Corrections and changes (minor change).

Release Name

Future planned releases should have names not to be mixed up with version names. Release names are basically not part of configuration management but of planning. Because of this you should separate between names for planned releases and versions of an existing configuration (real product). These are basically two different things and using the same names may lead to confusion.

Releases can be identified as such by a delivery letter, for example "R" (Release) and a sequence number. This indicates that this concerns a future release. The sequence number may be the same as the later used version number and thus corresponds to the functional content (according to earlier example). If preliminary releases are planned, a preliminary character is used. Releases can be named R3A, R3B, R3 etc. Planned release R3A can be released version 3.1 and release R3 can at the end be version 3.6.

The relation between (planned) release and version is illustrated in figure 4.7.

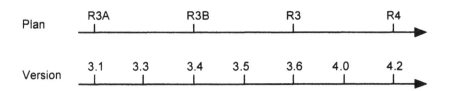

Fig. 4.7 Names for releases

Release name may also be composed of the parts; product abbreviation (ABCD), deliverymarker (R), version number (3), and optional preliminary character (A).

Final version name for unplanned releases, of the type bug-fix or preliminary has the form of type 3.5 (bug-fix) and 3.5A respectively. A pre-release can by definition not be planned. A released version (correction release), with stepped revision number, should justify the presumption that it is better than the one before.

4.2.2.4 Configuration Control

Development Status

Every Configuration Item (CI), and its included files, exists in different development states with successively higher status. For example, when choosing version of a software component you should not chose an "old with errors" or a "new untested", but chose "the right" version in between.

In CM theory, the following states exist:

- Working   - In continuous change (Development)
- Archived   - Stored version that can be retrieved (Frozen)
- Tested   - Measured ability, control and test (Verified)
- Released   - Can be used and distributed, internal maintenance (Released)
- Approved   - Part of configuration, base for further development (Baseline)
- Operative   - Delivered to customer, external maintenance (Delivered)

Baseline

The concept "baseline", is interpreted as "base for further development". The content of a baseline is established at a certain point in time and is after that changed only by formal change management. Every baseline represents a new, often more complete and more correct, platform for further development.

Establishing of a baseline means a sharp limit for going over from a more informal change of versions to a formal way of making changes and using new versions. In an established baseline only formally authorised changes are allowed.

A baseline consists of an amount of configuration items having reached a certain development state, and together they are the result of a certain development phase, and are decided to be part of a valid configuration.

The correct relation between baseline and configuration is:

	Latest established baseline
+	Made and approved changes
=	Now valid configuration

Too early and to closely established baselines means that formal management is started unnecessary early and leads to extra work having a slowing effect. Too late and to sparsely established baselines leads to a work difficult to control and inefficiency, due to uncertainty about what that is valid and bad control of what is happening.

Sometimes a number of named baselines are use within CM. Named baselines are partial "freezings" of a configuration, normally at a defined state of a product development. Often the establishment of baseline is related to different milestones or decision points. Named baseline indicates a configuration established to and with a certain "system level", for instance customer requirements. All changes under this level are thereafter done via formal change management. Changes above this level are done in a more informal way, until next baseline is established.

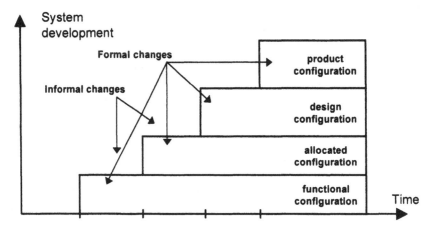

Fig. 4.8 Named baselines and configurations

The ISO10007 standard mention Functional- and Production Configuration Baseline.

The IEEE Std 610.12 standard uses Functional-, Allocated-, Developmental- and Product Baseline.

The following free interpretations are examples of relatively accepted usage:

- Functional Baseline describes the first requirement definition for the system.
- Functional Configuration encompasses what we are to build, in the form of the external requirements picture for the system and which starting from functional baseline is controlling the internal structure of the system.
- Allocated Baseline describes the first division into software and hardware.

- Allocated Configuration encompasses how we are to build, in the shape of the internal structure of the system and starting from the allocated baseline is governing the implementation of the components (top-down design).
- Design Baseline describes the first build of the system.
- Design Configuration encompasses what is in building, in the shape of implementing the system, and is governing for dependent development, builds and testing (bottom-up integration).
- Product Baseline describes the first complete system.
- Product Configuration encompasses what we have built, in the form of the complete system, and which starting from product baseline is governing production, installation, usage, maintenance and spare parts supply.

Decision Forum

Who is to decide on what is to be the parts of a configuration? A common procedure is to have a central forum where all decisions on changes of a configuration are taken. This forum is in theoretical literature called CCB (Configuration/Change Control Board), or CB (Configuration Board) according to ISO 10007.

There are two types of decisions, regarding:

- What future changes are to be made.
- Which made changes are to be approved in a configuration.

Practically it is not efficient to have too many persons participating in all kinds of decisions. It is better to identify different kinds of decisions and delegate these to suitable positions. As a principle – those having the best information base for taking the decision should take the decision. The division into decision types can be done according to document type, critical interfaces, component size and position in the hierarchy of the system.

Selection and establishment of final software configuration can be wholly delegated to a special organisation for integration and testing. One single changed software file can be taken directly into a final systems configuration, without previous testing, if this is a conscious decision based on a judgement that the quality of the total system (by the best of knowledge) is increased.

A problem regarding a wide delegation is that all configuration decisions have to be "recorded", which can be complicated. A good way is to have a central forum (CCB), but still delegate the decisions to for different kinds of decisions to prescribe a lowest number of participants to make such a meeting to be valid.

How configuration management is done more in detail should be described in a CM-plan. The more thought through and delegated this is described the smoother the decisions are taken. Lead-time to implement changes in a configuration is a measure of the efficiency of the process.

Change Control

Changes in an existing configuration are done via formal change management, often in the form of registered forms or reports, these can be:

- Trouble reports   (for instant observed deficiencies)
- Change proposals   (for instance performance improvement)
- Deviations   (for instance conflicting requirements)

Common names are System/Software Performance/Problem Report (SPR), Change Request (CR), Trouble Report (TR), etc. We name all those "Reports".

Such a report usually results in some type of change in the system. The same report can be acted on in several ways in order to get the right effect. For example a test case, which does not verify requirements in an as expected, can be fixed through modification in the software, changing the requirement or redesign of the test case.

Changes in existing configurations are managed and recorded in the form of a report, which can have different states depending on the further acting on it. In practice there are just three basic states for acting on a report which are interesting (n.b. not the state of a component here):

- Registered
  A change need has been noted and formally been registered in the form of a report. A report can be an error report, a change proposal or a discovered inconsistency.
- Fixed
  After a report has been registered an analysis is started on how to act on it and a decision on real action and the planning for this. The action is done and actual configuration items are archived with new releases. In their change history reference is made to actual reports.
- Verified
  When it has been proven that done actions really have had the desired effects the state verified occurs. This is the final state. To reach this state a test is done or a review. The verification is documented in review protocol or in test report. A note in the report links to this documentation.

A report is used not only to register troubles but also as the normal way of planning changes in the system. Reports can be used to register errors, propose improvements, distribute commands, note future changes, synchronise dependent changes, progress communication, etc.

To achieve traceability the report itself is updated in parallel to being acted on. It documents analyses and action proposals, taken decisions (CCB Protocol), development plans, and test report for verification. In the sections of document and program code where actions have been taken are placed references to the actual report, for instance revision history.

It is practical to manage all types of reports in the same process and forum, independent of type. It can also be practical to manage additions (new functionality) together with the trouble reports. They compete for the same resources and should be prioritised together. If you separate trouble reports and development in an early stage, you risk having parallel tracks. Also it is healthy for a development department to be confronted with its own errors.

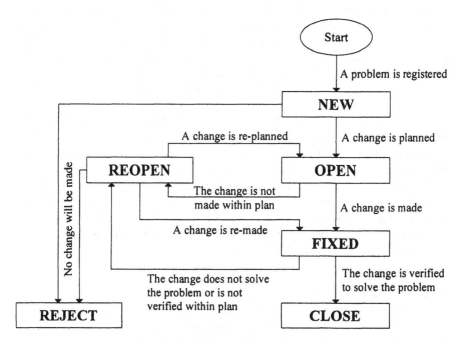

Fig. 4.9 State diagram for trouble reports

Classifying trouble reports is done in many ways and from several points of view. Usually you classify by "system impact" or technical obstacles existing. For instance:

- Fatal   - The system does to a big extent not work at all.
- Error   - Error that is possible to work around.
- Defect   - Can be improved, should be fixed.

Note that classification regarding system impact should not be the only basis for priorities when an action is implemented. A reported defect easy to fix may result in considerable performance improvement or reduction of future work. Prioritising of time between report actions and new functionality (additions) should be based on a rational investment calculation.

Note that the number of reports is not a measure of quality. If you measure the number of trouble reports you get a measure of discovered errors, not the real number of errors. A low number of reports can be the result of inferior testing.

Release

To release of a software component (configuration item) means both that it is made available for use in a wider circle, and a commitment about some future maintenance. Responsibility, authority and criteria for release are described in the CM-plan.

There is a difference between release and configuration. A release means that a version is made available for use. A configuration means that a version through a conscious decision is in use. Compare with Microsoft releasing its product Windows95 and a decision in Company X to base its client-server system on this product, with a specified version. The same principle exists internally in for instance a development project, but is often not used as clearly.

A release is normally done when some kind of testing result is known. A release can contain everything from quite untested changes to completely carry through tests. The important thing is to label the components with its status and possible restrictions of its use. This labelling is made in some form of release information (accompanying letter) or other attributes.

A release of a software component need not be complete with all documents and software units. It is the user needs that should govern the release. Early and many releases contribute to information distribution, which is a requisite for a successful project. A poor release, on the other hand, contributes to the spread of errors and thereby to increased quality costs.

A release of a component is characterised by:

- A new version is made available for use.
- It is published though updating of a "version index".
- It is decided by product/maintenance responsible.
- Delivery is made of a component from a supplier.

In an organisation with parallel development or reuse of components, the same component can at the same time be part of several different configurations. The relations between release and configuration are demonstrated by figure 4.10.

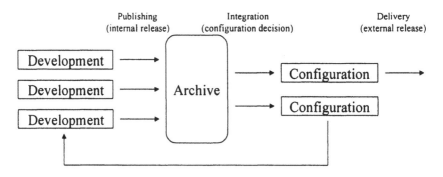

Fig. 4.10 Relation component version and configuration

4.2.2.5   Status Accounting

Record Keeping and Accounting

Record keeping and accounting is a base for configuration management.

Record keeping can comprise activities to register:

- Releases
- Configuration decision.
- Valid configuration

Accounting means activities to publish contents of current and valid configuration and to give overviews of development status.

Persons keeping a CM position in a project normally handle these activities. The initial information is configuration decisions, test reports, review protocols, change reports, decision on release, decision on configuration content, etc.

Version Structure

An archive structure, and its released configuration items, can be published through a structure of version descriptions. You can use VD (version description) as a document, which defines the content in all released versions of a component.

The version structure, with the help of which you can find what there is to be reused or decide to be part of a product (configuration), can be built with the aid of links (pointers). In this way you can easily "click" your way to the right information and see what component versions that are released and their relation to other components.

Configuration Index

The configuration of a product version, composed by a number of software components, is described as a list indicating identity, version and number of documents, hardware and software components.

In order to put together the content of a configuration you can use a configuration index. MCI (Master Configuration Index) is a document, which defines and publishes the valid content of a configuration. There is one MCI Document per configuration. A system can be described by several configurations, for instance one configuration per subsystem or separate configuration for hardware and software. Also hierarchies of MCI documents can occur.

A MCI Document can be structured in the following way as indicated by example:

```
MASTER CONFIGURATION INDEX
FUNCTIONAL CONFIGURATION
Item Identification:          SRS-100123 V1.3
Quality Control Record:       (Review meeting minutes)
Configuration Control Record: (CCB meeting minutes)
```

```
ALLOCATED CONFIGURATION
Item Identification:          ...
PRODUCT CONFIGURATION
Item Identification:          ABC-100123 V3.16
Quality Control Record:       (Test Report)
Configuration Control Record: (CCB meeting minutes)
Item Identification:          ...
```

Collected versions of this document make, together with referred documents, the collected account (Status Accounting).

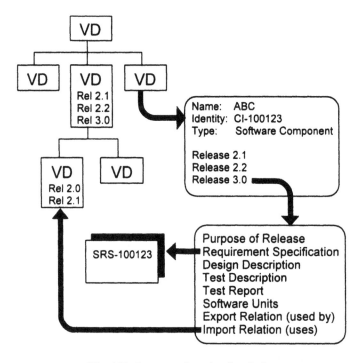

Fig. 4.11 Structure of version descriptions

The index, describing the configuration, can be completed with references to test reports and review protocols, and decision protocols. In this way you can handle publishing of the current configuration and at the same time facilitate for quality and configuration audit.

The traceability to trouble reports can be accomplished by that each:

- Component version state, for example in a release note, what trouble reports that are fixed.
- Test session state, for example in a test report, which trouble reports that are verified.

4.2.2.6   Configuration Audit

The purpose is to show how well a listed configuration (configuration index) and status (verification status) matches the real product. This is primarily done through checking status of components and status of current reports. Note that these checking do not comprise any evaluation of quality, it just checks the configuration content.

There are two types of configuration audits:

- Functional Audit
- Physical Audit

Functional Audit

Also called Functional Configuration Audit (FCA). Investigates evidence for the compiled product really containing specified functionality and performance.

In a final configuration of a finished product all change reports should be verified if they were planned to be verified. Checking of this is done on different configuration audits. Has a trouble report, which is indicated as fixed, really verified in an acceptable fashion. Evidence for this is searched in test reports and history for trouble reports.

This is comparable to that all functions described in a user handbook really are implemented in the product. Have for instance all specified functions been verified somewhere in a test case.

One example of a defect in a configuration audit is the product cc:Mail, release 2, from Lotus. It exists both for PC and Macintosh computers. The manual for the Macintosh version describes basic functions that are not implemented. This reported situation remained for at least one year.

Physical Audit

Also called Physical Configuration Audit (PCA). Investigates evidence for all parts specified to be parts of the product really are the ones used in the actual product, and that the parts indicated really have the version and status they should.

If some program module is used in several places, has the same version been used (consistency check)? I there any unauthorised or unknown "last minute" changes? Untested components can be part of a configuration, on condition that this is a conscious (authorised) decision.

4.2.2.7   Literature

Configuration Management Tools

A Detailed Evaluation, An evaluation report on CM-tools from May 1995, 363 pages in English [OVUM95].

The software tools administrate version management, changes, variants of installations, etc. It describes and compares 13 software tools: Adele, Aide-de-Champ, CCC/Harvest, Change Man, ClearCase, CMVC, CM/Vision, Continuos/CM, Endeavor, Endevor/WSX, Entry/Developer, PCMS and PVCS.

If you use or intend to invest in CM tools, this report may be a good help. You "slipper" a market investigation, though not all tools are covered. You get help with specification of detailed requirements. Judgements, and comparisons are already done. The content is also a good introduction to CM, a guidance for implementation, market prognoses etc.

The report is produced by Ovum Limited in the UK.

Capability Maturity Model

A model for evaluating processes for software development. Built as a level model of 5 steps, where level 2 among other things comprises Configuration Management. This part can be used to evaluate your own CM work. CMM is published by Software Engineering Institute (SEI). More information on Internet. [CMM]

Continuous Improvement of the Software Development Process via Maturity Models

A report from the VI (Association of Swedish Mechanical Industries), describing the role of maturity models in process improvement. Contains a description of CMM. [VI95a]

Architecture and Systems Building for Software

A report from VI (Association of Swedish Mechanical Industries), describing different principles for structuring systems. As a continuation of such a structuring, the physical CM structure is designed, for archiving and management as separate version managed building blocks. [VI95b]

Implementing Configuration Management

Describes the subject with the aid of different examples. Encompasses "hardware, software and firmware". Good figures and flowcharts. A book suitable for understanding and avoiding different problems. [Fletcher93]

Software Configuration Management Guidebook

Contains good checking questions and useful examples, for instance on how to formulate a CM Plan. Describes how the standards can be implemented. Focussed on software. A book suitable when designing processes and routines. *[Ben-Menachem94]*

Methods and Tools for Software Configuration Management

Treats the most common questions, in what concerns software development, with the aid of examples. Describes especially needs around build and make in a thorough way. Treats different relations between software components. A suitable book for the organisation of software into an archive structure. *[Whitgift91]*

4.2.2.8 Bibliography

[OVUM95]

Configuration Management Tools, A Detailed Evaluation, An evaluation report on CM-tools from May 1995, 363 pages in English by Ovum Limited, UK.

[CMM]

Capability Maturity Model, Software Engineering Institute (SEI).

[VI95a]

Continuous improvement of the software development process via maturity models, VI (Association of Swedish Mechanical Industries), 1995.

[VI95b]

Architecture and systems building for software, VI (Association of Swedish Mechanical Industries), 1995.

[Fletcher93]

Fletcher, J. Buckley, *Implementing Configuration Management* ISBN 0-7803-0435-7, IEEE Press 1993.

[Ben-Menachem94]

Ben-Menachem, Mordechai, *Software Configuration Management Guidebook.*, ISBN 0-07-709013-6, McGraw-Hill, 1994.

[Whitgift91]

Whitgift, David, *Methods and Tools for Software Configuration Management*, ISBN 0-471-92940-9, John Wiley & Sons, 1991.

4.2.3   Impact of Configuration Management

B. Kölmel, J. Eisenbiegler
Forschungszentrum Informatik FZI, Karlsruhe

4.2.3.1 Introduction

"Software Configuration Management is the backbone of the software development process, and when implemented correctly, helps ensure software quality and process improvement" [STSC94].

"Software Configuration Management involves identifying the configuration of the software (i.e., selected software work products and their descriptions) at given points in time, systematically controlling changes to the configuration, and maintaining the integrity and traceability of the configuration throughout the software lifecycle. The work products placed under software configuration management include the software products that are delivered to the customer (e.g., the software requirements document and the code) and the items that are identified with or required to create these software products (e.g., compiler)" [Paulk 93].

Configuration Management helps to keep track on the status of a software product, it answers questions on:

- Who made the changes in the software?
- What changes were made to the software?
- When were the changes made?
- Why were the changes made?

Software Configuration Management includes the following functional areas: Identification (configuration, version and components of the system), Change Control (controlling the release and changes to software), Status Accounting (recording and reporting of the change process), and Audit (verification that the software product is built according to the requirements, standards, or contractual agreements).

Typical state-of-the-art Software Configuration Management tools may have all or combinations of the following features:

- Release Management (Change Control, Version Control, Variant Control)
- Configuration Support
- Process Support
- Team Support
- Library/Repository Support
- Security/Protection
- Reporting/Query
- Tool Integration

- Build Support
- Customisation Support
- Graphical User Interfaces (GUIs)

4.2.3.2 Scope

Configuration Management (CM) attracted more and more attention among software-producing companies. Especially in projects where more than 6 personnel are involved the difficulties of working in the team are obvious. The problems get bigger, if the teams get larger or the working places are locally distributed.

With Configuration Management techniques and tools it is possible to manage all stages of development and maintenance and accompany the evolution of software products, since it spans all dimensions of the software lifecycle. Adopting Software Configuration Management in an organisation is complex, since both managerial and technical issues must be addressed. The complexity of possible Software Configuration Management solutions is very high and could easily get very costly. At the end almost all people, all data and all processes of the software-developing organisation are involved in this issue.

The purpose of this report is to provide motivation on why to introduce a Software Configuration Management solution into a company. Why should they spend a lot of money and reach a break-even only after some long time?.

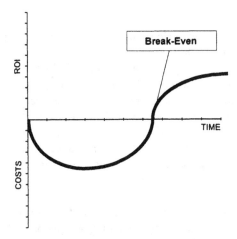

Fig. 4.12 Investment and ROI for SCM

This article should help to get an idea on questions like:

- Why should a company introduce a SCM-tool?
- What are the typical goals of software developing organisations, who started to introduce a SCM-system?
- What is the typical approach, when introducing a SCM-tool?

- What are the typical results and outcomes of a SCM-introduction?
- What are the lessons learned while introducing a SCM-tool?
- What are the possible pitfalls or leverages of such a project?

The information presented in this report concentrates on results gained out of the analysis of several Case-Studies. It will not describe specific technical issues but concentrate on experiences and lessons-learned during SCM projects.

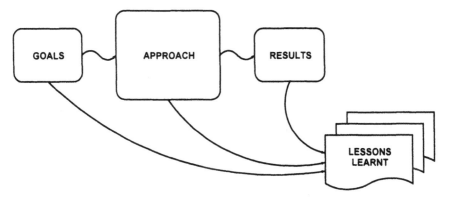

Fig. 4.13 Collection of Lessons Learned

The adoption of a Software Configuration Management system consists of several steps involved in introducing a SCM tool into an organisation up to the company-wide diffusion and using it on all projects. SCM adoption is a complicated and costly process, since it affects all levels of the organisation. At the beginning an thorough evaluation of the development process is necessary to determine how the activities and software developers will be affected. "SCM concepts are not difficult to understand, but are difficult to apply. The successful adoption of SCM technology becomes more of a cultural issue than a technical one" [STSC94].

It is important to recognise that purchasing a SCM tool will not solve all problems, there is no "silver bullet" SCM tool. A tool alone will not solve an organisation's SCM problems.

Gartner Group states in a study that the cost of the software tool represents only 10 percent of the total cost of implementing a solution. "Lost productivity accounts for 50 percent and the remaining 40 percent of the solution is derived from the cost of manpower" [Softool 92]. In order to guarantee the effective usage of a SCM solution, the software development unit must take complex factors, like technical, managerial, process-centred, organisational, cultural etc. issues into account.

Besides the technical problems, like how to operate and customise the tool, or how to install and maximise the performance of the tool etc., especially the managerial topics are very important: the planning, monitoring, making of schedules, and managing resources. Who will be allocated to fulfil the adoption activities or how will the product schedules be affected are crucial for the success of the SCM-adoption. All processes must be reconsidered and re-engineered according the requirements of the tool and activities. Moreover the organisational and cultural issues like communication and new or additional responsibilities or how to organise the change processes have to be taken into account. The human factor matters most, both in political and people-related aspects, resistance, re-organisation and promotion of skilled employees affect the SCM-adoption dramatically. One of the greatest barriers to overcome when introducing SCM into an organisation is to change how people view SCM. At first people react negatively toward SCM. Many software developers perceive the tool as intrusive and have little understanding of the long-term effects of not following SCM procedures. In many organisations, SCM has a low status, and SCM personnel are not trained or qualified to perform SCM duties. The person in charge of SCM needs a broad understanding of software engineering principles and the cultural aspects of the software-developing unit. Therefore training becomes an important aspect of ensuring that SCM principles are accepted and well-used within the organisation.

4.2.3.3   Goals of SCM-Adoption

The reasons of introducing a Software Configuration Management system into an organisation could be various. Besides the overall strategic goals to be BETTER, CHEAPER, FASTER, there are several specific objectives:

Fig. 4.14 Goal hierarchy of SCM

Change Control
To avoid repeated loops of changing things there and back again, it is necessary to know who and why things were changed. It is also very useful to keep track of the changes (error corrections, adding of features, etc.), to be able to plan resources and milestones. Without this knowledge it is hardly possible to get an overview of the state of a software project which is based on facts rather than on impressions.

Version Control

If there is more than one customer for a software product there is more than one version running at customer site. In this case it is necessary to keep knowledge on which version is installed at which customer. This includes knowledge about the different features and errors of these versions.

Variant Control

Most software products are highly customised. This means that almost every customer has a specialised variant of the product. Either different needs or environment of customers can force this. Detailed Knowledge of the variants available or installed at the customer not only helps to support the customer but also to keep track of the different variants of software modules and their interdependencies. A configuration support or build management can help to automate building of customised variants. An efficient variant control makes it possible to manage high flexibility.

Altogether, these possibilities of SCM strengthen the reproducibility, flexibility and custom orientation of the software process in the company.

4.2.3.4 Approach of SCM-Introduction

The introduction of a Software Configuration Management is an expendable task for every enterprise. Therefore it should be planned carefully. The introduction of SCM is generally carried out in phases. These phases could be as follows:

Preparation and Planning

The preparation and planning phase is very often underrated The purpose of this phase is to plan for the adoption activities, starting with an adoption plan and the careful selection of the right team members (right persons for the right tasks).

The benefits, the temporary schedule, the required resources, the responsibilities and the planned procedures need to be established. Anybody affected (even the management must be aware of the potential benefits) by the project must understand the strategic goals and help to define clear and precise requirements.

Very important is the development of an SCM plan, [STSC94] gives a possible outline of the structure:

- SCM activities over the software lifecycle
- SCM organisation
- SCM responsibilities and authority
- Resources needed to perform SCM functions
- Interfaces to other organisations
- SCM roles, policies, and procedures
- The change control process
- Level of SCM control
- Library requirements and activities

- Members of the Configuration Control Board.

Assistance for this crucial phase of a SCM-project can be found in [IEEE87] and [IEEE90].

Process Definition

The Introduction of SCM requires the definition of the processes of Software development and maintenance. In most cases this processes only had an informal or outdated description. An example for such a process is a change request: What happens if a client calls the hotline and wants to have an additional feature? These processes are subjects of change. For it's definition, future changes have to be taken into account.

Tool Evaluation, Selection and Customisation

The evaluation and selection of an adequate SCM-tool is an often-underestimated task. Having an accurate definition of the processes, which should be handled by the SCM-tool, is a useful basis. There are a lot of SCM-systems available, differing largely in their functionality. It is no solution to just by the most sophisticated one you can pay for. In most cases the customisation or downsizing of the SCM system to your needs is more costly than the software itself. An adequate SCM tool is capable of handling your actual process definitions and the future changes you are expecting for the next years. Additional information on tool-selection is available from the SEI WEB server (http://www.sei.cmu.edu/legacy/scm/).

Training of Users

SCM is a complex task. Most users, especially good software developers, refuse to use it, because they only see the extra work an not the benefits. Therefore the most important part of the introduction of SCM is to convince the people to use it. This consists of two parts: At first the users have to understand what SCM is, so they can see what the benefits are. Second the user have to be trained to work with the SCM tool, so the extra work gets as small as possible. If there will be a pilot project, it is a good idea to train the staff concerned with this pilot project first. The remaining staff can be trained before the roll out of the SCM to the whole enterprise, so the experience gained in the pilot project can be used.

Pilot Project Implementation

The use and impact of SCM should be investigated with a pilot project before SCM is rolled out to the whole enterprise. This makes it possible to correct errors made in the steps before. Additionally this pilot project should be used to collect hard facts about the impact of SCM. Therefore it necessary to analyse the starting scenario and the changes made by the introduction of SCM. These figures can be a good help to convince users as well as managers. It is necessary to distinguish between the effort of the project itself and the effort caused by the introduction of

SCM. If this distinction is not made people will not do a fair introduction of SCM since everything they do are additional costs for their project.

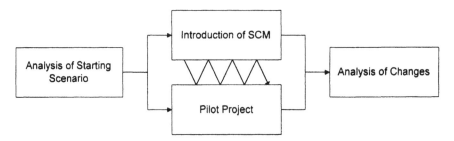

Fig. 4.15 Process Improvement Model for SCM

Review and Re-Engineering of Processes
The experiences gained in the pilot project should be used to review the decisions made in the previous phases. If you come to the conclusion, that there are too many changes to be done, it might be useful to do another pilot project to confirm these changes.

Rollout to the Enterprise
If you are convinced that your process definitions work and that you chose the right SCM tool, you can start to roll out the SCM to the whole enterprise. Be sure that all staff is trained adequately. Using SCM for more and more projects should do this rollout. The usage of SCM is not only a technical change like a new network or operating system. It changes the way work culture. Therefore it is useful that people who have already done this change pass on their experiences to their colleagues. An open discussion about goals and benefits but also about disadvantages facilitates this change.

4.2.3.5   Results of SCM

The results of a SCM-project could be various, [Zimm98] states "that a consequent usage of configuration management rules and procedures reduces the time from introducing a change request until it's incorporation by 50%. This leads to cost reductions of about 32%."

Several results have been observed in SCM-projects, among them are:
- Increased overall quality
- Development time reduction
- Fewer engineering changes
- Reduced time to market
- Increased team productivity

- Defined, repeatable development process
- Organisation wide alignment and awareness for changes
- Increased effectiveness of human teams

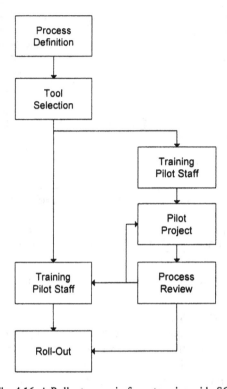

Fig. 4.16 A Rollout scenario for enterprise-wide SCM

The following illustration demonstrates statements from several projects, providing their view and experiences on SCM-projects.

4.2.3.6 Lessons Learned

There are lot reasons, why things can go wrong. Often the errors are very specific but some of them are typical and should be provided here:

Lack of Training

The main reason why SCM fails is resistance of the people, which are forced to use it. Especially the better Software developers tend to see SCM as extra and unnecessary work. The other reason for this resistance is that the people do not know how use the tools correctly and efficiently. Training about SCM and the tools used is necessary to overcome this. It must be clear that the costs of the training are an essential part of the whole costs for introducing SCM.

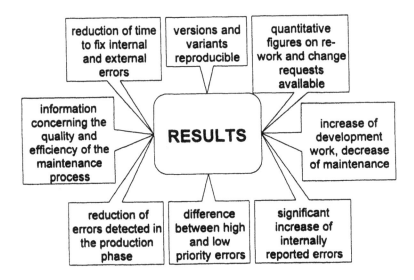

Fig. 4.17 The base model for version units

Management Commitment

The second most common reason is the lack of management commitment. The introduction of SCM is costly and resource consuming. In the very most cases it pays off after some time [Sissi99]. But it is necessary that this process improvement is seen as an strategic investment in the future. It is not possible to introduce SCM on the side. This would lead to an approach where the introduction of SCM only consists of buying some tools, which will never be used.

Work Culture

Using an SCM system changes the way you work, it changes the work culture in your enterprise. By defining processes things are formalised. But, informal ways can be more efficient than the formal ones, as long as they work. If people see SCM just as a formalisation of things, which formerly worked better the informal way, they see the new technology as something negative. The new processes have to be defined clearly and everybody should get an idea why things are better with them.

Underestimating of "Sideline-Tasks and Effects"

The Introduction of SCM is not just buying and using a tool. It must be clear that there are a lot of other things to do like tool evaluation and customisation, training, or process definition. A considerable amount of time and effort is necessary for the selection an customisation of the CM tools If these things are not taken into account at the beginning of the SCM introduction the project costs and time will explode. This leads to shortenings in tools and training and incomplete process definitions. The project will end with a situation that has not improved but confused, because nobody understands how to use the wrong tool for confusing processes.

Tool Selection

The tool selection is complicated and resource-consuming task. It is better to invest in a tool with more sophistication than you need, since with every project, where the SCM-tool is used, the expectations and requirements are increasing. The incremental deployment of the tool could be the winning factor for the acceptance within the software-developing organisation. But nonetheless people find always ways to get around a poorly implemented process, therefore it is useful to find tools (which are tools are difficult to customise or integrate into the prior processes) with which you need to accomplish the process.

Infrastructure

- Diverse machines, protocols, languages, software tools; no cross-platform coordination or standard use.
- Performance issues.
- Deployment costs, high cost of installing minimum and consistent process tools and technology on every relevant desktop.
- No integration of tools and data through co-ordinated hyperlinks or processes, i.e., how does this fit?
- Processes may not be tightly connected, mobile or disconnected users difficult to support, a lot of work happens offline.

4.2.3.7   Conclusions

The rapid changes in computing and application architecture, and the wide-spread development of applications at the departmental level are forcing a new level of awareness of team development in software organisations, and are pushing vendors to make their team development products more sophisticated and yet easier to use.

Version control and configuration management tools cover a wide range of approaches and functionality. A third generation tool is not necessarily "better" than a first generation tool. It all depends on which characteristics best match your needs and environment. Buying the most advanced product could be a mistake if you are only trying to handle a very simple situation. Therefore, the issue is not which product is best, but which one is the best match for you.

In closing, we want to acknowledge the pioneering work of dedicated professionals and vendors that through the last twenty years have succeeded in making software configuration management and team development a well respected and valued discipline.

4.2.3.8 Bibliography

[STSC94]
Software Technology Support Centre: *Software Configuration Management – Technology Report*, 1994.
[Paulk93]
Paulk, M. C., et al. *The Capability Maturity Model for Software, Version 1.1* (CMU/SEI-93-TR-24, ADA 263403). Pittsburgh, PA: Software Engineering Institute, Carnegie Mellon University, 1993.
[IEEE87]
IEEE STD-1042-1987, *Guide to Software Configuration Management*.
[IEEE90]
IEEE STD-828-1990, *Standard for Software Configuration Management Plans*.
[Softool92]
Softool Corporation, *Successful Software Strategies Seminar Series: Improving Your Configuration Management Implementation Strategy*, Washington, D.C., 1992.
[Zimmermann98]
Michael Zimmermann , *Configuration Management, Just a fashion or a profession? White Paper*, usb GmbH, 1998.
[Humphrey90]
Humphrey, Watts S., *Managing the Software Process*, Addison-Wesley Publishing Company, August 1990.

4.2.4   The Role of Control Boards in Configuration Management

J. A. Calvo-Manzano, M. García, T. San Feliu
Universidad Politécnica, Madrid
A. de Amescua
Universidad Carlos III, Madrid

4.2.4.1   Introduction

The construction, implementation and exploitation of any data processing system normally present a series of problems generally associated with co-ordination and control that will affect not only the development phase, but also the exploitation and maintenance phases. These can be classified as:

- Designation and identification of component elements
- Change control of such elements
- Library management
- Different products versions management utilised for and in the development, either own or third parties
- Systems construction to be delivered
- Support tools
- etc.

In summary, Configuration Management covers and deals with all these aspects. They mainly affect large or medium-sized complex systems. Although on a smaller scale, small systems or those that are not very complex, cannot be excluded.

In order to manage the aforementioned, it is necessary to control the influence and impact, as well as their possible variations of the following:

- Software elements over other software elements,
- Software elements over hardware/firmware elements, and vice versa.

This should give rise to the existence of a procedure which has the following objectives:

- Early and quick identification of these influences, impacts and their variations, and those of the elements that are impacted by these influences and their possible variations,
- Routing and reporting all the variations of the elements to the bodies concerned,
- Connection with other similar software/hardware/firmware "control systems" related to the system, and

- Connection among all the areas and departments that, direct and indirectly, participate and intervene in the execution, exploitation and maintenance of the system

The control systems established to carry out the previous objectives are called Configuration Control Boards and Change Control Boards. But, what do these terms mean or imply? The response is given in the sections that follow.

4.2.4.2 Control Boards

In the related literature on this subject, every author has his own concept and definition of Control Boards. For this purpose, only the "official" definitions are presented. By official definitions, we understand those offered by the ISO and the IEEE.

ISO

Configuration Board: A group of technical and administrative experts with the assigned authority and responsibility to make decisions on the configuration and its management. This group is frequently known as the Configuration Control Board.

IEEE

Configuration Control Board: A group of people responsible for evaluating and approving or disapproving proposed changes to the configuration items, and for ensuring implementation of approved changes.

Change Control Board: It is used as synonym for the previous definition.

In this respect, it should be noted that in most Software Engineering literature, all the authors accept that both concepts are synonyms. It is worth pointing out that the first has a more extensive scope than the second due to the fact that it encompasses the process carried out to determine the composition of a specific version of a data processing system. This would include:

- Modules in the different hierarchical levels
- Version number of same
- Source situation
- Construction method of system from the modules
- Differences with its predecessors (what? and how?)
- Tools used
- Etc.

The IEEE definition presupposes the existence of specific elements, already defined, and that the control established refers to any modification of it. In these sections the Control Board (CB) definition, embracing both concepts, will be used.

During the life of these control boards, *formal aspects* can be considered as those that specify the functions, objectives and composition of same, the private functions of each of their components, and the *functional aspects* are those that specify the way and form in which such control board work.

4.2.4.3 Formal Aspects

The formal aspects of the procedure would be carried out through the previously mentioned body, and are described as follows:

Definition

If we apply the previous definitions, the Board would have to be a body with delegated authority from all the Departments or Divisions involved in the execution, exploitation and maintenance of the software. They would receive, study, process and approve, if necessary, the changes received from the different Departments related to the system software product, before the Software Design and Development Department, the only one entrusted and responsible for its realisation, implements it.

The managers of the department involved should establish the CB levels of authority, within which, they would have full power over decisions.

Objective

Efficient implementation of all the required changes inside the system software should be assured according to the following criteria:

- Product quality improvement.
- Minimum impact in the production of products or packages.
- Minimum alteration in the functioning of the already operating products.
- Minimum cost.
- Maximum normalisation of the product.

These criteria should not have pre-established weight, since in each case, depending on the policies of the organisation, they would have one priority or another, depending on the appraisal of the CB.

Functions

Besides the basic functions, included in the definition, the following could be added:

- Make and send the comments considered opportune, once the changes have been analysed, as well as following them up to their definitive completion.
- Interact with the previously mentioned appropriate departmental levels or with any other department, either in the same or in the client's organisation which might be directly or indirectly involved to recommend actions, reach decisions in cases beyond their competence or for consultations
- Establish the necessary contacts with other Change Board (hardware changes and support software) to co-ordinate actions or procedures.

- Consider and define the application and treatment of changes related with other Change Boards, both internal and external, as well as those that affect the systems that are in the exploitation or great production phase.
- Bear in mind that, as the change management does not only affect specific parts of the life cycle but its totality, everything related to the continuity of the *design revisions* and/or *audits* (results, pending action points, requirement modifications, technical specifications, etc.), which can affect the system to be developed or under development, should be considered included in the functions of the CB. The CB is the only forum in which all those questions will be dealt with and will becoming part of their documentation and processing.

The CB decisions shall be unanimous. Should there be any further comments, whether for clarification or consultation, this should be recorded in the corresponding minutes.

All members will have a vote of equal value, except for the President who could have will have the qualifying vote, and the Secretary or Administrator who, due their functions, have no vote.

Composition

The CB should be composed of members appointed by the different areas involved. They should appoint a president (obligatory), a vice president (optional) and a secretary or administrator (obligatory), from among themselves.

To prevent inequality/discrimination, all the members should have the sufficient level of authority and knowledge with regards to the area they represent, be able to take as many operating and technical decisions as required for the execution of their assignment during the Board meetings.

All the areas involved throughout the life cycle of the system should be represented. These main areas could be:

- Quality.
- Software Factory.
- Engineering.
- Marketing.
- P/D.

Any area could be able to be represented by more than one member, should it be considered necessary for the good and smoothing functioning of the CB.

Other areas not mentioned, could be consulted, called or informed provided that they were involved in any matter to be dealt with or in any decision to be taken. It could be possible to extend the representation at any time to another/other area/s, understood to be included in the "P/D" definition, different from those described. The same consideration would be given to appointing new members or substituting current ones.

As changes are dealt with and approved in the board meetings, attendance should be compulsory. Consistent absence of any member would be his direct responsibility and indirectly, that of the person in charge of his area. Given the frequency, with which meetings may be held for a particular issue, it could be suggested that if a member was unable to attend, he should send a delegate to represent him, fully and totally, with all the implications inherent.

In general, all members should have identical functions and assignments, except the president, vice president and secretary who, because of their positions, will have some extra functions as described below.

Member General Functions

These functions could be:

- Attending CB meetings or, in his absence, appointing a suitable substitute.
- Supervising and ensuring that all decisions taken and action points assigned by the CB are being carried out as agreed, in his area.
- Preparing and delivering, mainly in writing, all the information or appraisal required by the CB according to the action points assigned or on matters to be dealt with.
- Presenting the changes (when necessary) in his area or department. He will also have to give any explanation requested by any other member of the CC to clarify any doubts regarding the change suggested, including requesting assistance, if necessary, from anyone in his area.
- Supervising all the changes and notes in his area to ensure compliance with the required norms and procedures set out in the organisation's "Design Procedures Manual."
- Studying and revising the content of all the changes in order to verify that the impacts mentioned correspond with the functionality modified or to be introduced, or with the anomaly that it intends to correct, as well as to detect those impacts that the said change may have in his area and make them explicit, either before or during the CB meeting.
- Taking note of the action points assigned and initiating their execution, independently of when the minutes in which they appear, is received.

Specific Functions of the President

Besides those of a general nature mentioned in the previous section, the president could have the following functions:

- Overseeing the smooth running of all the meetings.
- Ensuring that all the areas are adequately represented in each meeting.
- Acting as moderator in any discussion that may arise and assigning, accordingly, the corresponding action points.
- Obtaining the adequate technical assistance.
- Deciding whether to hold or postpone a meeting for reasons which could affect the running of the CB.

- Taking the proposals to a higher level in the areas concerned in order to reach a unanimous decision, in cases of disagreement where the qualifying vote should not be applied.
- Co-ordinating the actions of the members, in order to prevent job duplication and gaps between actions in the different areas.
- Informing the CB of any possible external or internal data that could affect any decision to be taken by its members

Specific Functions of the Vice President

Given that this post is optional, his only function as such, could be to:

- Substitute for the President in cases of absence or need and assuming his functions.

Specific Functions of the Secretary

Since he is the basic "nucleus" of the Board, his functions would consist of:

- Assuring CB meetings are held on the agreed date, place and time, and that the meetings had been recorded in the minutes of the previous meeting and will be noted in the respective summons.
- Publishing and distributing in advance the changes for study and analysis by the Board members, ensuring that the design norms in force are complied with.
- Calling any extraordinary meeting that for any serious reason, the relevant areas consider opportune, as well as calling the Emergency Board or Mini-Board to present and discuss changes that, because of the urgency, cannot be wait until a subsequent ordinary meeting of the CB.
- Preparing and distributing the minutes of each meeting well in advance so that every CB member receives it before the date of the following meeting.
- Receiving, co-ordinating and distributing all the information on changes in associated organisations.
- Facilitating reports to all areas on the general situation and state of all existing changes, they be approved or not, they be from associates or one's own.
- Being responsible for everything related to the functional aspects of this norm.

4.2.4.4   Functional Aspects of the Procedure

The functional aspects would include the activities to be carried out by the Board, such as:

- Change Control.
- Change Edition.
- Summons, agendas and minutes of the Committee meetings.
- Board Meetings.
- Presentation and approval of changes.

The term "activities" include not only the activities of all the components of the Board as a whole, but also those of some of their individual members.

Change Control

The control, processing and supervision of changes could normally be carried out through a series of inter-related libraries, to which areas involved could have free access (reading, writing, writing/reading as convenient). They could be:

- Free access to reading/writing containing the changes pending approval, in process of execution or approved but perhaps still be susceptible to modification.
- Free access to reading containing the latest approved version of the changes and used as a control for the delivery of elements.
- Free access to reading containing all the changes closed, rejected, withdrawn, etc.

In addition, there could be a fourth library for the use of and of exclusive access of the secretary or administrator and under his entire responsibility. This fourth library may contain the changes that are in the editing phase or those pending approval that may undergo modification, and those that have no reference in any of the other libraries.

Periodically (weeks, days, hours, etc.) a check would be made on the library which offers free access to reading/writing to detect the modifications or alterations. This would be to verify the elements affected and whether the norms established in the corresponding procedure manual, which should contain a chapter dedicated to the CB, were followed. The possibility of anomalies in compliance with the norms and the actions to be carried out, depending on the type of anomaly and its reiteration should be predicted.

Editing Changes

Periodically, or depending on the number of existing changes, changes, either new or modification of some already existing ones, would be edited and distributed.

Previously, in agreement with specifications in the existing Method, the following tasks could be carried out:

- Notify, publicly and sufficiently in advance, that the change is officially in the editing process and that any variation to same should be discussed directly with the office of the secretary of the CB.
- Review:
  - In the case of a new change: all the formalities of same (number, date, author/authors, title, context of application, requirements, functional description, etc.). Likewise, verify that:
  - to every impacted element corresponds an element to deliver (patch or new code and/or variant and/or version of the element).

- in the specific files expressly created for this purpose, every related element is specified according to the official names they are registered under.
- all the main impacted elements are accompanied by all their related elements.
- if the element is impacted by a patch, such a solution, the main impacted element and the reference to the identity of the patch, should be explicitly specified as soon as possible,
- if a change has already been published, in addition to all of the previous verification, the formality of all those parts that are only susceptible to modification according to specification in the design norms, and that no alterations were made on fixed parts of same, would be checked out. Similarly, verifications would be made to ensure that the identifier of the corresponding modification, as well as the justification of this new modification accompanies any modification, large or small.
- Send a copy of the changes to all the members of the CB and persons nominated, for study and revision. The revision of the functional aspect and its impacts is personal and exclusive of any area and person that receive the information. They cannot allege ignorance or subsequent lack of knowledge for any undetected impact.
- Update the historic log with the relative annotations of the change request, as well as the previous version of it, once the changes are distributed. Likewise, they would become part of the matters to be discussed at the following CB meeting.
- Revise periodically, the libraries of the official element delivery to detect inconsistencies, false deliveries, deviations, anonymous delivery that are not protected by a change to be able, therefore, to stabilise the product.

Summons, Agendas and Acts of the Meetings

The CB to should meet by means of express SUMMONS, normally in writing, with sufficient advance notice so that each one of its members or guests could prepare the matters to be discussed. In exceptional cases, this summons could be: verbal, without any time interval, urgent cases between summons and meeting. The place, day and time of meeting, as well as the agenda, should be clearly specified.

This AGENDA should be prepared by the secretary of the CB and submitted to the president for approval before posting and distributing it.

The agenda should contain, by product, the following sections:

- Pending action point revision from previous meeting/s.
- Revision of changes pending approval, mentioned in the previous action points (time permitting) or up-dated with the functionality impacts, strategy or elements (specification of each one of them).
- Presentation of new changes (specification of each one of them).

- Other matters related to the system or product (mention to changes approved or in state of execution, situation of the system, etc.).

Therefore, there would be as many sections as systems or products, with specific mention in each section of the said system or product, to be discussed. Likewise, there could be a final section, dedicated to "any other business" that covers general aspects of the operation of the CB, requests and questions, etc.

The MINUTES would be the official document that compiles and reflects the development and result of the meeting. It would have a similar structure to that of the agenda, and would be composed of various sections:

- A section dedicated to the formal aspect of the meeting: the place, day, time of meeting, designation of members without making a distinction between whether they are members or not of the CB, or whether their attendance was partial or not.
- Another section repeating the agenda but including the specific matters, not contemplated in the summons, introduced during the course of the meeting. This should be made evident in the minutes.
- As many sections as products discussed as stated in the agenda. If necessary, the following should be made explicit:
- The fulfilment or not of the action points and forms of their fulfilment accompanied by the necessary support documentation in each case, and also, if they result in new action points.
- The state and situation of each change and if specific action points have been assigned, adding, when necessary, clarifying information on the subject.
- A section, dedicated to various matters in which each of the subjects discussed, and the action points assignment, if any, are clearly explained in sub-sections.

The assigned action points should reflect the action to be taken person/s or area/s responsible and the date of their completion. If no date is stated, it is assumed that the completion date is the as that of the next meeting. When a point of action has been completed before the date anticipated, it should be explicitly communicated on completion instead of waiting until the next meeting.

Meetings of the Change Board (CB)

To give stability to the CB meetings it would be convenient to fix its periodicity, date and venue, as well as determine attendance.

- PERIODICITY: Under normal circumstances, the meetings would have a fixed and determined periodicity, with the possibility of changing to another periodicity when circumstances demand it. In case of unexpected events, festivities, etc. it will go over to the following day or week.
- DATE: Within the periodicity, a day of the week and a fixed time will be indicated. This should not be an impediment to holding it, due to circumstances, on any day and time.

- VENUE: It would be convenient to have an adequate and permanent venue. This does not mean that, due to unforeseen circumstances, it cannot be held at another venue.
- ATTENDANCE: Attendance should be compulsory for all CB members. They could, on occasions, nominate a representative of recognised authority and prestige in their area who could give their opinion, take decisions, point out difficulties, list the problems that a particular solution presents, etc.

Optionally, and as support to the CB, other persons of the same or different areas would attend it for consultations or to provide information, etc.

Presentation and Approval of Changes
Two types of changes could be presented for approval: normal and extraordinary:

- Normal: these would take place during the CB meeting. The changes would be approved or rejected, after all the areas involved study, analyse and consider the impact, the opportunity for its introduction, the time and place for its implementation, as well as the form of its introduction. The above-mentioned evaluation should be reflected in the minutes, as well as in the corresponding sections of the change. Likewise, the comments or limitations that affect the introduction of same, should be reflected, as much in the minutes as in the change. In identical circumstances, it should be noted whether the change is withdrawn, cancelled, rejected, pending, etc.
- Extraordinary: these would take place when an urgent need necessitate them and a CB meeting cannot be called at short notice. Options such as: calling an extraordinary meeting with only the parties involved and identical to that of the normal process; or a personal consultation with the secretary of the CB, after agreement with the president, and with all those involved. Once the consensus is obtained and the impact is recognised and assumed, the change would be approved, clearly marked with the phrase, "APPROVED OUT OF COMMITTEE" and stating the occasion, the circumstances that obliged it and the name of the persons consulted. Likewise, in the corresponding index of changes, a note could be made relating to the change approved. If there was no consensus for its approval, for whatever reason, it should be presented at the earliest CB, be it normal or extraordinary.

Figure 4.18 reflects the processing flow of the change requests for approval or refusal.

In accordance with section 3, regarding Functions of the Board, the requirements could have the same treatment as the changes.

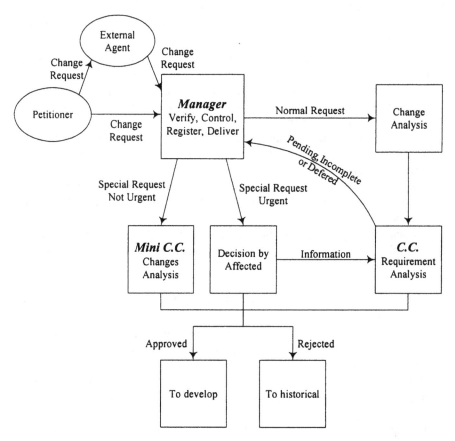

Fig. 4.18 Change requests for approval or refusal

4.2.4.5 Implementation

Independent of the size of the organisation, and of the size and complexity of the systems or products to be controlled, the keys to the success of a good configuration management should be kept in mind in order to implement the control board:

- The commitment of the entire organisation to applying the theory and practice of configuration management.
- The availability of a defined and concrete plan.

Similarly, the same factors of success that require a good configuration management would be applied and required of the committee, in the execution of their assignments:

- Pro-activity: not so much as a solution to problems but anticipating on top of them.
- Flexibility: sensitivity in the working environment, keeping in mind that different data processing systems (projects) have different requirements and, therefore, different needs and processing.
- Integration: not to be an administrative overload, considering what designers have to face daily in their job, but an aid that notifies and helps them when there are problems.
- Visibility: to leave visible tracks of all the work done, since most problems are originate from the ignorance and lack of knowledge of the designers and not their bad faith.
- Automation: use of tools in the execution of their job, always taking into account that are tools never the panacea and that systems do not have to adapt to tools.

These control boards should act according to some principles that regulate their activities and that can be summarised as:

- Principle of Authority: to have sufficient capacity to evaluate and to direct the implementation of a product change, or constituent part of the same, within one's sphere of activity.
- Principle of Sole Responsibility: existence of only one person who assumes or has been assigned the responsibility for taking decisions, supported by the other members.
- Principle of Specialisation: limited only to a predetermined area of the development of the product.
- Principle of Sensibility: the capacity to admit, manage and inform about the requests received

As has been previously mentioned, the implementation of a "practice" of this type will be affected by the size and complexity of the product and by the person who is going to assume each one of the main "roles": president, vice president and secretary or administrator. If the product is large and a considerable number of persons intervene in its execution, and specific persons can dedicate themselves to carrying out this type of control, above all for the functions of secretary or administrator which require great dedication, then there should be no problems in its implementation. The problem exists when the systems or products are small, and they are carried out and developed by a small number of persons, since this type of implementation, bureaucratic in appearance, could stifle its execution.

The previous development does not mean that all the administrative load that an implementation of this type implies, be assumed by the small projects, since it is thought for large organisations or for very large projects. What it does intend to do is to draw attention to the fact that there has to be a control of all the changes carried out. In the cases of small systems or products, with small number of persons involved in its development, the project leader can assume the "role" of the president of the committee and, if there are various projects, the role of the secretary or administrator can be common to all.

In conclusion, the use of tools should never substitute or push aside all the problems that the uses of the control board for management and control entail. The tools could and should help them, but not bring about their elimination, since they are necessary to analyse carefully what parts of the control boards' job could be automated without confusing the automation of Configuration Management with the substitution of their Control Boards.

4.2.4.6   Bibliography

[Ayer92]
   S.J. Ayer, F.S. Patrinostro, *Software Configuration Management: Identification, Accounting, Control, and Management*, McGraw-Hill, 1992
[Berlack92]
   H.R. Berlack, *Software Configuration Management*, John Wiley & Sons, 1992
[Bersoff80]
   E.H. Bersoff, V. Henderson, S. Siegel, *Software Configuration Management: A Tutorial*, IEEE Computer Society Press, 1980
[Bersoff84]
   E.H. Bersoff, *Elements of Software Configuration Management*, IEEE Transactions on Software Engineering, Vol. SE-10, No. 1, pp. 79-87, January, 1984
[Bersoff91]
   E.H. Bersoff, A.M. Davis, *Impacts of Life Cycle Models on Software Configuration Management*, Communications of the ACM, Vol. 34, No. 8, pp. 104-117, August, 1991
[Harvey86]
   K.E. Harvey, *Summary of the SEI Workshop on Software Configuration Management*, Technical Report CMU/SEI-86-TR-5, Software Engineering Institute, Carnegie Mellon University, Pittsburgh, December, 1986
[Whitgift91]
   D. Whitgift, *Methods and Tools for Software Configuration Management*, John Wiley & Sons, 1991
[Ben-Menachem94]
   M. Ben-Menachem, *Software Configuration Management Guidebook*, McGraw-Hill Book Company, 1994
[Bryan80]
   Bryan, W., Chadbourne, C., Siegel, S., *Software Configuration Management*, IEEE Computer Society Press, 1980.

[Dart92]
S. A. Dart, *The Past, Present and Future of Configuration Management*, Proceedings of the IFIP World Congress, Madrid, Spain, September 1992.

[Krane89]
Krane, Steven P., *Modeling the Configuration Management process*, University of Colorado, Boulder, Dept. of Computer Science, 1989.

[SEIBridge90]
SEI Bridge, *Configuration Management: State of the Art*, Software Engineering Institute, Carnegie-Mellon University, March 1990.

[Wingerd98]
Wingerd, L., Seiwald, C. *High-level best practices in software configuration management System Configuration Management*. ECOOP'98 SCM-8 Symposium. Proceedings. Springer-Verlag, Berlin, Germany; 1998

[Rahikkala98]
Rahikkala, T., Taramaa, J., Valimaki, A., *Industrial experiences from SCM current state analysis*. System Configuration Management. ECOOP'98 SCM-8 Symposium. Proceedings. Springer-Verlag, Berlin, Germany; 1998

5 Resources for Practitioners

G. Cuevas
SOCINTEC, Bilbao

5.1 Methods and Tools

Selecting a particular method or tool to solve the problems associated with the configuration management aspects of software development and maintenance can be a very complex problem in an of itself. The final decision to choose a particular tool is going to depend on the budget available as well as the tool's capabilities. To assist with these problems, several different methods and tools are presented in the following sections. In the case of tools, we distinguish between commercial tools and public domain tools.

5.1.1 Commercial CM Systems

The capabilities provided by these tools will be examined from three perspectives: configuration management as a complete process, software version control and problem tracking control. The product description information included in the following sections has been derived from marketing and commercial literature.

5.1.1.1 *Process-Based Configuration Management*

True Software

TRUExchange is the only product to fully implement Change-Sets across its complete functional scope.

Change-Sets group all related modifications across multiple files in a single, self-contained, reusable object: SCM personnel add or remove specific fixes, enhancements and features (Change-Sets) to software releases and variants in the natural context in which they plan and implement them.

Using Change-Sets, you will apply, move, merge and undo all changes in a given feature or enhancement in a single pass.

You will be able to support realistic life cycles, designed by you to optimise concurrence of effort and instant availability of the correct features and enhancements.

TRUEchanges encapsulates all changes made to any number of entities for a given purpose. It gives more choices, and better opportunity.

Table 5.1 Automatic Tools for CM

Vendor	Tool	URL
McCabe & Associates	TRUEchange	http://www.mccabe.com/products/truechange.htm
Intasoft	Allchange	http://www.intasoft.co.uk/default.asp
Computer Associates	CA-Endevor Unix	http://www.cai.com/products/endevor_unix.htm
Platinum (recently adquired by C.A.)	CCC/Harvest	http://ca.com/products/ccc_harvest.htm
Rational	ClearCase with ClearGuide	http://www.rational.com/products/clearcase/index.jtmpl
ExpertWare	CMVision	http://www.cmvision.com/
Continuus	Continuus/Cm and WebSynergy	http://www.continuus.com/
SERENA	EChange Man	http://www.serena.com/html/echange.htm
Merant	PVCS	http://www.merant.com/pvcs/index.asp
Tower Concepts	Razor	

Intasoft

AllChange provides a Configuration Management system. Provides an active supportive environment for your development, but does not impose throttling constraints or unacceptable bottlenecks.

AllChange provides information about the make-up of your product or project and actively helps project managers and developers by:

- Ensuring that your procedures are carried out according to your specification.
- Tracking the progress of change.
- Securing components of a product against unauthorised access.
- Allowing your developers to work together but without getting in each others way.
- Making information available to those people that require it.

AllChange ensures that you remain in complete control of your own processes. Taking this a step further, we made a positive decision to allow you to specify the levels of control that suit your specific needs. We recognise that different projects will require different levels of control.

AllChange has at its heart a database holding information about all the configuration items that you want to manage.

Computer Associates

Endevor for UNIX is a powerful software configuration management (SCM) system developed specifically for distributed UNIX development projects.

Endevor for UNIX visually tracks, manages, and automates the workflow of software development projects, supporting the needs of both managers and developers. Endevor for UNIX fits seamlessly and transparently into your organisation.

Endevor Workstation automates the entire software development process, tracks and manages changes, categorizes software assets and ensures application integrity. Endevor Workstation is part of an enterprise-wide SCM solution, providing high flexibility and capability.

Platinum

CCC/Harvest is a repository-based change and configuration management solution that synchronises development activities across heterogeneous platforms during the entire application development lifecycle.

CCC/Harvest allows users to create a repeatable process through which they manage application development. CCC/Harvest scales up to serve project teams working on your largest enterprise systems and scales down to meet the needs of your smallest groups.

CCC/Harvest provides functionality to help you more easily manage your day-to-day configuration management (CM) activities.

The most significant new feature available is the new user interface, the Harvest Explorer. Based on the Microsoft Windows Explorer, the Harvest Explorer provides users with a more intuitive way of executing day-to-day CM tasks.

CC/Harvest support for multi-site concurrent development

Rational

The ClearCase Product Family ClearCase, configuration management, is part of an integrated change management solution from Rational that supports both Windows and Unix platforms.

The product family ClearCase, ClearCase MultiSite, and ClearQuest – provides a comprehensive solution for configuration management ClearCase), distributed development (ClearCase MultiSite), and defect tracking (ClearQuest).

ClearCase provides a comprehensive configuration management solution, including version control, workspace management, build management, and process control. ClearCase offers a transparent, non-intrusive approach, and supports multiple platforms and IDEs, making it easy to deploy and maintain, without forcing you to change your existing environment, your tools, or the way you work.

Enables parallel development – even across geographically distributed sites.

ClearGuide offers a highly collaborative approach to software process management. Providing a flexible framework for defining tasks, prioritising activities, allocating resources and tracking project progress, ClearGuide particularly suits the needs of organisations implementing ISO 9000 or higher levels of the Capability Maturity Model.

ExpertWare

CMVision is a robust software product consisting of an integrated family of modules that automates the many different functions of system configuration management, change management, and problem tracking, including software, hardware, and documentation.

CMVision supports all phases of the system life cycle and provides process automation and tracking for all these phases.

CMVision uses graphical techniques to provide a functionally rich core of capability and has been designed for ease of installation. It requires little knowledge of the underlying Operating System to use or administer.

CMVision provides powerful and easy to use interfaces designed to help the user apply the tool to the diverse situations that may be encountered.

Continuus

Continuus/CM is a workflow centre approach to configuration management.

Continuus/CM is the configuration manager component of an easy comprehensive change-management system for Windows and UNIX software development, the Continuus Change Management Suite. With its team oriented, workflow approach to configuration management, Continuus/CM is a "smart CM" tool for software development.

Continuus/CM delivers a truly comprehensive set of change management capabilities. In addition to tracking critical history and status information for all project components and activities, Continuus/CM co-ordinates and communicates the software development activities of all team members with groupware efficiency.

Continuus/CM offers all the necessary components for: Version Control, Component/Object Management, distributed and Remote Development, Parallel Development, Build Management, and Work Area Management

Intelligent conflict detection identifies inconsistencies caused by incomplete or

Continuus/ CM provides a complete software change management solution to automate tracking an communication of logical changes across development teams. The task-based capability of Continuus/CM simplifies the change management process through an evolutionary integration between configuration management and change management, resulting in lower overhead and, consequently, higher development productivity.

With Continuus/CM developers need not be connected to the repository in order to work. Continuus/CM's reconcile operation updates the central code repository with changes from the remote work area when remote developers reconnect to the repository.

Continuus/CM supports real-time transfer through nightly scheduled operations allowing source changes and other information to be shared on demand.

Continuus/CM manages all types of parallel development: Concurrent development – making changes to different versions of the same objects at the same time variant releases – creating different variations of the same release, Parallel releases – preparing two different releases of the same product simultaneously.

Within the Continuus/CM environment each developer creates software in an insulated work area, updating with outside changes at their discretion. Developers work on checked-out versions of objects to prototype, edit, build and debug before making their changes available to other developers. Locating and resolving problems is easy because each developer has control over changes to his work area.

Continuus' graphical user interface (GUI), puts all the tools a development team needs at their fingertips. Checking code in and out, making code changes, and getting on-line help are as easy as pointing and clicking, with version history and project structure visible at a glance. Additionally all commands and capabilities are available from the command line.

Continuus/WebSynergy™, the latest addition to the Continuus enterprise change management suite, supports the collaborative development, management, approval, and deployment of all types of web content and software. Continuus/WebSynergy solves the two most critical problems facing organisations struggling to build and control ambitious web applications. These problems are:

- Co-ordinating diverse and distributed development teams working at web speed.
- Ensuring the quality and accuracy of web-based information, in the midst of escalating growth, increasing complexity and accelerating change.

Continuus/WebSynergy empowers all members of the web development team to build, maintain, and deploy web changes. By providing a browser-based client for content developers, WebSynergy supports the collaboration, management and deployment of all web content seamlessly and efficiently.

Continuus/WebSynergy ensures the highest quality, timely web content by eliminating bottlenecks. WebSynergy provides task-based change management for the webmaster so the latest set(s) of approved changes can be deployed to any web server, and individual tasks may be added or removed from a web server in a single operation.

Continuus/WebSynergy provides webmasters with a powerful, flexible, task-based workflow for making changes from assignment to deployment. Webmasters can set up different testing and approval workflow for departments. They can also add or remove any or all of the changes associated with a task in a single operation. They can also update multiple live web servers with only the newly approved changes and reproduce any previous configuration with guaranteed accuracy.

Serena

Echange Man manages your software's lifecycle in a distributed heterogeneous environment. It helps you to: Control software development and maintenance activities, reduce bugs, meet budgets and deadlines, pass the audits, increase the productivity of software developers.

Echange Man provides an integrated solution addressing such issues as: software Inventory / Impact Analysis, automatically analyses your software located on distributed hosts.

Maintains an inventory repository describing objects and their components. Supports most programming languages and formats. Instantly identifies objects that may be affected by a proposed change.

- Eliminates conflicting software changes by multiple developers.
- Supports distributed development activities across multiple platforms.
- Provides sophisticated parallel development (branching, merging) functionality.
- Provides graphical Process Flow configuration.
- Facilitates implementation of flexible SCM design.
- Ensures that all file transfers are authorised by the management and security personnel.
- Maintains comprehensive audit trail information for the distribution activities.

Automatically saves old versions of changed files and executables. Identifies the difference between multiple releases. Reinstates old releases, should the new versions become inoperable. Uses the reverse delta technology to minimise the disk space requirements.

Merant
PVCS provides the people, process and products that help your teams deliver quality software faster. PVCS integrates the three disciplines of Software Configuration Management (SCM): Version and Build Management, Issue Management, and Process Management, to make your entire development operation more competitive.

PVCS easily scales from the project team to the enterprise and supports the widest range of platforms and development environment.

Tower Concepts
Razor, an integrated tool suite which offers both configuration management and problem tracking, and at a very aggressive price.

The issues program could be considered the heart of the Razor package. It's a highly configurable problem tracking system; locally defined problem forms can use text fields, radio buttons, check boxes, choices etc, for whatever information is important to your work.

Through the versions program, Razor provides an intuitive and insightful window interface to all of the standard version control needs; checking files in/out for edit, parallel development, reporting changes, viewing differences, browsing, etc.

Your final product is actually the culmination and integration of innumerable changes spread across a wide number of files. The threads program provides an easy mechanism for managing all of this. With this tool, users and teams easily manage the releases they're generating.

Through a simple GUI/mouse manoeuvre, users are able to easily relate their check-in, check-out, and thread activities directly to problem reports in provides the greatest power of the package. Both managers and engineers have direct insight into not only the changes that are being made but also the issues which drive them.

5.1.1.2 Configuration Management and Version Control

Table 5.2 Automatic Tool Information for Version Control

Vendor	Tool	
Aldon	Aldon/CMS	http://www.aldon.com/cms_overview.html
Industrial Strength Software	Change Master	http://www.industrial-strength.com/
ThompsonAutoma-tionSoftware	Corporate RCS	http://www.tasoft.com/
Lockheed Martin	EagleSpeed	
JavaSoft	JavaSafe	http://www.javasoft.com/marketing/collater al/java_safe_ds.html
Lucent Technologies	Sablime	http://www.bell-labs.com/ project/sablime/index.html
Microsoft	SourceSafe	http://msdn.microsoft.com/ssafe/
SoftLanding Systems	TurnOver	http://www.softlanding.com/sourcecode.ht ml
Softlab	Visual Enabler	http://www.softlabna.com/Products/VE/ve. htm
Sun	WorkShop TeamWare	http://www.sun.com/forte/teamware/

Aldon

Aldon/CMS is an AS/400 software change management system designed to bring control, automation, tools and information to the software maintenance and development process.

You decide: What testing must be performed and what standards must be met, what documentation must be done, who is authorised to perform which object movement functions and any other rules you want applied to the move to production process.

Once you identify the process you want code to follow on its way from concept to production, Aldon/CMS will automate and enforce that process and ensure all of your standards are met. Improve Productivity. It is time to free programmers from the repetitive, clerical tasks like change documentation, data file conversions, object copying and creation, etc., so they can focus on application development and innovation.

When you are ready to move an object or group of objects, Aldon/CMS knows: Where to find them and where to move them. You just specify the object selection criteria, how to create them and what authority assignments are necessary, what dependent or prerequisite objects also must be created or moved, what data conversions must be performed (and does them automatically), whether change documentation is required (and automatically creates the documentation) and who is authorised and accountable for the move.

Aldon/CMS will find the right copy of each object and do all of the work. Programmers, operators and managers are freed to perform more important and more interesting tasks – like creating new applications!

Industrial Strength Software

The configuration management tool ChangeMaster, is a good change management and version control solution for AS/400s. It contains an on-line history module in order to help the identification of past changes responsible across different AS/400 platforms. It does some automatic decisions and actions based on the code test results regarding information and data flow control.

It has a high degree of customisation in order to meet particular requirements. For this purpose, the APIs are documented to make easier the interfaces programming task. All the information and source code archived on its database, has been compressed.

Thompson Automation Software

Corporate RCS Multi-Platform Revision Control System.

Corporate RCS is the Solution when:

- Changes made by one author are lost when the file is accidentally over-written by another author who was modifying the file simultaneously.
- You need to recreate an older version of a product or document. Did you even remember to make a back-up? Which files are required? And where are they? Maybe on a tape back-up somewhere?
- You fix a bug in one version of your product, and surprise! Its back again in the next version through a simple over-sights.
- You find yourself maintaining two different versions of a product, for example, for different customers, or for different operating systems. Each new change has to be made in each version, and your workload grows exponentially.
- A customer demands to know which version of your product fixes a particular bug.
- You simply deleted a file by accident! RCS stores multiple revisions of a file in what is called an RCS Archive.

The RCS Archive contains:

- The file itself and all the revisions made to the file, stored in a very compact manner.
- An optional description of the file and each revision made to the file.
- The date, time, author, and state (or status) of each revision.
- The name of the person currently working on each version of the file.

RCS can store both versions (called "branches") and revisions in a single archive file. For example, you may have a file that has three different versions for customers A, B and C; or a program file with different versions for DOS, Windows and Windows 95. On top of that, each of these versions will have multiple revisions, representing bug fixes and new features you have added over time. RCS allows you to maintain all these versions and revisions in a single RCS archive.

Features of RCS are:

- Resolve Access Conflicts among Multiple Users.
- RCS allows multiple users to access files simultaneously. An option to enforce "strict" locking means that two users can not accidentally work on the same version of a file simultaneously.
- Merge Changes. A merge utility allows you to merge changes. For example, if you let two authors work on the same file simultaneously, you can merge both sets of changes back together into a single file. Any over-lapping areas of change are flagged for your inspection. You can also merge changes made in one branch version into another branch version.
- Maintain a Complete History of Revisions.
- Each revision includes the time, date, author and state (for example: experimental vs. release) of the revision, as well as a comment solicited from the author when the revision is checked-in. Now you can identify exactly when a bug was fixed, who fixed it, and what changes were made to effect the fix.

Lockheed Martin

What is EagleSpeedTM? Consider the environment of the world's most advanced submarine. To say that it is complex and demanding is an understatement. There is zero tolerance for system failure. These extreme conditions have given birth to a new paradigm in software development. Lockheed Martin is proud to be the developer of these advanced naval systems and the software that makes them possible. Now, this software technology is available commercially in an affordable package.

EagleSpeedTM can:

- Simplify management of multiple configurations.
- Easily incorporate real-time database management processes.
- Greatly reduce the risk of unplanned software changes.
- Allow you to gain early insight into proposed changes and impacts.
- Dramatically reduce learning curves.

Javasoft

JavaSafe provides a flexible source management and revision control system. It gives developers, working alone or in teams, control of their software development projects. JavaSafe software builds, maintains and safeguards directories or "repositories" that provide a centralised, secure environment for Web content, source code, or any other type of file that is associated with a project. The JavaSafe server manages the repositories and concurrency issues, while the JavaSafe client provides file versioning, file check-in and file checkout.

JavaSafe is designed to keep the members of a development project synchronised. That means JavaSafe not only manages your source code, binaries, and executables, but that it also handles all your Web-related code including binary files, JavaTM technology applets and associated source code, pictures, CGI and HTML code. You can even manage memos, notes, and documentation, so that all your valuable project-related knowledge is preserved for reuse.

Lucent Technologies

Sablime system provides comprehensive configuration management to track changes to software, firmware, hardware, and documentation from origination through maintenance, delivery, and support. Sablime provides tightly integrated version, configuration, and change management to enforce an effective and proven software development process.

The Sablime Product Administration System has a long proven record of effective use in over 400 projects within Lucent Technologies and AT&T, accounting for over 12,000 domestic and international users in a variety of businesses.

Microsoft

Visual SourceSafe enables users to work at file and project levels while also promoting file reuse. Its project oriented features increase the efficiency of managing day-to-day tasks associated with team-based software and Web content development.

Its major features are oriented to resolve conflicting file updates, differentiate among projects work spaces and an archive utility.

The differentiation of projects work spaces, helps keep team members in synchronisation by comparing local project work spaces with the current shared server project, and graphically illustrating the differences while providing easy resolution option.

The archive utility helps projects among separate Visual SourceSafe-based databases, or archive unneeded project history to a compressed file that can be reintroduced later.

SoftLanding Systems

Turnover helps you find the right source quickly TurnOver finds the right source for you, protects your changes from being overlaid, co-ordinates concurrent development, helps you perform emergency changes safely, keeps track of where each program lives and all its attributes, and gives you the information when you need it. It remembers all the details so you don't have to.

Turnover adjusts to your way of doing your job while keeping your work organised and the development tools you prefer readily available.

You customise to your working style. It shows you only the objects you need for a given task or subtask and tells you at a glance where each object is in the change cycle. It lets you move easily between projects as your workflow demands, all the while giving you direct access to your choice of development tools such as source editors and cross-referencing packages. Like a well-engineered machine, you'll appreciate how all of the pieces fit seamlessly together to make even complex tasks appear amazingly easy.

Turnover helps you keep mistakes from happening, and helps you recover if they do.

Softlab

Visual Enabler provides key new features that help streamline the development process and improve time to market.

Enterprises that develop applications for Windows platforms had limited choices for version control until now. Before Visual Enabler, Enterprise Windows development teams had a choice between low-end solutions that didn't quite meet their needs, and expensive high-end solutions that have too much of a Unix feel.

Visual Enabler fills this gap by delivering the feature set that allows a smooth migration path from the low-end version control solutions without the expense or hassle of the high-end solutions. It does this in the Project-oriented approach that most Enterprise Windows development teams have become accustomed to. Visual Enabler helps Enterprise Windows development teams with four important issues:

Build Management, concurrent development, parallel development, and team co-ordination.

Visual Enabler delivers this capability in an unprecedented easy to use version control solution with tight integration to the most popular integration development environments (IDEs).

Visual Enabler uses breakthrough object repository technology to create advances in Version Control that are difficult, if not impossible, to achieve with conventional technologies. Visual Enabler's repository uses Object Classes, Relationships, and Attributes to define the underlying Information Model that supports the feature set required of Enterprise Windows development teams.

Sun

WorkShop TeamWare provides a powerful multiplatform software configuration management toolset for development teams that enhances your team's co-ordination and lets you:

- Easily manage your team's software development activities.
- Increase your team's productivity immediately.

- Improve your product quality.
- Get your product to market faster.
- Easily distribute and grow your team.

Sun WorkShop TeamWare allows you to conveniently co-ordinate development across SolarisTM SPARCTM and Solaris Intel environments. Sun Work-Shop TeamWare is fully compatible with all Sun WorkShop language systems and development tools. It is included in Sun Visual WorkShopTM C++ and Sun Performance WorkShopTM Fortran packages, or can be purchased as a stand-alone product.

Sun WorkShop TeamWare provides your team with software configuration management, version control, change control, build management, integration, and release support that will improve your team's productivity and your product's quality. Sun WorkShop TeamWare is completely scalable and can be used effectively by teams that are centrally grouped or widely distributed. Your team members will like Sun WorkShop TeamWare because it fits seamlessly into their present development environment and is easy to use.

Sun WorkShop TeamWare enables your team to work effectively and concurrently on files, configurations, and releases. It significantly reduces elapsed time for software builds by enabling you to utilize the power of your entire network by distributing your build jobs. Sun WorkShop TeamWare does not require lengthy setup, time consuming education, or separate administration. The day you install Sun WorkShop TeamWare is the first day of improved productivity for your team.

Sun WorkShop TeamWare automates software development's most error-prone process – change integration. It keeps track of conflicting changes and automates the resolution of the changes to help you eliminate costly integration errors. With the complete history of all changes made to your software provided by Sun WorkShop TeamWare, you can more easily identify areas where your product quality can be improved.

5.1.1.3   Problem Tracking Systems

Table 5.3 Automatic Tool Information for Problem Tracking

Vendor	Tools	URL
MetaQuest Software	Census 2.0	
Rational	ClearDDTS	http://www.rational.com/products/clear_ddts/index.jsp
Rational	ClearQuest	http://www.rational.com/products/clearquest/index.jsp
Clarify	ClearQuality	http://www.nortelnetworks.com/products/04/cqual/index.html
Continuus	Continuus/PT	http://www.continuus.com/products/productsB.html
MERANT	PVCS	http://www.merant.com/pvcs/products/index.asp
Tower Concepts	Razor	

Most of these tools, with the exception of Census, are modules or subsystems of the previous identified tools. There main feature is the configuration and use of problem queues within an organise process. They also provide a number of report layouts out of the problems status tracked.

MetaQuest Software

Census is a sophisticated but easy-to-use Defect tracking System. An intuitive graphical interface gives you quick access to predefined queries, reports, and more. Tailoring Census to the way you work is easy with Census point-and-click editors.

Census capabilities can be adapted to any organisation's needs whether for defect tracking or for tracking other types of issues, such us requirements, notes, tasks, etc.

5.1.2   Public Domain or Free CM Systems

The following tools, available at no cost, cover many of the basic capabilities required for software version control and problem tracking.

5.1.2.1   Version Control

Table 5.4 Tool Information for Version Control

Aegis	http://www.canb.auug.org.au/~millerp/aegis/aegis.html
CSSC	http://mirror.ox.ac.uk/rpm2html/Development_Version_Control.html
CVS	http://www.loria.fr/~molli/cvs-index.html
ODE	http://www.accurev.com/i_prod.html
PRCS	http://www.XCF.Berkeley.EDU/~jmacd/prcs.html
RCS	http://www.cvshome.org/cyclic/cyclic-pages/rcs.html
SCCS	(free implementations) http://www.cvshome.org/cyclic/cyclic-pages/sccs.html
TCCS	http://www.oreilly.com/homepages/tccs/
TkCVS	http://www.cvshome.org/cyclic/tkcvs/

5.1.2.2   Problem Tracking Systems

Table 5.5 Tool Information for Problem Tracking Systems

The Bug Database	http://world.std.com/~rsh/robert2.html
GNATS, GNU Bug Tracking System	Web resources on GNATS: http://www.alumni.caltech.edu/~dank/gnats.html
California Institute Of Technology – CALTECH)	Mort Bay Consulting –Issue Tracker
JitterBug	http://samba.anu.edu.au/cgi-bin/jitterbug
Open Track Defect and Enhancement Tracking System	http://www.accurev.com/ot/

Problem Tracking System	Project Tracking System
	Requires an e-mail based request tracking system
	http://www.ccs.neu.edu/software/ccs/req/
RUST	http://www.cvshome.org/cyclic/cyclic-pages/rust.html
WISE	http://research.ivv.nasa.gov/projects/index.html

5.2   Books

[Pressman97]
   Roger S. Pressman, *Software Engineering: A practical Approach*, McGraw-Hill, 1997
[Paulk95]
   Mark C. Paulk; Charles B Weber; Bill Curtis and Mary Beth Chrissis, *The Capability Maturity Model: Guidelines for Improving the Software Process*, Addison Wesley, 1995
[Watts89]
   Watts S. Humphrey, *Managing the Software Process*, Addison Wesley, 1989
[Dymond95]
   Keneth M. Dymond ,*A guide to the CMM: Understanding the Capability Maturity Model*, Process Inc., 1995
[Mazza96]
   C. Mazza; J. Fairclough; B. Melton; D. De Pablo; Scheffer; R. Stevens;M. Jones and G. Alvisi, *Software Engineering Guide*, Prentice Hall, 1996
[Berlack92]
   H. R. Berlack , *Software Configuration Management*, John Wiley & Sons, 1992
[Whitgift91]
   D. Whitgift , *Methods and Tools for Software Configuration Management*, John Wiley & Sons, 1991
[Ben-Menachen94]
   M. Ben-Menachem , *Software Configuration Management Guidebook*, McGraw-Hill, 1994
[Compton94]
   S. Compton and G. Conner , *Configuration Management for Software*, Van Nostrand Reinhold, 1994
[Brown99]
   William J. Brown, Hays W. McCormick, Scott W. Thomas, *Antipatterns and Patterns in Software Configuration Management*, John Wiley & Sons, 1999
[Lyon99]
   David D. Lyon, *Practical CM: Best Configuration Management Practices for the 21st century*, Raven Publishing Company, 1999

[NRC Staff90]
National Research Council Staff, *Configuration Management and Performance Verification of Explosives-Detection Systems*, National Academy of Social Insurance, 1990

[ESA91]
European Space Agency, ESA, *Guide to Software Configuration Management*, Software Engineering Standards Issue, 1991

[IEEE90]
IEEE/ANSI Std. Computer Society Engineering Technical Committee , *Standard for Software Configuration management Plans,* Software Engineering Standards Subcommittee, 1990

[IEEE87]
IEEE/ANSI Std. Computer Society, Software Engineering Technical Committee, *Guide to Software Configuration Management*, Software Engineering Standards Subcommittee, 1987

[Ecoop98]
Proceedings (Lecture Notes in Computer Science), *System Configuration Management – Ecoop '98 SCM-8 Symposium Brussels*, Springer Verlag, 1998

5.3 Organisations

Table 5.6 List of Organisations

Name	URL
International Society of Configuration Management (ISCM)	
Association of Configuration Management and Data Management (ACDM)	http://www.acdm.org/
Configuration Management BCS Specialist Group	http://www.bcs.org.uk/siggroup/sg57.htm
Institute of Configuration Management (ICM)	http://www.icmhq.com/index.html
Software Engineering Institute (SEI) –Software Configuration Management (SCM) area	http://www.sei.cmu.edu/legacy/scm/
Software Productivity Center Resources: Configuration Management	http://www.spc.ca/

5.4   Important Conferences

Table 5.7 List of conference

Name	URL
ACM Symposium on Applied Computing USA International Symposium on System Configuration Management (SCM-9) France	http://www.cs.ucy.ac.cy/
Conference on Quality Engineering in Software Technology Germany	http://www.asqf.de/
The International Conference on Practical Software Quality Techniques. USA	mhanna@softdim.com
The Association for Configuration and Data Management Annual Conference: C out of the Box. Atlanta, Georgia. USA	http://www.acdm.org/meet.html
Annual CMII Conference. Canada	http://www.cmiiug.com/conferen.htm

5.5   Web Sites

In addition to sites listed previously when referring to a specific topic, the following web sites are related to configuration management.

Table 5.8 List of Related Webs

Name	URL
Comp. Software Config-Mgmt FAQ at IAC Honeywell Inc.	http://www.iac.honeywell.com/Pub/Tech/CM/index.html
The Configuration Management (CM) Resource Guide	http://www.quality.org/config/cm-guide.html
Configuration Management & Project Engineering	http://www.configuration.org/
A software Engineering Resource List for Software Configuration Management	http://seg.iit.nrc.ca/English/index.html
Configuration Management Tools	http://www.loria.fr/~molli/cm-index.html

6 Experience Reports

S. Rementeria
SOCINTEC, Bilbao

This chapter presents the experiences of eight companies that either implemented configuration and change management from scratch or improved their existing practices in these areas. Seven of them did so in the context of the European Systems and Software Initiative (ESSI) funded by the European Commission in the Calls of 1993, 1995 and 1996, whereas the remaining one corresponds to an internal, privately funded process improvement project. The list is not exhaustive, but it represents a sampling of similar actions taking place in software development organisations worldwide. It is hoped that this sample offers a glimpse of real configuration management implementation experiences and the associated potential benefits, as well as the risks and practical aspects to consider during the adoption process.

The case studies are listed in table 6.1. Each case begins with a short summary followed by some background information and a description of the work done, and concludes with a list of lessons learned during the implementation phase and a brief statement of intended future actions.[12]

Table 6.1 Reference information of the eight Configuration and Requirements Management adoption experiences

Sec-tion	ESSI Project N.	Acronym	Name	Organisation	Contact person	e-mail address
6.1	21244	MIDAS	"Applying GQM to Assess CM Practice for Better Interbank Services"	S.I.A., Società Interbancaria per l'Automazione S.p.A. (Italy)	Roberto Soro	so-ro@sia.it
6.2	21379	ICONMAN	"Introduction of a Configuration Man-agement in a Very	Event AS, TSC AS and Aktuar Systemer AS	Tor Vidvei	tor.vidvei@sn.no

---

[12] The following sections are based on information provided by the projects for publication.

Sec-tion	ESSI Project N.	Acronym	Name	Organisation	Contact person	e-mail address
			Small Organisa-tions"	(Norway)		
6.3	21568	CMEX	"Configuration Management Expe-riment"	Sysdeco GIS AS (Norway)	Leidulf Alnes	lal@gis. sysde-co.no
6.4	10564	AUTOMA	"Introduction of Configuration Ma-nagement"	S.p.A. (Italy)	Gianfranco Del Duca	Deldu-ca@data mat.it
6.5	21531	PITA	"Electronic Docu-ment System"	AMT.SYBEX (Ireland)	Katherine Voss	Sy-bex@iol .ie
6.6	21269	SOCCOMA	"Configuration and Change Manage-ment to Rising Quality of Service "	Istiservice S.p.A. (Italy)	Corrado Chierici	Msitbm 01.qzyb ws@eds .com
6.7	21547	MSI_QBP	"Build-up of a centralised software quality management function"	GEPIN Engi-neering S.p.A. (Italy)	Maurizio Esposito	Gepi-neng@ti n.it
6.8	N/A	MPS-SCM	"Enhanced Version Integrity with Soft-ware Configuration and Change Man-agement"	Iberdrola Siste-mas (Spain)	Isabel Blanco	Isa-bel.blan co@iber drola.es

6.1   Applying GQM to Assess CM Practice

Applying GQM to Assess CM Practice for Better Interbank Services

S.I.A. succeeded in the implementation of the MIDAS project aimed at improving the reliability and availability of services of the National Inter-bank Network of Italy, by establishing an effective Configuration Management (CM) process and defining a suitable measurement program based on the Goal-Question-Metric (GQM) technique. This led to a higher visibility and the ownership of the software maintenance process, supported by precise weekly anomaly reports.

Measuring and analysing collected data is hard work, yet one of the best ways not only to gain insight over complex products, but also to gather objective infor-mation to support the decision process.

6.1.1 Background

Società Interbancaria per l'Automazione S.p.A. (Interbank Company for Automation, S.I.A.) is a public utility providing data processing and telecommunication services to the entire Italian banking system. S.I.A. shareholders are the Bank of Italy (40%), ABI (Italian Bankers Association), STET (the Italian national Telecommunication holding) (5%) and about 200 Italian banks. S.I.A. products and services are classified in: Network services, Banking services and Financial Markets operation. It employs 280 people and the turnover for 1997 was 90 M ECU. and manages one of most important infrastructures of the Italian economy.

A big part of the interbank payment traffic, including cash withdrawal transactions through the Bancomat circuit, passes across the S.I.A. network.

In recent years, S.I.A. has experienced a variety of problems:

- The management of subcontractors was becoming more and more difficult as the dimension and criticality of the applications increases. It is difficult to estimate costs and track projects. Moreover, it is difficult to have full control of the source code developed by subcontractors.
- The interaction between S.I.A. customers and S.I.A. departments was difficult because there were basically different responsibilities and interaction points for the same customer. In particular, software development was separated from operation and, therefore, the evolution of an application was managed separately from its daily operation.

The banking and financial markets were demanding higher quality systems, especially as far as availability and reliability of the services were concerned.

6.1.2 Improving Service Quality Through New CM

To address the above issues S.I.A. carried out an assessment of the software process, according to the SEI's Capability Maturity Model (CMM).

Following the assessment results and recommendations, further to the reorganisation of the company in three divisions – Banking applications, Financial markets and Network infrastructure –, the management decided to start a project aimed at establishing an improved configuration management process supported by state-of-the-art tools. A goal-oriented measurement program based on the GQM approach was applied, in order to provide management's questions with objective answers.

The most visible impact, or tangible result, has been the introduction of a weekly report that allows the Board of Directors to monitor the behaviour of the NRO ("New OSI Network") product in production. The report, prepared with the information automatically retrieved by the CM tool, along with the historical series of anomalies is a valuable source of information for monitoring the service level to the ultimate user compared with the information retrieved from the Call Management system.

6.1.3   Work Performed

MIDAS project involved S.I.A.'s Network Division, which provides the Network services. It started in January 1996 and lasted 18 months.

6.1.3.1   Technical Environment

To support the S.I.A.'s software development process and to evaluate the benefits obtained by the introduction of CM practices into this process, two tools were used: CCC and the GQM Tool.

Developed by PLATINUM Technology Inc., CCC is a commercial tool that provides a unified framework to support all the core functions in the software development and maintenance process.

The GQM Tool, developed by CEFRIEL, provides support for a measurement program based on the Goal Question Metric (GQM) approach.

Through its easy to use Windows GUI the GQM Tool user can store the GQM goals, questions and metrics; each question can be related to the goals it allows to achieve and each metric can be related to the questions it allows to answer to.

Further to the internal database used by the GQM Tool, it is possible to use Microsoft Access to store and manage the data collected during the measuring process. This latter solution, allowing maximum flexibility, was adopted in the MIDAS project.

6.1.3.2   Baseline Project

The project selected as baseline was the NRO (New OSI Network). The NRO project was considered the most representative project for S.I.A. since it merges characteristics like:

- Complexity. It provides a full range of services for the management and operation of the S.I.A. network.
- Large sizes. The products are about 5 million LOC. There are several sub-teams working on NRO.
- Multi-platforms: range from MVS to UNIX.
- High level and number of customisations.
- Phases of the Experiment.
- Hereafter the main project activities are reported.

6.1.3.3   Phases of the Work

Measurement Program

A GQM plan was defined, and two goals were selected:

- Goal 1: Analyse the maintenance process for the purpose of characterising, with respect to effort and duration, from the points of view of the project managers and testers, in the environment NRO project.

- Goal 2: Analyse the maintenance process for the purpose of characterising with respect to the anomalies and rework, from the points of view of the project managers and testers, in the environment NRO project.

Data collection, for the evaluation of the initial situation, was outlined as part of the results of the CMM assessment performed before introducing CM.

Data, regarding the situation after the introduction of CM, were collected and stored with the support of the GQM tool. Most of this data is extracted from the CM system itself.

CM Policies and Tools
CCC, the CM Tool, was customised to implement the CM process and procedures defined for the MIDAS pilot project.

Pilot Project
The activity of support deployment has been carried out through interviews and meetings with S.I.A. managers and project people to gather information for:

- The GQM plan definition.
- The collection of data concerning the situation before CM.
- The CM process definition.
- The CM tool customisation.

S.I.A. prepared the data collection environment setting up the GQM tool and the database in order to store collected data and providing automatic procedures to extract data from the CM database. Furthermore S.I.A. was weekly gathering and maintaining data according to the metrics defined in the GQM plan.

6.1.4   Results and Analysis

6.1.4.1   Technical

The measurement plan was executed quite smoothly, and the resulting data was analysed and interpreted jointly by the data providers (i.e. the process agents) and the measurement team. A brief list of the conclusions from the first measurement session follows:

- The MIDAS project has been the first serious approach to measurement performed in the company, as far as the software production process is concerned.
- Maintaining software integrity in presence of plenty of changes during the entire software life cycle was a very complex task before the introduction of CM practice.

The first tangible result of introducing CM is the availability of the repository containing all the information related to the development and maintenance process.

This is very important since people can retrieve information and software configurations from a unique central location.

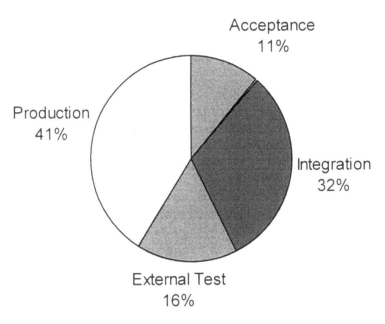

Fig. 6.1 Anomalies by detection phase over a one-year period

Data analysis provided valuable information concerning the quality and efficiency of the maintenance process in the NRO project.

6.1.4.2 Business

The most significant benefit, as stated by S.I.A.'s management is the fact that the company has now a real Measurement System and a centralised anomaly and change collection system.

Figures 6.1 and 6.2 show the distribution of anomalies versus Detection Phase considering the first period June 96 to June 97 and the second period from June 97, on the whole software products under development for the NRO project.

The data represent how the distribution of the anomalies has been modified after taking some managerial decisions between the first and the second period.

It can be clearly observed a clear reduction (from 41% to 18%) in the percentage of errors detected in the production phase, that is during the operation of the released products at the customer site.

Many other types of data are collected to measure other metrics; most of them automatically supplied by the Configuration Management tool itself, then retrieved from the database.

For instance great importance is given to the errors discovered at production time versus the mean time to correct the correspondent anomalies, (as reported weekly with a value for each anomaly and with an average value, indicating the duration in days) to closely monitoring the maintenance process.

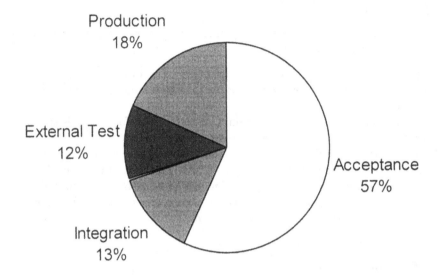

Fig. 6.2 Anomalies by detection phase over a 16-month period

Another valuable report is the time (days) and effort (man-days) spent on each phase of the process, available for each product and for each release.

Nonetheless a remark must be made in the sense that it is not possible to know the contribution of the MIDAS project to the improvements shown before, due to the fact that there isn't another similar project to compare with (i.e. to make the measurements "without MIDAS improvement").

In any case, the opinion of S.I.A.'s management is that the value of this PIE responds to the prime objective for the company: to have installed a Configuration Management environment and a Measurement system, as it is the case today.

6.1.5   Lessons Learned

Among the most interesting lessons learned in the running of the SPI project, the following can be outlined from a technical and business point of view.

6.1.5.1   Technical

Establishing a CM process is not a trivial process. Therefore it has to be accurately managed; in particular modelling the production process is very critical, especially for companies – like S.I.A. – that were at level 1 of CMM.

A considerable amount of time and effort must be dedicated to the selection and customisation of CM tools, because there is a great number of complex tools available and rarely the features provided perfectly fit the company needs.

6.1.5.2   Business

The experience gained in the MIDAS project suggest the following hints for a successful establishment of CM:

• Management support is constantly required in order to convince the reluctant ones, mainly when the people responsible for introducing CM are not in a leading position.
• Constant support after the initial training must be given for CM tools and practices, otherwise people could revert to the old way of working.
• Incremental deployment of the tool was a winning factor. In this way, only relatively small amounts of software at a time were moved into the CM environment, and only a few people at a time had to be assisted in their initial impact with the new procedures. Moreover, the experience gained from the first users was exploited as soon as it was available.

6.1.6   Future Actions

The main actions foreseen or already undertaken are:

• Deployment of the CM process in other departments of S.I.A. This action (which has already been prepared by the internal dissemination actions) will be organised in phases, corresponding to MIDAS results more or less readily reusable (for instance, porting issues related to the different platforms existing in S.I.A.).
• Enhancement of the measurement process. The measurement environment established for MIDAS will be retained and used to continually monitor the performance of the process, and the quality of the software products.
• Enhance CM. In the near future the CM process will be extended to a wider set of artefacts (in addition to those developed for the NRO project), including several types of documents, test case definitions and results, and much more.

It can be said that the Configuration Management has been used, at S.I.A., to generate a Cultural Revolution in the company.

6.2   Introduction of a Configuration Management

Introduction of a Configuration Management in Very Small Organisations

Through the introduction of configuration management three small Norwegian companies – Event AS, TSC AS and Aktuar Systemer AS – were able to increase customer confidence in their products, as well as decreasing the time taken to find and rectify errors.

Implementing configuration management is a very complex process. To succeed things need to be kept simple. Companies should be prepared for revisions.

6.2.1   Background

Event AS delivers systems for stochastic modelling and analysis based on a proprietary statistical method. The company presently has two employees.

TSC AS´s main product is a system simulating oil reservoirs. The company consists of 5 employees, all working as software developers.

Aktuar Systemer AS produces a family of systems for managing pension funds and their members. A large insurance corporation has recently purchased the company.

6.2.2   Response to Change Requests

Due to changing customer requirements, software developers, be they large or small, are finding themselves with multiple versions of their product in the market. To complicate matters further, these versions could also be running on different operating platforms. This makes it very difficult to ensure that problems that are reported are being fixed on the correct version and operating system. In order to alleviate this problem, software developers are realising the benefits of having a well developed and managed formalised procedure for tracking the diversity of their products.

Through this approach, even the most sophisticated software developer is able to improve their responsiveness to customer needs.

6.2.3   The Approach Taken

In this case study, Event, TSC and Aktuar Systemer, with the assistance of the Norwegian Computer Centre (NCC), addressed the problem of configuration management in very small organisations.

The approach taken was to make an initial assessment of each of the companies software practices and their customer relationships. The NCC performed this. The strategy for the rest of the project was developed based on the results of this assessment.

6.2.4 The Initial Scenario

At the start of the project, all three companies had a very rudimentary understanding of the principles behind configuration management (CM). However, none of the companies had CM embedded as part of their organisations operational culture. This caused much wasted time when customers reported errors with their systems, as it was difficult to track what version they were using and on what platform.

Event AS's software development is based on one fundamental software library. Before ICONMAN, this library was developed and maintained by one developer. The developers use this library as a resource to develop specific applications. Both developer and user documentation was rudimentary.

TSC AS realised the importance of CM and testing as quality assurance measures, and as an important part of their development process. However, they had no formal or documented routines for CM of their main product, FrontSim.

Aktuar Systemer AS had implemented a very rudimentary version control system. However, this meant that only the current and previous production version of their main product ABAKUS were kept readily at hand. Earlier versions had been reconstructed from these versions, which was slow and cumbersome.

6.2.5 Work Performed

The ICONMAN project was divided into three main phases.

Phase 1 lasted 6 months. This phase included:
- The development of CM procedures. These included the management of change requests, and the development of metrics to measure the outcome of the project.
- The selection and introduction of an appropriate tool. This also included the development of all the relevant procedures, and a configuration library.
- Phase 2 lasted 7 months. This phase consisted of:
- The training of developers in the operation of the CM tool.
- Refining the CM procedures based on feedback from the developers.
- Initiation of the process of collecting metrics data.

Phase 3 lasted 5 months. During this phase the collection of data was continued, and the project evaluated.

Due to the different technical platforms used by the three companies, two different CM packages were chosen. Event AS and Aktuar Systemer AS chose and adopted Visual Source Safe from Microsoft. TSC chose the low number of version control system SCCS that is included in the UNIX environment. To increase its user friendliness, shell software had to be utilised.

6.2.6   Results and Analysis

In order to measure the success of ICONMAN in the three companies, various metrics were designed. These show several significant areas of improvement, both in terms of reaction times to customer requests, and the availability of both procedural and product related documentation. Particular improvements are:

- Routines for CM have been established, implemented, and refined.
- Software support in the form of configuration item libraries, change request databases, and systems for logging effort data have been developed, and established in all companies.
- All companies have their own CM "Users Guide".
- Metrics have been developed to measure the impact of CM.
- All companies have noted that, due to the improved documentation of the CM procedures, developers daily tasks have been simplified and the time spent on correcting errors and generating production releases has been significantly reduced.
- Confidence in the quality of the final products produced by the three companies has also increased since the implementation of CM.

6.2.7   Lessons Learned

There were many lessons learned during this experiment. The main lessons were:

- The process of implementing CM routines is a very complex and time-consuming process. It is an iterative process that requires continuous refinement.
- CM routines need to be tested in a controlled, but real-life environment before implementing on a large scale in the whole organisation.
- The identification of appropriate data to quantify possible improvements in the software development process was difficult. Existing information should be used as a basis for defining metrics.
- An operative CM system has a concrete impact on customer relations. TSC has experienced positive feedback from customers inquiring about their CM routines.
- Document every stage of the process followed during implementation and ensure that clear procedural documents are produced. This will establish a practical way of operating the system within the company.
- Make sure that all personnel using the system are fully trained before using the system. This will ensure that once the system goes into operation, all personnel

are comfortable with it and know how to operate it. This will ease acceptance of the system.

6.2.8   Future Plans

EVENTS AS will be building on the results of ICONMAN through a new PIE project, "A Statistical Approach to Support Project Estimation and Management". The main objective of this project is to do statistical analysis of data from the change request database established in ICONMAN.

6.3   Implementing Configuration Management in Small Enterprises

Through the introduction of a common configuration management system within their development department, Sysdeco GIS A/S vastly decreased the number of errors in their software products prior to release, as well as reducing the time-to-market. The overall effect of this exercise was to raise the awareness of the true cost of correcting errors, as well as to reduce product development costs.

Implementing Configuration Management software is only part of the whole story. The mayor components of the whole exercise are to implement supporting CM procedures, to get CM accepted as an integral part of a company's culture, and to establish the correct measures.

6.3.1   Background

Sysdeco GIS A/S (SGIS) is a company developing mapping applications for the international market. The company has subsidiaries in Europe (England, Norway, Germany, Sweden, and Italy) and in Asia (Singapore and Malaysia). All together, there are approximately 150 employees world-wide. 40 of these are employed at the headquarters in Norway, 40 in the UK and 40 associated with the Singapore office.

Software producers, be they small or large, have realised that there is a need to be able to track customer and change requests. This need has arisen from the need for shorter product development cycles in order to meet the constantly changing needs of customers and to maintain competitiveness. Due to the complexity of the products offered by producers, and the number and variety of versions it is efficient tracking of versions and customers is an impossibility without some form of systematic approach. This situation is further compounded when the various versions and products are offered on totally different platforms.

6.3.2   The Approach Taken

In this case study, Sysdeco, with the assistance of the Norwegian Technical University (NTNU), addressed the problem of configuration management over multiple, and differing development platforms, as well as the development of relevant metrics.

The approach taken was to introduce configuration management software that could be utilised on UNIX, Windows NT, and Windows 95 development platforms within their GIS development department. Additionally, new procedures to support the use of the new software were also implemented. With the assistance of NTNU, metrics were defined to measure the success of implementing the new configuration management software and procedures.

These metrics were defined in such away as to be able to measure the before and after situations, in order to determine whether the implementation was a success. A third party was used to provide impartiality.

6.3.3   The Sysdeco GIS Product

Sysdeco GIS's (SGIS) development department delivers two main products; Tellus and Tellus Vision. These are tool-kits that are used by a product group to make the end-user products.

Tellus was originally developed in the late 1980's for various UNIX environments. Tellus provides developers with a hybrid raster and vector tool-set for layered colour maps and includes a proprietary programming language (TCL) for application dependant code.

Tellus Vision is the newest product. This offers Tellus mapping technology on Windows NT/Windows 95.

The Tellus family of products consists of more than 20 different variants depending on platform (UNIX, Windows) and database system. The system consists of more than 600,000 lines of code. In view of this, the management of the different variant of the products was a complex and arduous process.

At the start of the project, an old configuration management system, SCCS, was used. This was satisfactory for UNIX products, but was not available for Windows NT. As a result of this, configuration management for the Windows products was a manual process, which was fraught with errors and inconsistencies.

6.3.4   Work Performed

The CMEX experiment was carried out by a project team co-ordinated by SGIS' Technical Director. A sub-contractor, NTNU was utilised to develop and track all relevant metrics. All experiment related dissemination and administration was performed by the SGIS team.

The configuration management system chosen for this experiment was Clear-Case. This tool was chosen based on a previous study undertaken by another development group within Sysdeco. The choice of tool was decided upon by management and not by the developers themselves. As a result of this decision, scepticism and resistance were anticipated from the development staff, all of who were highly qualified computer specialists. In view of this decision and the possibility of resistance, a questionnaire was developed to track and document user acceptance of the system, before, during, and after implementation.

The experiment itself was divided into three work packages. The first work package (WP1) was the preparation phase. During this phase, SGIS' experience data base was studied and analysed. This formed the basis of the metrics used throughout the experiment. In all 16 different metrics were defined. However, due to the lack of sufficient data only five of the metrics were used to identify the results of the experiment. WP1 also included the installation of the ClearCase configuration management software. The second work package (WP2) concerned change control.

The objective of this work package was to:

- Train team members in the configuration management (CM) system.
- Use the CM system to develop new releases of a product.
- Collect process data during the experiment.
- Provide services to the team.

The key milestones and deliverables for the project were:

- Documentation defining metrics and procedure.
- Installation of configuration management tool.
- Collection and analysis of data on Phase 1 of the experiment.
- Collection and analysis of data on Phase 2 of the experiment.

6.3.5   Results and Analysis

In order to assess the on-going success of the experiment, thorough measurements of quality and process were taken at project mid-point. These were used as a basis for quantifying improvements. Toward the end of the experiment, data collected during the second phase of the project was processed. At this stage, it was discovered that data for some of the metrics originally defined were not consistently recorded. This resulted in only the following metrics being used:

- M01 – Defect arrival rate.
- M03 – Defect priority.
- M07 – Defect fix time.
- M13 – Resource usage.
- M14 – Maintenance effort.

From the measurements taken during this experiment (Figure 6.3) the following can be shown:

- In terms of experiment aim to reduce the number of reported errors from customers (SQR) by 10%, this has been achieved and surpassed. SQR errors have been reduced by 35.7%.
- Development work has relatively increased by 21.8% and maintenance relatively decreased by 33.3%, leading to a shorter time-to-market for products.

Other observations made as a result of this experiment were that:

- The number of high and low priority errors have been significantly reduced.

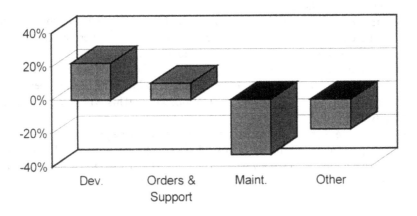

Fig. 6.3 Relative Change of Work Areas

- The number of internally reported errors – errors reported on alpha and beta versions – have significantly increased. This is a wanted development since the costs associated with correcting an internal error are much less than those for correcting an external error.
- The time taken to fix both internal and external errors has decreased. For external errors, a 5.5% reduction has been noticed and for internal errors, a reduction of 56% has been noted.
- The cost of errors had been underestimated and was higher than was originally thought. The estimated average is around 5000 ECU.
- Personnel acknowledged the need for a new configuration management system and process.

6.3.6   Lessons Learned

There were many lessons learned during this experiment. The main lessons were:
- To implement a configuration management system takes a long time. For the implementation to succeed then it should not be rushed. SGIS's initial estimate for the implementation was that it would take two months. In fact, it took twelve months.
- Do not underestimate the cost of implementing and maintaining a configuration management system.
- Do not underestimate the number of licenses required. Plan on one license per developer.
- Ensure that the hardware on which the system is to operate is powerful enough. Rather have excess capacity than not enough, as this will influence the performance of the system.
- Document every stage of the process followed during implementation and ensure that clear procedural documents are produced. This will establish a practical way of operating the system within the company.
- Make sure that all personnel using the system are fully trained before using the system. This will ensure that once the system goes into operation, all personnel are comfortable with it and know how to operate it. This will ease acceptance of the system.
- Do not assume that by implementing configuration management (CM) software package performance will be improved. Improvement will only be obtained through the adoption of a new way of working which revolves around CM and related processes.

6.3.7   Future Plans

Sysdeco GIS A/S intends to continue refining their configuration management process.

They will also be introducing an automated testing tool as part of an EC sponsored experiment – ATEX – Automated Testing Experiment.

6.4   Introduction of Configuration Management

By introducing configuration management into the development process of their financial application products, Datamat Ingegneria dei Sistemi S.p.A. vastly decreased the time-to-market and the number of errors in their software products. The overall effect was to decrease development costs in order for Datamat to gain a competitive edge.

By being able to respond quickly and accurately to customer request for change, we have greatly increased customer satisfaction levels, as well as reducing product development costs.

6.4.1 Background

Datamat Ingegneria dei Sistemi S.p.A. (Datamat) is a large system integration company based in Rome, undertaking turn-key software projects in a number of sectors including defence, aerospace, finance and public administration. The Datamat group employs over 1,000 people with a turnover exceeding 110 MECU.

6.4.2 Response to Change Request

Software producers need to be able to respond quickly and accurately to change requests from customers. In addition, there is continual pressure for shorter product release cycles in order to meet customer requirements and to continue to be competitive.

Many companies deliver complex software systems to a number of clients, each of whom requires customised variants of the basic system, who require their supplier to be able to amend their systems when market or legislation changes demand it.

Even sophisticated software developers are able to improve their responsiveness to customer needs, by formalising their procedures for keeping track of the product components (such as source code modules, libraries and documentation).

6.4.3 The Approach Taken

In this case study Datamat addressed the problem of configuration management, and achieved shorter delivery times for software, which also had less errors. In addition, they found their responsiveness to customer requests for change was greatly increased.

The approach taken was to introduce configuration management techniques and tools into Datamat's software development process for financial application products. In this project, this was carried out for one of Datamat's new products, Datasim.

Any software producing organisation can benefit from configuration management, although it is particularly suited to those development projects which are large enough to benefit from formal management. Suggested bounds are an application development team of more than eight people, and an application which consists of more than one hundred modules.

6.4.4   The DATASIM Product

One of Datamat's most recent products is called DATASIM, an information management system for Italian financial services companies.

The nature of the DATASIM product and its clients meant that this product was an ideal one in which to introduce configuration management into the maintenance and development phase of the product's lifecycle.

Recent changes in legislation relating to financial service companies meant that Datasim's customers were required to change their legislative framework and consequently their software. Since both the software and the legislation were new, adjustments needed to be made not only to reflect the latest legal interpretations but to correct any software errors.

Failure to deliver the product in a short time could have meant that customers would face suspension of his operating license.

DATASIM has many real-time functions and system failure often means that the company ceases to operate for the duration of the system problem. For this reason, high levels of quality assurance are essential. This project addressed two particular quality issues – firstly, reducing configuration delivery problems, as it was often difficult to create or recreate a specific instance of the product and secondly, reducing installation problems for new releases, where sometimes new problems were created and old problems re-emerged in installation of the software.

6.4.5   Implementation

The nature of the project objectives had already focussed attention on configuration management as the area to be addressed. This was confirmed by an independent assessment of Datamat's software development process for financial products using the SPICE methodology. The SPICE assessment showed that many key procedures relating to configuration management were informal, unplanned, and not documented.

The first step, therefore, was to plan and document the procedures defining the lifecycle for objects to be managed by the configuration management system. These objects are typically program modules, but can also be libraries, compilers, or user manuals for example.

Datamat then selected a suitable configuration management product to implement and automate these procedures. The product chosen was PCMS, a flexible tool capable of being adapted to support a variety of software development approaches. In order to implement the tool, the tests were:

- Modifying the control parameters in the PCMS database in order to define information specific to Datamat's software development process.
- Customising the user interface in order that the programmers did not interact directly with PCMS, but selected one of a number of standard "scripts".

- Loading of the DATASIM product, in order to put it under configuration management.

Testing the Model

The model which had been implemented was then tested by carrying out typical maintenance activities and many changes were made to the parameterisation to discover the optimal approach. After this period of parallel running, the database was reloaded with the latest DATASIM code and development stopped to permit a cut-over to the new system. This period of two days was then also used to train the development team members.

6.4.6   Project Results

In order to formally measure the results of the project, a second SPICE assessment was carried out on the development process for financial products. This showed several significant areas of improvement, where Datamat's software development processes were now closely conformant to industry best practice. Particular improvements are:

- There is now an overall *change control* function, which authorises modifications to objects such as code and documentation only where there is a validated change request.
- It is now possible to *reproduce* all the current and past delivered versions and variants of the system, taking into account the specific differences of individual customer installations.
- Deliveries to customers are prepared by a configuration management team; and only in the case of an emergency can the system be modified at a customer site. Each delivery is rigorously *tested* before release.

Impact on Business

As well as the technical benefits of the project, a great impact on Datamat's business has been achieved. In addition to higher product quality, there is a much improved responsiveness to customer needs and legislative requirements.

This has resulted in greater customer satisfaction and therefore an increase in repeat business. Another benefit which has resulted is a greater overall software development productivity due to project team members being able to spend a higher proportion of their time on directly productive work, rather than on solving problems relating to incorrectly configured releases.

6.4.7   Lessons Learned

Introducing formal processes where there used to be none can often generate opposition. Before seeing the benefits of introducing configuration management, it is first necessary to introduce what may seem like useless bureaucracy for a time. Top level management support is necessary in order to make some team members believe in the importance of the task.

In order to see the pay-off from implementation of configuration management, it is advisable to choose a project with at least a moderate degree of complexity where the development team is big enough to benefit from a formal system of collaboration.

It is easy to get carried away with the possibilities of a sophisticated software process model, risking failure due to its unworkable complexity. Datamat learned that it is better to start with a basic number of object states and roles, and then elaborate upon that basis later if necessary.

The wrong configuration management tool can become a strait-jacket, forcing your developers to follow a process model designed on the basis of "one size fits all". It is better to invest in a tool with more sophistication than you need (in terms of customisability) rather than less.

These lessons learned throughout the experience of the practice can be resume in the following concepts:

- Top Management support is essential.
- Choose a significant project.
- Take a realistic view of working practices.
- Buy a configurable product.

6.4.8   Future Plans

Datamat intends to continue building on the success of their software best practice project. The configuration management system will be implemented company-wide for all future in-house product development projects under Unix.

6.5   Electronic Document System

AMT·SYBEX is a medium sized software company that wished to improve its present Quality Management System (QMS) and its Configuration Management tools. By converting from a paper-based to an electronic system, AMT·SYBEX have noticed improvements in a variety of areas including a reduction in the amount of reworking.

The overall acceptance of the automated processes has been very high, therefore we expect to see additional benefits of shorter development times scales and reduce re-work.

6.5.1 Background

AMT-Sybex is totally focused on developing and implementing Business Management, and Asset Management solutions through the application of consultancy services and highly functional software.

6.5.2 Improved Evaluation

For any software development company, the monitoring of processes and management of quality is an important aspect of the business. Historically this activity has been performed using paper-based systems. There are many problems with this traditional method of operation, especially when the company produces large pieces of software and has long project duration. For these reasons, a company, which fits these criteria, would spend its time profitably by implementing an automatic documentation system.

Some of the advantages of introducing an automatic document system are more measurable than others; for example, it can be seen that less time is spent rewriting existing code under a new system. On the other hand, it is difficult to measure the amount of time an engineer might waste looking for a paper-based project file when he could find an electronic file immediately on computer. There are further issues, such as the fact that a team member can work more confidently and plan his time more effectively when he knows that he will definitely be able to get hold of a relevant piece of information.

The experience gained during this project will be of use to any medium size software company that is looking to convert from a paper based QMS to an electronically based one.

6.5.3 Operating Efficiency

There are many reasons why a company might wish to switch to an automatic documentation system. In the case of AMT, one of the main triggers was the fact that the company wanted to relocate its paper-based system. This was proving to be a major task due to its size; obviously the problem would be eliminated if the records were stored electronically. Also the tracing back of problems and location of their source was enormously difficult when using a paper archive.

There are more day-to-day improvements noticed with the implementation of this type of system. Managers find it much easier to keep track of projects when they are on electronic record since they are much more "transparent." Additionally, there is less work assigned to the managers, and projects can flow more continuously.

This is due to the fact that projects consist of a number of stages, each of which is completed by a different member of the team. When using a paper based record of the project, the record must be returned to the manager upon completion of each stage of the project in order that it can then be re-allocated for the next stage of development. However, when the record is controlled electronically, it can be passed automatically on to the next team member, thus saving time and increasing continuity.

6.5.4   Work Performed

There were three senior staff involved on the Process Improvement Experiment; one project manager, one quality supervisor and one senior analyst and lead developer. In addition to these personnel, there were further team members who became trained in the operation of the new methods during the project.

The PITA encouraged the company to upgrade much of its hardware and software technology sooner, and to a higher standard, than it would otherwise have done.

The training of staff was carried out in two separate sections for the two projects, which were being undertaken:

- Training for the Configuration Management section was carried out by Intersolv. Two members of the team were trained in the use of the PVCS, which was the chosen configuration management tool. These people then provided training to eight other developers within the team.
- For the Workflow and Document Management, four members of the team were trained it the use of the relevant applications.

The PITA application was used to train five members of the software development team. After the pilot, all of the software development team was trained in use of the PITA software.

Project assessments etc. were done by monitoring timesheet records before and after the experiment.

6.5.5   Results Achieved

The results of this PIE have still to be seen in financial terms; there has been little concrete evidence as yet to point towards any improvement. The company has not yet attempted a calculation of its return on investment.

On the other hand, it is the feeling within the company that the project has been a success. The managers believe that due to the PIE, the amount of time, which was spent, on the automated project was smaller than the amount of time spent on the baseline. There are a couple of causes cited for this increase in efficiency. The first, which has been mentioned, is that projects are passed automatically from one team member to the next, without going through the manager each time.

Secondly, under the new system, outstanding work is reminded to them electronically each time they open their PITA "in box."

The project managers believe that there has been a 10% reduction in the overall cycle time for a project. In addition to this there has been a 5% increase in productivity, which is due to a reduction in the amount of rework. This was occurring because engineers were repeating work, which had already been performed by other team members, the increase in information provided by the new documentation system, has eliminated this.

There has been a reduction in the amount of paper usage and as a result a reduction in the amount of storage space required.

The new system makes the progression of projects more transparent to the project managers; as a result, they can monitor problems associated with particular aspects of the project. They are able to build profiles for specific types of project, this helps estimate costs and manpower required in the future.

The company tried to convert the existing documentation system, which supported their ISO 9001 certification directly into digital format. There were a few problems encountered with this, including the difficulty of engineers creating digital signatures using a mouse. Also the company found that their existing documentation and process flow diagrams were not sophisticated enough to support Workflow process maps; quite a lot of effort was required to make the transition possible.

6.5.6   Lessons Learned

AMT.SYBEX discovered that in order to carry out a project such as this, a company needs to have some breathing space. The company was undergoing a period of growth during this PIE, and due to the high demand upon their staff, they found it difficult to get, as much benefit out of the PIE as would have been ideal. They recommend undertaking a project during a period of stability, or excess capacity.

The company learned some lessons with regard to the change in procedure that was not expected. They believe it is important that any company doing an experiment such as this be prepared for the appearance of unforeseen information.

The people at the company discovered that just because they had obtained the ISO 9001 certification, this was no guarantee that their documentation system would be easy to automate. In addition, they found that ISO did not necessarily entail a methodical approach either. The Workflow software requires understanding of the process; this is not required by the system needed for ISO certification.

The company found that to implement the workflow system, they had to perform significant upgrades to their software and hardware facilities.

There were three main weaknesses in the project in the eyes of Configuration Management Tools:

- The initial proposal identified too many objectives for the project. They found that a lot of time was consumed by the early objectives and that little was left for the later ones.

- They applied for a project, which was outside their frame of reference. This meant that the staff who was working on the project had little knowledge of the new area and hence adaptation was problematic.
- There was too much time pressure exerted on the project from other fee earning projects at the time. This led to resources for the PIE frequently being cut in favour of the commercial projects.

6.6   Configuration and Change Management

Configuration and Change Management to Rising Quality of Service

The implementation of this PIE, focused on the Software Change and the Configuration Management system (SO.C.CO.MA), has led to establishing a centralised Change Management Process that really works and allows the management of environments with a combination of internally and externally developed software. Furthermore the introduction of quantitative measures about the new process represents the starting point towards a management by metrics.

The SO.C.CO.MA project pushed the company to set up a new measurement system, it never existed before. That will allow to build a database for improving the processes. After the project, once the Software Configuration Manager is exploiting, the company will reduce rework and improve time-to-market.

6.6.1   Background

Istiservice S.p.A. is a 100 people Italian Company founded in 1989 by ISTBANK, and now controlled by EDS (Electronic Data Systems) since 1995. Currently EDS-Istiservice, based in Milan, offers Total Outsourcing and Facilities Management services primarily to finance insurance and banking companies. Turnover for 1997 was 16 MECU.

6.6.2   Outsourcing Services for the Financial Market

Istiservice S.p.A., a EDS Group Italian company, based in Milan, provides outsourcing services to financial and banking companies.

The services can be classified as:

- Total Outsourcing, when the customer gets from Istiservice the whole Information system service. The software is acquired from external suppliers.
- Specific services (partial outsourcing), when the service content deals only with particular applications. In this case the software may be developed also by Istiservice.

One peculiar characteristic of the software development environment at Istiservice is the combination of internally and externally developed software, with a high degree of integration.

An analysis of the starting scenario pointed out special considerations such as:

- Lack of formal procedures in the application software change management, and in problem tracking.
- Service supplied was suffering from significant delays in the delivery, from uncertainty in the residual defects, from extra costs, and from overload in the involved people.

6.6.3 Improving Product and Service Through CM

Taking into account the above-mentioned product and market considerations, Istiservice carried out an internal diagnostic, further supported by the management's concern towards software quality, resulting in the launching of the SOC-COMA project, focused on the software change and configuration management process.

The PIE project aimed at setting up a centralized change management process, allowing the definition of the whole lifecycle of the software change, and a Configuration Management System supported by formal and defined rules.

The definition and implementation of a measurement system to allow monitoring the whole change management process, was an expected outcome as well.

Achieved results have been the centralisation and the control of the Change Management Process, with all objects satisfactorily treated by the tools, and the introduction for the very first time of quantitative measures, representing the starting point towards a management by metrics.

6.6.4 Work Performed

The SO.C.CO.MA project started in February 1996 and lasted for 14 months, affecting Application and Scheduling Groups, and, even if marginally, the teams involved in the promotion of application software to the production department: Systems Engineers and Shift Operations.

6.6.4.1 Technical Environment

Main changes to the existing technical environment were the adoption of the following tools at the purpose, running both under MVS operating system:

- Endeavour, in order to manage the configuration environment and the software changes.
- JCR, in order to manage the JCL changes and the related documentation.

6.6.4.2   Phases of the Experiment

The project was organised according to the following main phases:

Start up Activities

During this phase a seminar was held with the purpose of raising the awareness of the employees towards process improvement and quality management topics.

Then, a preliminary analysis of the current Change Management Process and Configuration System was carried out through a series of interviews performed by the consultant team and the Quality Staff. The document issued from this analysis was used as the basis for the following phases.

Set up of the Change Management Process

The new configuration system consists of two main environments: Test and Production.

The Test Environment consists of two Stages:

- Stage of Application Test, where programs are tested as single elements. Actions allowed: moving elements to the Stage of System Test.
- Stage of System Test, where programs are tested in connection to the applications to which they belong and to the whole Information System, if necessary. Actions allowed: promoting elements to the Stage of Production.

The Production Environment consists of the two following ones:

- Stage of Emergency, where programs are quickly recovered, having retrieved them from Production and fixed them in the Development Library. Actions allowed: moving elements to the Stage of Production.
- Stage of Production, where production applications are stored and executed.

The "Development" Library is kept out of control of the tool for not overloading the development and the updating process.

Tool Selection

The following step was the definition and the choice of the most suitable tools supporting the change management process (see above Technical environment).

Set up of the Measurement System

This task was particularly delicate considering the fact that for the very first time Application Areas were asked to collect data concerning their job on a regular basis.

The measurement system, simple but effective, has been set up by carrying out the following steps:

- General goals definition.
- Metrics definition.
- Design and accomplishment of the data collection analysis, which are full compliant with ISO 9000 standards.

Application to the Selected Baseline Project

The experiment was conducted over three banking application procedures representing the Baseline Project:

- Bill Portfolio (acquired from external supplier).
- Branch Bank application (acquired from external supplier).
- Payment Provisions (Interbanking Bill Payment Terms Modification, developed by Istiservice).

The main approach for the selection was the "change rate".

6.6.5   Results and Analysis

Some points regarding technical, cultural and organisational results are hereafter treated under a qualitative point of view.

In order to get a more effective experimentation, the number of monitored applications has to be extended massively after a brief period checking of the new process. Therefore it is not possible at this moment to show a real improvement of the defined quantitative indicators in the experimentation period, as expected.

6.6.5.1   Technical

The centralisation of the Change Management Process can be considered achieved regarding both the software lifecycle and the roles/responsibilities involved.

For the very first time quantitative measures about the activities carried out and about the new process have been introduced. This represents the starting point towards a management by metrics.

It must be said, nevertheless, that the setting up of the measurement system has been a very important achievement, although it requires further refinement regarding the indicators taken into account. Figures 6.4 and 6.5 show some examples of metrics collected for the Failure Distribution.

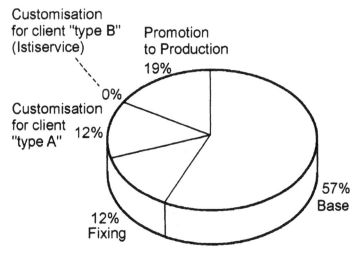

Fig. 6.4 Failure Distribution (by Phase)

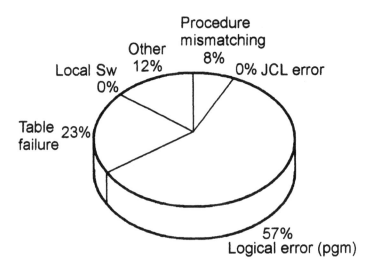

Fig. 6.5 Failure Distribution (by Type)

6.6.5.2   *Business*

The new process becomes an important selling point in the presentations to prospect clients, giving them an immediate perception of the service level attainable from Istiservice.

6.6.5.3 *Organisation*

Roles and responsibilities involved in the Change Management Process have been better outlined, accomplishing one of the starting goals of the PIE. Therefore it is expected that measurable goals will be soon given to the people involved in software development and promotion to production areas, reducing the hidden costs of non-quality.

6.6.6   Lessons Learned

The following lessons learned can be stated, among the most significant ones:

- The approach can be taken to other processes (e.g. development, testing), by defining a set of proper metrics, establishing similar collection of procedures and defining quantitative goals to achieve.
- If the project were to be repeated, before the starting the experimentation, the indicators to be taken into account should be more clearly identified.
- A continuous sensibilization action shall be promoted through specific actions in order to minimise the most frequent risks, like loss of interest, perceive the project as a bureaucratic overhead, etc.
- The new process cannot be considered established; therefore a project review is mostly advisable at the effective start of the application phase.

6.6.7   Future Actions

Istiservice expects to spread the new process to the remaining applications of the information system as soon as possible. The new procedures will be applied gradually in accordance with times scales and general project planning set up by Quality Function together with Scheduling and Application Areas and monitored by the person Responsible for Scheduling.

Another important activity to carry out in the future points out to measure topics such as timeliness, stability, effort and defectiveness, in order to settle the newly introduced culture towards management by metrics

Istiservice is also planning to utilise the measurement results as systematic feedback towards its software suppliers, in order to help them to work better, so as to get from them more consolidated software products.

6.7   Build-up a Centralised Software Quality Management Function

The improvement achieved by GEPIN Engineering S.p.A in the areas of Configuration/Change Management and Documentation Development Management has definitively contributed to obtain the ISO 9001 certification, which in turn has allowed GEPIN to expand their business by accessing the large turn-key project marketplace.

The improvement of Document & Configuration Management support processes has driven to a direct improvement in Information System & Workflow Management (by using the PIE tools in normal activities) and an indirect improvement of company capability of planning and tracking primary processes.

6.7.1   Background

GEPIN Engineering S.p.A., a 300 people System House founded in 1987 in Naples, with branches in Milan and Venice, is part of the GEPIN Group (650 employees), which includes another two companies: one in Rome and GEPIN International in South America. The turn-over for 1997 was 9 MECU.

GEPIN Engineering S.p.A, is a lead company in the areas of software systems, projects and consulting. Employing more than 300 people, GEPIN activities cover the software system development and integration in the following main sectors: telecommunications, special systems, real-time systems, management systems, computer based training.

The company develops its activity in a competitive and fast moving market – the high technology value market facing the continuous demand for higher quality software products.

GEPIN's business expansion strategy has led to the need of entering higher risk markets, of which the requirements to select software project suppliers (usually through call for tender procedure) involve strict System Quality Assurance to control the software process and products.

In this context, GEPIN started in 1993 its route to the Quality, facing the evolution from a Time & Material type of activity towards a Turn-key project oriented company.

6.7.2   Improving the Software Quality System

The above-mentioned market exigencies made GEPIN Engineering aware of the increasing relevance of the quality requirements to enter into the *riskier market* of large turn-key projects in big companies, such as Telecom Italy, where access to the Primary supplier list requires high technical qualification, including the ISO 9001 certification.

Thus, committed to Quality since 1993, GEPIN Engineering carried out this PIE as a first step to build up a centralised Software Quality Management function, focusing on the Software Life Cycle supporting processes perceived by GEPING as the most critical: Configuration and Change Management (CCM) and Documentation Development Management (DDM), resulting in:

- The obtention of the ISO 9001 certification.
- The expansion of business activities to new market opportunities (large turn-key projects), which has contributed to Turnover increase (more than *three times* in a two year period).

6.7.3   Work Performed

The MSI-QBP project started in February 1996 and lasted until December 1997 occupying part of what is known at GEPIN as the "ESSI-PIE period", running from July 95 until May 98, at the end of which an important qualitative achievement for GEPIN has been that of transforming people's competence into Enterprise Competence.

The PIE team was composed of:
- the PIE Manager, responsible for all the activities of the experiment.
- the Documentation Management Co-ordinator.
- the Configuration Management Co-ordinator.
- the Baseline Project Manager.

6.7.3.1   Baseline Project

The baseline project concerned a new release of a GEPIN automated system for the treatment of M*aritime* Safety Information (MSI), whose major functions were acquisition, classification, selection and publication of news, bulletins, etc. Originally in full text screen technology, the new release was developed in a visual object technology, by adopting a prototype approach effectively ruled by the documentation and configuration procedures defined during the PIE.

6.7.3.2   Technical Environment

The most important change was the introduction of a Client/Server architecture in a multiserver local network and adopting the TCP/IP standard to have the possibility of using new Intranet/Internet technologies.

6.7.3.3   Support Tools

Lotus Notes was installed and customised to produce all the documents on the basis of defined templates and to manage them in terms of workflow.

For Configuration Management the CCC/Harvest environment was adopted.

6.7.3.4   *Methods and Standards*

For the management of the PIE, the external consultant used its own approach, named PRIMO (Process Improvement Method and Organisation), which has been validated in several in-field improvement projects and has been adopted by other ESSI projects.

ISO 15504/SPICE was used for the initial and final assessments, and the AMI method for the implementation of a measurement framework.

6.7.3.5   *Phases of the Experiment*

Formal Qualification of the PIE

An initial assessment using the SPICE method was conducted for the CCM and DDM processes. A measurement plan was produced to monitor the achievement of the PIE objectives and a final assessment of the reached process capability was carried out at the end of the PIE.

Training

The consultant company conducted the training on the Quality standards (ISO, IEEE) and on methods and techniques (SEI CMM, AMI, ISO 15504/SPICE). In particular, seminars and exercise-lessons were attended by a relevant number of GEPIN's people, to disseminate internally the culture on Quality and Process Improvement.

Training on the support tools was conducted by the selected tools providers.

Experiment Deployment

This has been the core of the PIE and its main activities – Baseline Project Start, Design, Development, Integration and Post-production – were developed on top of the baseline project.

All the related project documents were produced in Lotus Notes environment on the basis of the templates previously defined, and put under configuration control in the CCC/Harvest environment.

The sub-phase Post-production produced the initial nucleus of the Quality Manual, incorporating the procedures and templates derived from the previous activities.

6.7.4   **Results and Analysis**

6.7.4.1   *Technical*

The implementation of the PIE resulted in the following outcomes from a technical view:

• SPICE initial and final capability profile of GEPIN in CCM and DDM practices.

- DDM and CCM standard procedures and templates.
- the customisation of the Lotus Notes and CCC/Harvest environment to the requirements defined in the CCM and DDM standard procedures.
- all the work products made according to above mentioned standard procedures.
- the implementation of a measurement framework, according to the AMI method.

Figures 6.6 and 6.7 show the capability profiles of the process for Documentation Development Management. We can observe that initially the Capability Level 1 (Performed Informally) practices were covered Largely (50%) and Partially(50%) with no practice fully covered.

The final assessment instead shows that this Capability Level 1 was Fully performed (100%), thus giving evidence, in an objective way, of the improvement obtained from the PIE execution. A similar meaningful improvement was reached for the CCM process (Level 4 and 5 practices were not assessed because they were not among the goals of the PIE).

Develop Documentation

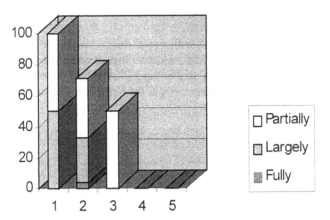

Fig. 6.6 SPICE initial Process Capability Profile

Develop Documentation

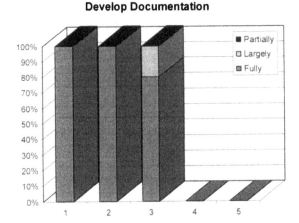

Fig. 6.7 SPICE final Process Capability Profile

6.7.4.2 Business

The implementation of the PIE resulted in the following outcomes from a business view:

- Although not easy to quantify, it can be said that the SQA (software Quality Assurance) has contributed with more than 15% in the Turn-over increase. From its side, the PIE has had a positive influence on the Quality system (estimated in a 50% contribution to the required effort for the certification).
- Confidence of the top management in the reduction of costs in the management of the project work products.

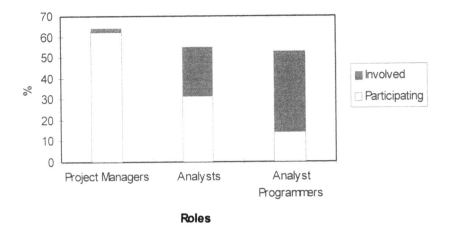

Fig. 6.8 Dissemination of the software quality culture in GEPIN

6.7.4.3 *Organisation*

The implementation of the PIE resulted in the following outcomes from an organisational view:

- SQA function was set up on top of the procedural and technological framework produced by the PIE.
- Both DDM and CCM procedures have been adopted as standard in all the projects.

6.7.4.4 *Dissemination of the Software Quality Culture*

The histogram, Fig. 6.8, shows the percentage of people (by roles) involved in the diffusion of software quality culture.

6.7.5 Lessons Learned

The main lessons learned are described hereafter with respect to the different points of view, technical, organisational and business.

6.7.5.1 *Technical*

The technical aspects achieved throughout the project can be summarise in the following most important ones:

- SPICE and AMI can be effective complementary frameworks for Software Process Improvement (SPI) strategies.
- Care must be taken during the installation of the tools (example: portability problems).
- Careful analysis and training in the selected tools is very important: the customisation of Lotus Notes has been made easy, but there were initially some difficulties with CCC/Harvest due to the novelty of the technology. The difficulties have been overcome during the PIE, but there are still some problems to be adjusted.
- The set-up of a PIE (Initial assessment, measurement plan, training, etc) requires a relevant effort, which must be spent over a restricted time period (1 year around) before the start of the baseline project, representing potential difficulties to manage the experimentation of the results of such an important PIE step. GEPIN solved this problem adopting a *prototyping approach* in the baseline project.

6.7.5.2 *Organisation*

The organisational aspects achieved throughout the project can be summarise in the following most important one:

The same procedures cannot be applied to the different types of projects. These were classified according to their size/complexity in: small, medium and large projects, then adapting the Documentation and Configuration management procedures to these three types of projects.

6.7.5.3 Business

The business aspects achieved throughout the project can be summarise in the following most important ones:

- The Top Management is well aware that the improvement process undertaken in the PIE is the first cycle of an evolutionary SPI process.
- Improvement of DDM and CCM processes positively influences the improvement of both Software Life Cycle engineering and management processes.
- Customer involvement in SPI training and dissemination actions increases customer confidence in the software quality policy of their software providers.

6.7.6   Future Actions

The actions planed to be taken, once the benefits of the project has been achieved are as follow:

- To extend the ISO 9001 certificate to Rome, Venice and Milan subsidiaries.
- To spread over the other projects of the company the DDM and CCM practices and technologies experimented during the PIE.
- To evolve the SPI program in two directions:
  - Enforcement of the process capability in CCM and DDM towards a higher SPICE capability level .
  - To initiate a SPI project on Risk management of software projects.

6.8   Enhanced Version Integrity

Enhanced Version Integrity with Software Configuration and Change Management

As part of an ongoing internal software improvement initiative, the software development area of Iberdrola defined and established standard configuration and change management processes, together with a versioning policy, documentation and data management procedures, as well as guides and templates to prepare documents like configuration management plans, configuration reports and problem reports. The existence of a standard approach has helped this electric utility improve the integrity of product versions and reduce the number of delivered errors due to a more orderly documentation, change and work product management.

6.8.1   Background and Work Done

This initiative took place in Iberdrola, a electric utility in Spain, as part of a global project for internal software process improvement. It was carried out as an internally funded project whose objective was to understand and improve the way in which the organisation conducted software development and maintenance.

The first activity was a SEI Capability Maturity Model (CMM) appraisal. Although led by external consultants, the assessment team included 8 people from the department that had been intensively trained for the task. As a result of this exercise an improvement plan was produced covering the three prioritised areas of project management, configuration management and quality assurance.

Three working groups were created, one per improvement area, with the objective to define the new processes to be applied. The members of these working groups were staff from the development projects, working part-time, and support personnel from the SEGP and SQA groups, as well as external experienced consultants. Both the Software Engineering Process Group (SEPG) and Software Quality Assurance (SQA) function had been set up as the first action after the assessment. The former's role is to act as an improvement driving force and to provide support on software engineering issues, whereas SQA is in charge of external quality assurance tasks in software projects. Working groups were managed like any other project in the organisation, defining their teams and required infrastructure, the specific objectives and plans for each one of them (always within the scope of the overall action plan), and tracking their evolution in terms of schedule, deliverables, etc.

In particular, the objectives established for the improvement project in the area of configuration management were:

- Have the projects manage their products by versions.
- Reduce the number of errors in deliveries due to the improved integrity of product versions.
- Authorise a repository for work products.
- Ensure the control of problems and changes to software products.

6.8.2   Resulting Scenario

As a result of the improvements in the configuration management area a series of documents were produced which were established as standards:
- Configuration management procedure.
- Problems and change management procedure.
- Documentation and data management procedure.
- Guide to prepare configuration management plans.

6.8.2.1 Policies

Although it is the management's responsibility to establish policies, these were obtained as a result of the work group who defined the policies based on directives established by the management.

The Configuration Management policies estates the basis to establish and maintain the integrity of the software products of the project.

Despite the fact that the management of versions forms part of the configuration Management, it was thought to be convenient to define a specific policy about this point due to its repercussions within the organisation.

Historically work is done in the organisation with continuous working deliveries, in some cases even daily, this generates great problems mainly due to problems of planning, possibility of running behind time, and above all making tests more difficult due to lack of time to carry them out and at the same time having to repeat a lot of them. The versions policies are defined with the objective of getting the organisation to work with planned deliveries to fundamentally improve the control of the said deliveries and make it easier to plan and manage the requests of the projects.

6.8.2.2   Guide for the Definition of Configuration Management Plans

This document establishes the general guideline of the contents of a Configuration Management plan project. In the guide we find the following sections:

- Characteristics and activities of the configuration control group that should exist for every project.
- The elements that the basic product guidelines should contain. Because of the existence of different levels of development, objectives are established that should form part of the mentioned guideline, afterwards every project will have its basic guideline defined and it will be specifically included it in the configuration management plan.
- The management of libraries, establishing the libraries that should exist and their management. The physical implantation of these libraries and the management activities that they carry should be specified as a basis of this minimum in every project plan depending on the level of development at which it is working.
- Also defined in this document are the audits and status monitoring reports that should be included in the plans so that they are generated by the project.

6.8.2.3   Guide for the Definition of the Document that Describes the Versions

This document defines how the delivery of a version should be documented. It describes the document for the description of the delivery of versions and establishes its format and contents.

6.8.2.4   Procedure for Change and Problem Management

This procedure defines how problem management and requests for changes in the software should be achieved.

6.8.2.5   Problem Management

The format and contents are defined that should contain a "Report of the Problem", as well as the flow of the process which is established for its management.

6.8.2.6   Change Management

The format and contents are defined that should contain a "Request for Change", as well as a flow of the process which is established for its management.

6.8.2.7   Automatic Tool Support

To carry out the defined processes the PVCS tool was selected. This tool is basically composed of two modules:

- PVCS Version Manager, that fulfils version management and libraries of those development platforms with distributed environments, therefore allowing maintaining the elements of the basic guidelines and automating most of the information about the document that describes the versions.
- PVCS Tracker, which supports the report of problems and requests for change, and implements the defined process flow.

6.8.3   Lessons Learned

Management support is a must for the success of a process improvement project, both in its initial stages as well as later during the procedure development phase and, most of all, in their implementation.

It is important to maintain a balance in the working groups between people from actual software projects and staff specifically focused on improvement actions (like the SEPG in this case).

The resultant processes of an improvement project with these characteristics have to be simple and operative, covering the steps strictly necessary so make that the initial implementation is simple enough. Process maintenance should be easy to perform in order to allow for further improvements as the adoption of new practices proceeds.

It is important to define improvement objectives, indicators and success criteria in order to monitor the evolution of the initiative and be able to decide if the desired levels of performance have been achieved.

Although the objective of the improvement is the process itself, one should not forget that the success in the adoption of new practices often depends on the support tools selected. This is especially true of software configuration management, which covers tasks that are difficult to manage manually.

6.8.4   Future Work

The experience described was first implemented on a pilot project and later extended to all software development projects. Although it was originated as a genuine internal improvement initiative, it happened to be very useful as some months later the software development area conformed Iberdrola Sistemas S.A., a new Information Technologies company separated from the corporate business. In this way, improved practices turned into the standard ones in the new context (which included new staff), and helped pave the way for the ISO 9001 certification obtained in 1999.

After project and configuration management, improvement efforts concentrated in requirements management and the definition of software indicators from business objectives. Software testing is next in the list. The scope of SQA is also widening as new process areas are standardised. As of this writing, a pilot experiment is being concluded on the adoption of the Function Point technique for project estimation.

7 Lessons from the EUREX Workshops

S. Rementeria
SOCINTEC, Bilbao

In this chapter we present results from the EUREX Workshops of Bilbao (Spain), Milan (Italy) and Karlsruhe (Germany), each of which addressed the subjects of Configuration and Change Management and Requirements Engineering. Following the workshop descriptions is a summary of the opinions, results, and conclusions derived by the authors from the complete workshop experience.

Fig. 7.1 EUREX workshop locations

7.1   Bilbao Workshop

This workshop was held at the Parque Tecnológico de Zamudio, in the European Software Institute installations. The meeting place was a hall with large enough for approximately 30 people, who attended the seminar, and could be converted into four smaller meeting rooms, so the four specific working groups could work independently during the afternoon.

36 persons attended the event, from which 15 persons representing 8 PIEs, four of them as speakers. The other attendants were: two persons as speakers thirteen people from SMEs and large organisations, and six organisers. The workshop started with a general presentation of the EUREX project. The structure of the workshop and its objectives were explained in 10 minutes at the end of the presentation.

The first technical presentation was made by the invited Expert Ms Concha Díaz of ENOSA on Configuration Management. It consisted of a general overview of this particular domain, but very much adapted to the specific situation of the Spanish SMEs intending to start working in the domain. This first module was followed by four PIE presentations (LANTIK, Iberdrola Sistemas, Eroski, B-Kin) and a speech by Alcatel.

After lunch, four groups were formed to discuss on the presentations made, each one focusing on one of the following aspects :

- Methodologies and processes.
- Technologies and tools.
- Change Management.
- Business area.

The synthesis session was a summary on the conclusions of the four working groups made by the expert from Enosa.

From this workshop, we include the raw material corresponding to the main aspects presented by the Enosa expert and Alcatel, the conclusions derived from the Working groups after the projects were presented, and the general conclusions and lessons learned as seen by the expert.

7.1.1   Expert Presentation

The expert presented an explanation about Software Configuration Management focus, concepts, activities and selection criteria , giving the following conclusions:

Software Configuration Management facilitates the elimination of physical and organisational barriers among Clients, Project Management, Software Engineering, Manufacturing, Logistics and Services, assuring:

- Increase in the quality as a whole.
- Reduction of the development time.
- Less changes in engineering.

- Reduction in the Time-to-Market.
- Increase in software productivity.
- Defined and repeated development processes.
- An organisation that knows about changes.
- Increase in the efficiency of the human team.
- Transparency and communication of all the information and data.
- Elimination of frustration and increase in motivation.

"Software Configuration Management does not control, it keeps you informed, and helps achieve the level of quality required, and is the key to success", was stated by the Expert.

7.1.2   Alcatel Presentation

The title of Alcatel's presentation was "Product Configuration Management in Global Environments".

It described the conditions and strategies applicable to product configuration management with a high software content throughout the length of its life-cycle in an organisation where many of the functions are of a global character.

Alcatel established a definition of the product life-cycle that includes various phases, milestones, responsibilities and associated decisions. These phases are not necessarily fixed; their definitions include a certain degree of precise formality and control that govern their interrelationships. Below are listed briefly, the most important phases and milestones of the life-cycle to be considered:

- Identification. Formality of market requirements, of economic objectives and availability needs , taking into account the suitability of the company strategy and position.
- Definition. Definition of the product mix that satisfies market requirements and business objectives. In this phase, the parts defined will be developed and/or acquired from external suppliers.
- Development and Acquisition. This phase has the final objective of obtaining a valid prototype and evaluation of the product. In addition to the different development activities , the preparation of the industrialisation and collection takes place within this phase.
- Commercial Preparation. This phase, parallel to development, involves the definition and starts the product launch.
- Evaluation. This phase assesses the completion of specifications and manufacturing process, and validates the operational processes (logistics, configuration, installation, after-sales...).
- Delivery (manufacture). Manufacturing phase of the products by volume, including installation and maintenance.
- Phase-out. This phase, includes actions and strategies associated with the gradual withdrawal of the obsolete products.

In Alcatel, Configuration Management is essential to, or affects, a great part of the organisation areas. From the management of product requirements to the installation and maintenance, the implementation of processes guarantee the error elimination, and at the same time are adapted in the best way possible to the environment and environments that it affects, are obligatory.

Until now, Alcatel considers the problem and strategy have been worded without mentioning the space dimension.

This dimension, when it appears in an important form in any process such as in Configuration Management, provokes a big impact, as it leads to conditions that may limit the application of any methodology or tool, and forces a very careful design of later implementation strategy, as well as adding complexity. Its intrinsic strategic importance increases due to the fact that the spread of errors and mistakes have a greater impact.

7.1.3   Conclusions of the Working Groups

Four areas or layers have been established in the work methodology of theEUREX project for the discussions in the Regional Workshops. These layers group together the findings and conclusions related to the positive as well as negative aspects of the presentations made by the different PIE speakers.

The four areas of interest used for the exchange of ideas and opinions are the following:

- Methodology and Process area.
- Technology area (tools used/implemented).
- Change Management area.
- Business area.

The Work groups were made up of approximately 8/10 people.

Previous to the Workshop, the people responsible for the organisation with the collaboration of an Expert in the area analysed and processed the information received from the PIEs. Their aim was to obtain the preliminary conclusions and findings, which would serve as discussion topics and dynamizers in the Work group meetings.

On the other hand, a person from the organisation and one from each of the four PIEs joined the Groups with the aim of helping discussion.

Summaries of the conclusions presented by each of the Groups after a work session of approximately 75 minutes can be found below.

7.1.3.1   Group A – Methodology and Process Area

Starting Point
Establish clearly the business objectives and have a well defined method.

The method for Software Configuration Management (SCM) and Requirements Management (RM) should be defined in accordance with the type of organisation.

There are differences in the context between organisations with only internal and/or external clients.

Also to be taken into account are the different rates of market influence and apply common sense to different situations.

Objectives

The objectives can be classed into two types:

- Knowledge of the current situation.
- To implement improvements.

It is also important to evaluate the current situation (assessment).

Also there is the need to verify external assistance to interpret the results of the evaluations.

Management plays a critical role in establishing short term and measurable objectives, and establishing pilot projects.

It is interesting to establish models in order to motivate the Management.

It is important that there are specific groups dedicated to these improvement projects that also lead the improvements.

The order of implementation of the improvements (SCM, RM) will depend on the objectives, on the needs, on the products, etc.

Reference Models

References are made to the criteria for the selection and application of the Reference Models.

It is important to apply common sense, the adaptation in every context, to a combination of objectives, to the "what" versus the "how" and to external assistance.

There exists a risk of relying on the Reference Model and wasting time on obvious aspects that, at the same time, should be covered initially independently of the chosen Model.

7.1.3.2 Group B – Technology Area

User Requirements

The capture of user requirements is an activity for which there are no automatic tools. They remain the same as 20 years ago.

The development requirements have had different sources and techniques, but the risk is in the loss of information.

A prototype is very useful for Client credibility.

SCM and RM Tools

The benefits of applying SCM and RM tools are not always quantifiable. However it is generally agreed that culture is fundamental.

The biggest problem of SCM tools is the adaptation to the company culture. A tool should be able to be adapted to the said culture.

CASE tools are of limited benefit, in that they do not avoid the correct working-out of the requirements catalogue.

The availability of a tool that covers the complete software cycle is missing.

7.1.3.3   Group C – Change Management Area

Improvement Organisation

The support of the Management is necessary in order to shift resources from other departments to the improvement project.

It is not sufficient to leave the implementation of an improvement project exclusively in the hands of an external company.

Work Groups

- Client participation is fundamental (internal and external clients).
- It is necessary to set realistic and achievable goals.
- Credibility in Management commitment should exist.
- Freedom of initiatives.

Pilot Project:

- Should be of low risk, representative and of a medium size.
- With a guarantee of success.
  - Personnel prone to change.
  - Client participation.

Institutionalisation

Should be carried out in three phases:

- Incorporate the staff prone to change (approx. 20% of the personnel).
- Incorporate the main body of the staff (approx. 50%).
- Incorporate the hard core of the staff (approx. 30%).

Communication and Training

It is of prime importance to use the communication and training to overcome resistance to change.

7.1.3.4   Group D – Business Area

Investment in SCM and RM

There exists a conviction of the positive contribution to the ROI, of the investment in RM and SCM improvement.

The requirements catalogue has an influence mainly in the first phases of the software lifecycle.

The Requirements Catalogue can guide the design of a Test plan (Note. – In some projects, e.g. mission critical, the tests can represent up to 80% of the development time).

The SCM is important, above all, in the final phases of the Life-cycle: construction, Implementation and Maintenance.

There are strategic factors that, by themselves, globally justify the investment in this type of improvement projects.

An example of Ratio for the ROI (Return on Investment) is:

Ratio = ROI + intangible benefits / project cost + maintenance + acceptance risk

Quantification

The quantification of savings is not easy due to the difficult availability of historic information (measurements), and to the lack of interest in recognising own errors.

Comparison Between Improvement Projects

The lack of comparisons between improvement projects (historic data) is an obstacle to evaluate the investment risk.

Product Acquisition

It is fundamental to have an adequate Requirements Management in the Software acquisition process.

The diagram below shows how Requirements Management has a major impact in the early phases of the Life-cycle, whereas Configuration Management is more important in the final phases of the Life-cycle.

Relationship between RM, SCM and the software life-cycle.

7.1.4   General Conclusions

As a result of this working day, the following conclusions can be drawn:

The level of assistance as well as the participation within the different working and discussion groups that were followed, showed the interest that arose in many companies about the topic.

Despite this interest, the experience present was very limited to the large companies. For the small and medium enterprises, and in the majority of cases its use is referred to in some phases of the SW life-cycle, without the real existence of implementation projects throughout the SW life-cycle, with some clear management objectives defined and supported by the management of the company.

In the cases presented by the participating companies all of them showed that the results have been positive (better offer of services and improvement of competitive position) demonstrating that SCM and RM are useful. However, some companies do not have specific plans to continue the development and the application of SCM and RM throughout the SW life-cycle.

The use of SCM and RM in certain phases of the SW life-cycle and in small companies is still found to be in an immature state (pilot projects). In general, it is the difference between the large and small companies that has been verified in order to facilitate the use of these techniques.

The result of this recent lack of experience and interest in the market, the number of consultant companies that can offer experience, knowledge and products in this scope of knowledge is very limited.

The SCM and RM techniques are considered very important as a means to allow alignment of the technological objectives with that of the business, helping to determine the value that SW engineering adds to the company and to improve the quality of the SW products.

One introduction project of a SCM and RM program in the company is a strategic project and should not, exclusively, be considered as a cost/benefit analysis of investments. The quantification of the savings is difficult due to the difficulty of the availability of historic measurements, and due to the lack of interest in recognising errors. The lack of comparison between improvement projects (historic data) that allows the knowledge of investment risk. To obtain success in the implementation an adequate plan, the organisation and necessary resources have to be available.

It is fundamental to have adequate requirements management in the process of tracking the project.

It is not possible to improve the quality of the software with out implementing the SCM and RM techniques.

In general, it can be affirmed that this working day has allowed an advancement in the awareness of the participating companies in the need to introduce SCM and RM techniques in SW engineering as a basis for of SW product quality.

7.1.5   Lessons learned

There are results of an unquestionable interest that exists for this topic (SCM and RM), although the level of use continues to be very limited.

In all cases the use of SCM and RM has been made clear, resulting as essential in many cases.

The business objectives should be taken into account throughout the process of identification and implementation of the SCM and RM methods.

An adequate balance should be found between the cost of implementing SCM and RM and the benefits that are hoped to be obtained, making it necessary to define a SCM and RM policy within the company. It has to be taken into account that it is an investment, therefore resources have to be assigned in order to obtain benefits in the medium term.

The method for implementation of SCM and RM should be defined in function of the type of organisation. The differences in context and the market influences between the different organisations have to be taken into account.

It is important to start with a previous evaluation of the present situation (assessment). Also the needs for external assistance to interpret the results of the evaluation is verified. The management plays a critical role establishing and supporting pilot projects and defining short term and measurable objectives. It is important that there are specific groups dedicated to these pilot improvement projects and who also lead the improvements. The order of implementation of the improvements (SCM and RM) will depend on the objectives, on the necessities, on the products, etc.

For the organisation of improvement, it is necessary to have the support of the Management in order to be able to remove resources from other departments, it is not sufficient that an external company assigns an improvement project to you, or to copy the proceedings of other companies, individual proceedings have to be carried out in every organisation.

In the work groups client participation (internal and external) is fundamental, realistic and achievable objectives have to be established, credibility in management guarantees and freedom of initiatives should exist.

The election of a pilot project does not have to be ambitious, this should be of low risk, representative and of medium size, should have a guarantee of success with personnel that are motivated, prepared and prone to change and participate clients and should have more success than is hoped for.

Communication and training has to be used to overcome the resistance to change.

The captivation of user requirements is an activity for which there are no tools. The development requirements have had different sources and techniques, but the risk is in the loss of information. The prototype is very good for Client credibility.

The benefits of applying SCM and RM tools can not always be quantified. However it is generally agreed that culture is fundamental. The biggest problem with the SCM tools is their adaptation to the business culture. A tool should be able to be adapted to the culture of the business. The CASE tools are of limited use, in that they do not avoid the correct elaboration of catalogue requirements. There lacks the existence of a tool that covers the complete software life-cycle.

The SCM and RM procedures allow change in the perception that clients have of SW processes in the long term. The procedures used should form part of the business culture.

7.2 Milan Workshop

The PIEs, which took part in the workshop panel, gave a brief presentation of the main objectives and results of their project. The presentation follows:

7.2.1   Measurable Improvement of Development, Deployment and Operation

The MIDAS project aims at a measurable improvement in the reliability and availability of interbank services offered by SIA, the organisation in charge of running, developing, and maintaining the National Inter-bank Network of Italy. Such improvement is achieved by establishing an effective CM process, i.e. to define CM procedures and policies, to select and customise automated tools supporting CM activities and to experiment the new CM process in a baseline project. A suitable measurement program was defined – using the Goal/Question/Metrics (GQM) technique – and executed in order to objectively assess the effectiveness of the new CM practice.

Work Done

CM policies and tools were the core activity of the project, since CM is the main innovation introduced in SIA with the experiment. The following steps were performed:

Definition of the CM Process for the Pilot Project

The pilot project is the NRO project. NRO will provide a full range of services for the management and operation of the SIA network. It also provides APIs and interfaces to allow SIA customers to interface their own applications with SIA services. It is one of the most strategic products that SIA will deliver in the next five years.

Selection and Customisation of a Supporting Tool

The tool selected was CCC/Harvest. Within the deployment of the CM system for the NRO software, training of NRO project people and establishment of an on-line support service (help desk) took place. Optimisation of the CM system was also done, according to the results of measurements, monitoring, problem reports and spontaneous feedback.

Definition of the GQM Plan and the Measurement Plan

The aim was to assess the effectiveness of introducing CM in SIA.

Execution of the GQM Measurement Program

The results obtained were analysed, reported and briefly outlined in order to discuss them with the managers.

External Dissemination

The MIDAS project, its objectives and results has been presented in several conferences and meetings.

Internal Dissemination

MIDAS objectives and technical and managerial implications were discussed in SIA, involving both people from the pilot project, people from other projects and departments, and also some suppliers.

7.2.2 Scout Software Configuration Usable Techniques

The SCOUT Process Improvement Experiment – conducted by Infosys S.r.l. with the support of the Commission of the European Communities within the European Software and Systems Initiative (ESSI) – has dealt with the definition and trial of a Software Configuration Management process based on available standards and best practices.

The experiment goals were both technical (reach CM managed level; improve capability to make reliable estimates for change implementation and verification) and of business operation (reduce effort associated to changes deriving from specification problems; minimise change cycle time).

The experiment has shown significant results the most noteworthy being the achievement of level 2 – largely achieved capability profile of the configuration management process.

Apart from the result above, the main key lessons from the experiment have been:

From a technological point of view we learned that an appropriate and comprehensive improvement effort, with well defined goals and measures, and continuously collected actual values from all professionals involved in the project, needs of a mix of tools both off-the-shelf (project management, "office automation") and ad-hoc developed (measurement database). Moreover, the technological environment to support configuration management procedure needs of a proper customisation in order to implement the established formal procedures.

From a business point of view, the experiment made evident that a controlled management of software artefacts during development significantly improves time and effort in implementing changes and in testing activities, thus resulting in a better quality of the final product. Nevertheless, the application of tools and methods is not for free and thus it is crucial for the experiment success that people involved in project being convinced that the additional work eventually imposed on them will be for their own benefit.

The success of experiment makes it evident to continue to use the devised practices and supporting tools in all the other company software development projects.

The results of our experiment are of main interest to small and medium companies involved in software development as well as to software engineering consultants.

7.2.3 Automated Corrective and Evolutionary Maintenance for Database Intensive Application Products

The AUTOMA experiment has concerned the improvement of maintenance activities for complex data management applications, through the formalisation and automation of:

- Requirements management.
- Configuration management.
- Regression testing.

The project has selected the appropriate tools and technologies, and has used them to build two complementary experiment scenarios, based on the maintenance activities of two project groups (one for each partner).

The project has been fully successful in the experimentation of Configuration Management and Requirements Management.

In the first case, the whole maintenance line of a complex system has been put under fully automated control, developing (on top of the selected tool) a CM environment and related procedures capable of ensuring full control while avoiding any extra effort for the maintenance teams (actually contributing to improve the overall efficiency).

On the second aspect, the specifications of another system (in continuous evolution due to changing and increasing user requirements) have been formalised and are now under tool-supported control.

The results obtained on testing shows some problem; at the beginning, more resistance has been experienced on these aspects by the development teams, despite the reduced involvement requested (the preparation of test procedures was performed by dedicated resources), due to the difficulties of showing the advantages of the approach.

The preparation phase has been however successful, and allowed to derive interesting lessons on how to extract and formalise the functional knowledge required to prepare good, effective functional tests.

Once an initial set of automated test procedures has been prepared, its exploitation suffered problems related to the high level of changes that the two systems are still experiencing from one release to the other; this has prevented, till now, a real deployment of automated testing on one of the two systems, while a partial automated testing approach is currently operational for the other.

Despite these difficulties, however, the need to formalise test procedures has injected a radical organisational change in the two maintenance teams that now handle testing-related activities in a quite better way. This is demonstrated by the comparison of the process assessments conducted before and after the experiment.

7.2.4 Summary of the Final Discussion

Provocative intervention. The final discussion was initiated by a provocative intervention by a member of the organisation who asked the PIEs and the audience to react to some provocative points showing how CM can be incompatible with the way things are done all the time in the industry.

The participants asked questions to the PIEs and to the external experts and participated very actively in the debate.

During the debate the main issues emerged were as follows.

Tools are not a guarantee against errors. They cannot solve problems caused by a wrong process or a non adequate organisation. No tool will ever prevent a programmer from dispatching the software one has just modified without any change control, and even if you had one it would be necessary to keep the possibility to bypass procedures in a crisis. For example when critical business processes are blocked due to a software problem your intervention must be immediate. CM procedures should cope with this situation or allow for temporary bypassing of the procedures.

Tyranny or democracy, which is the best? A debate opened between two opposite positions, which were dubbed "democracy" and "tyranny":

- Democracy. Those who maintain that everybody should be involved in the rules setting process and in general rules should be light and flexible (rules suffocate creativity and tend to come down from the top with no real consultation of those who do the work)
- Tyranny. Those who maintain that a software development organisation should have rules to be obeyed by everybody and enforced by top management, Programmers tend to hide behind urgency to avoid the procedures because they do not like rules, but the results of a rule-free environment is simply a disaster.

Probably both "dictatorship" and "democracy" should be applied at different times. When one introduces a new set of practices and a tool one has to be more rigid – even if you should not forget to involve people as far as you can –, later on, when people understand the benefits, they will accept the rules as part of their routine and will not complain any longer.

Are there data in the PIEs showing whether CM pays off or not? can these data convince senior management to invest in CM?.

The PIEs answered that it is very difficult to gather data in an early phase when you just introduced the new practices and don't have quantitative data on the past. This is a critical point: when you don't have data to compare with it is difficult to quantitatively assess any benefits. It is exactly during the first SPI experiment that you start collecting data.

However it is certain that introducing CM technologies and methods means accepting a high level of investment. Some benefits are evident: software components are managed in an orderly way, people are more interchangeable, reuse is facilitated; these are facts but still it is very hard to put a quantitative value on them.

If measuring benefits can be hard evaluating the ROI appears to be almost impossible. How to link the revenues of the company to SPI remains hard to tell, probably it is better to measure what can be really measured i.e. an improved efficiency in the process, higher quality in the product, etc.

Even if we recognised that. It is difficult to assess the ROI, if you had not had the EC funding would you have done the same investment?.

It was clear that all the PIEs were already planning an investment on CM when the ESSI call was issued, but probably they would have done a more limited investment, the presence of the EC funding allowed a wider and more complete experiment. Conversely, funding by itself, without a strategic commitment of the company, does not guarantee that the experiment would be done.

7.2.5   Workshop Findings and Lessons Learned

The following lessons could be gained from this EUREX workshop:

- Some of the critical success factors of a CM implementation project rules, process definition and enforcement come before the tool developing a clear idea of the requirements before buying new technology.
- Do not expect on one single tool bought on the market to solve your problems, a more complex solution based on a mix of market and in-house tools is often necessary.
- A careful inventory and sometimes a restructuring of your software assets is a preliminary and essential step before introducing a CM tool.
- Do not expect that programmers will immediately buy into the new practices, they will resist change claiming that it suffocates flexibility and requires more time.
- A disciplined CM process has many benefits but apparently it will not be as quick as the old way of doing things: you should be ready to assess and give evidence to the benefits compensating for such apparent drawback.
- There is not only one universal solution to CM. Each company should take the approach that suit best its problems and its capability The most relevant parameters to be taken into account are: size of the company, size and structural complexity of the software systems, development environments involved, organisation and localisation of the software producing unit, life cycle model (both for new development and for maintenance), resources available.

7.3   Karlsruhe Workshop

7.3.1   Domain Covered

The title of the fourth workshop was Software Best Practice: Configuration Management. The subject domain was selected on the basis of the results of the classification of the PIEs, which determined that 11 out of 70 German PIEs are related to configuration management.

The workshop focused on the following aspects of configuration management:

- Who is responsible for configuration management? What role does management play? What role does the developer play?.
- What tools support configuration management? Are there any differences between state-of-the-art and state-of-the-practice in this area?.
- How much does configuration management cost? Is it worth it?.

These were identified as significant questions arising from the PIEs' experience. In addition, PIEs were invited to be part of a workshop panel, which gave a presentation as summarised below.

The workshop began with a comprehensive discussion of configuration management by a recognised expert in the field [Editors' Note: This presentation is omitted here. It may be found in its entirety in Chapter 4]. Presentation of some real-world PIE experiences lent a practical basis. With this information as background, an open discussion, moderated by Michael Haug, provided an opportunity for all attendees to discuss the foregoing in an open forum.

7.3.2   PIE Presentation

7.3.2.1   Background

After having successfully completed our Process Improvement Experiment, we believe that we have implemented configuration and change management processes that approaches to the state-of-the-art. The motivation for this effort was a desire to achieve ISO 9000 certification. This led to an overall Quality Management System, incorporating both configuration and change management processes.

ProDV Software AG, Dortmund has 150 employees, including 130 software engineers. Of these, 90 employees are devoted primarily to customer-specific application software development on projects that typically last between 6 and 18 months. The remaining 60 employees are involved in product development.

During initial development phases, change management is somewhat informal. However, after deployment a very formal procedure is followed.

What happens in practice when a customer has request for enhancement or bug fix? The typical procedure was to pick up the phone and call a developer. Perhaps he will write a note, perhaps not. There is mostly verbal communication among teams. The request may even be forgotten or lost.

7.3.2.2   Change Management

As a starting point, a change database was developed. ProDV informed its customers of the database and provided forms that the customers for reporting problems (an MS Word template with fields). This input is emailed as an attachment to ProDV at which point a dedicated person transfers the data to an Access database This transfer is performed automatically, i.e. the association between template fields and database fields is used. Programmers may also enter additional requests or data.

This information is supplemented with things such as software application, component, version, O/S, test data set and so on. Then a request number is generated. An email is automatically sent to the Configuration Manager, the Project Manager for this customer, plus all people assigned to the indicated problem component or components that interface to that component.

Next, the request is analysed. As a result, the requested may be rejected.

If accepted, the Change Manager asks the programmer to propose a suitable change together with an estimate for the effort. If this proposal is accepted, he is nominated as the problem owner. Project Manager and others are informed of this assignment.

The programmer issues a change report and, once the Change Manager accepts the change, the status is set to "done", which triggers notifications to the appropriate people.

This procedure has been fully implemented.

7.3.2.3   Using Change Management Information

There is a significant amount of data generated during the change management process. We use this information in several ways, including:

- Defect diagnosis check whether new error request corresponds to a known problem already resolved? Or, many requests in the same "area" might imply that it should be fixed soon!
- Statistics for quality measures defect rates per component how do new methods or tasks (e.g. testing) influence the defect rate?
- How mature is a product?
- Documentation of lifecycle which customer has sent in what, when, how addressed? Product liability is a driving force.
- Change history and release notes still manually done but now based on change database
- Support of project management estimation numbers, effort used actually, effort tracking
- With a change order, the programmer receives a "change budget" i.e. the estimated effort.

7.3.2.4   Experiences with Change Management

We can organise our experiences with our change management process into several distinct areas. The first and most important is the organisational change. We now have a Change Management manager who is responsible for every software component. Our experience is that this new organisation prevents the chaos that we formerly encountered in this area. Responsibilities are clearly defined and the process is spelled out in detail, including changes rules, when to do changes, when to write a report, and so on. It is clear to all parties involved, including the customer, who did what when. Our procedures are clearly documented.

We also are pleased with the coupling of the change flow process to email. Nobody can avoid being informed of ongoing activities. There is no loss of information, everybody is equally informed. Currently, MS Word documents are attached to automatically generated emails.

The new system is also helpful to programmers because it supports diagnosis of problems and indicates possible sources of defects.

Finally, although there was some resistance in the beginning, both on the part of programmers as well as customers, the benefits have become clear to all and resistance has all but disappeared. Programmers and customers alike thought that it was too much effort to fill in the forms or that it was too formalistic. We can now say that only 3% of the total effort for defect report handling and bug fixing is consumed by change management activities. The programmers can see that customer satisfaction has obviously improved. They can also see that they are better informed; they accept that fact that to receive better information, they must also contribute information. We did experience some performance problems with the MS Access database (for example, to generate an email), but these problems have not caused major difficulties.

7.3.2.5 *Further Enhancements*

As a result of our experiences, we would like to implement several enhancements to our change management process, including:

- Support of diagnosis. A phonetic or thematic search is required. Search for "similarity" (actually: Access SQL query).
- Expert knowledge. If a programmer leaves the company, his knowledge should be kept in database.
- Release management. Today, release notes are extracted manually from the database. They should be generated automatically from entries, simply excluding internal entries.

Link to PVCS. It would be very useful to indicate in Configuration Management (PVCS) that the change process for a given component has not been completed yet. At the present time, there is no interface between these two programs. This means that a baseline might contain modules that not yet finished! To date, "careful release management" on the part of the programmers has avoided problems.

Replace the MS Word document. Instead of Word document, an email entry should be filled in directly, also for the customer. A web interface would be even better. Online forms could do direct input to the database. This would not change the process, but it would save effort. This would also simplify the ability to get a status report, using an online query of the database would require no interaction with programmers or other personnel.

7.3.2.6 Future at ProDV

Our ChangeFlow process is not a commercial tool, largely because the effort for enhancement too big. PVCS Tracker may be an alternative in the future. At the present time, however, the cost is too high.

7.3.3 Q&A Highlights

Dr Tichy: what interface between your ChangeFlow process and PVCS would be necessary?.

Cronau: I don't know, because today the internal users are completely separated. The tools are used in different project groups.

Attendee: Does you system include hierarchical rights or roles?.

Cronau: There should be role based rights: Change Manager, Configuration Manager, customer, programmer, and so on. This could be based on views, using state-of-the-art database systems. But this feature has not been implemented.

7.3.4 Moderated Discussion

The last segment of the workshop consisted of an open discussion moderated by Michael Haug with comments from Prof. Dr Tichy. The debate began with a presentation by Eric W Olsen intended to stimulate the participants into further thought. Following Mr. Olsen's presentation, a free-form discussion was held during which most of the participants shared in a spirited give-and-take.

The goal of Mr. Olsen's presentation was to provide some ideas, observations, and experiences derived from encounters with many companies. The presentation began with a simple survey of those present. Virtually all of the participants indicated that they had used CM, but many fewer were pleased with the results. Most also said that, despite some difficulties, they had used CM successfully. A few said that they used it only because it was required by management and nobody would admit to trying to avoid the use of CM on their projects.

In reviewing common complaints about CM and supporting tools, Mr. Olsen indicated that many people said it was too difficult to use properly, takes too much time, is not easily understandable, or is too vendor-specific.

Mr. Olsen also mentioned some organisational issues. In particular, smaller organisations often cannot afford CM or there is no time for it. Large organisations have difficulties managing CM because of its complexity. Medium size organisations often have both problems.

With respect to CM support tools, Mr. Olsen described a range of costs and problems. Costs range from freeware with no support up 5000 DM per seat. For a small company, cost is a significant factor in the choice of tool. Tools are not, as a rule, integrated with the development environment and there is often poor support from the CM tool vendors. (Unfortunately, this problem is not limited to CM tools.) There has been a significant consolidation in recent years (for example, Rational Software has been buying every CM company in sight in the last two years). If we are lucky, this consolidation will lead to better support and/or integration, including all of the features mentioned by Prof. Tichy in his presentation. But it still won't be cheap.

There are a number of people issues associated with CM, according to Mr. Olsen. In particular, developers generally have little or no understanding of CM because it was not part of their education or training. Contrary to the attitude expressed by Star Trek's Borg, resistance is not futile! People can destroy the usefulness of tools.

In spite of all of these difficulties, Mr. Olsen stated that CM is a necessary part of software development and we must do it. Furthermore, he believes, we have already built all of the simple software products and the things we have to build now and in the future are complex. This increases the need for CM and its benefits.

The most important message from Mr. Olsen was that configuration management is essential to the proper management of software projects and that its introduction should carefully address the experiences and needs of the people involved.

The following added value is gained from EUREX workshops:

- A wide audience is given the opportunity to hear competent practitioners talking about an important topic.
- Comparing and contrasting the experts with the real-world experiences of the PIEs is a real benefit to those investigating the topic for the first time.
- Open, lively debate improves confidence that all of the relevant issues have been addressed and not just the favourite ideas of a few experts.

7.3.5   Open Discussion Highlights

An edited transcript of the discussion follows. Conference organisers and presenters have been identified by name.

Haug: Is this the typical view of an American? Do we Germans accept the problems associated with CM more easily? Because we are aware of our customers, do programmers accept CM better in Germany?.

Attendee: Apparently only programmers are meant to do CM. However, there is no difference between specifications and programs. Quality management means that we need to bring together the various phases and processes. Sometimes this means using several CM systems for different aspects of the same project!

Cronau: Why several?

Attendee: Well, we have problems with legacy systems at my company. Many product variants have been developed and must be maintained. This is not so easy because, over time, we have used many different host systems, development environments, and specification procedures.

Haug: How many people involved?

Attendee: Several thousand.

Tichy: What is the biggest problem that you have encountered when linking between document types (specifications, code, etc.)?

Attendee: We have political problems. It is impossible for all projects to use the same tool. Projects in progress can't change. Over time, step by step, the software has been built upon previous versions. We have technical problems as well. We are testing the limits of the tools with the number of people and associated configuration items.

Haug: Are you looking for a single tool?

Attendee: You are discussing the difference between software configuration management and system configuration management. In our environment, working in banking and air traffic control systems means heating, cooling, hardware, plus some software. This is very different from a batch or online transaction application.

Haug: Dr Cronau, do you have problems using a single tool for everything?

Cronau: We are only dealing with software and our company is much smaller, around 130 people. Specifications, source, test data and so on are being managed by one system; but not at all perfectly. We cannot afford to purchase PVCS for every employee: we would go bankrupt! That's why we partly developed our own software to manage CM.

We developed a tool to manage change flow ourselves. PVCS offers a tool called Tracker, but there is no interface to the Change Management available! For example, you must enter the people responsible for various activities in both tools, separately. Also, each tool adds to the price.

Haug: This means that there are integration problems not only between different suppliers but also within the products of a single supplier.

Fr Tichy: As you notice, it is very important that tools are platform independent! Use an RCS-based tool. RCS runs on many different platforms. Some customers use it on a large set of platforms. Customers are grateful for the homogeneous approach.

Attendee: There are organisational issues to be concerned with: coaching large projects in big companies, you still have to explain what CM means. This is not always easy to do. You must explain the process, tailor it for the organisation, and implement it. Even in big companies with significant resources, this is difficult.

Tichy: That's true! You hear this everywhere.

Attendee: There are already enough process models, e.g. V-model, to use as a template for development. But two-thirds of people do not know much about CM!.

Tichy: My students studying software engineering have a week of CM as part of the curriculum.

Attendee: There are also problems with hardware manufacturers. They do not view themselves as programmers, even though they produce large amounts of software. They are not trained in CM and have even less understanding of the need for it than typical software people.

Tichy: ChangeFlow is simpler to use than Word. Why is it complicated? Is the assertion of complexity meant to hide some other problem?

Attendee: Perhaps so. One possible answer is that using such tools means that work and work products are more visible. Some people might not want this.

Haug: Existing processes may not be easily adaptable. Processes have to be described, documented and finally programmed. (Continuus e.g. is a programming language and compiler to program processes!)

That's why they fail, if they start with a more naive approach!

Koelmel: We should also mention the notion of software as art rather than an engineering discipline. FZI has experience with a lot of PIEs, projects funded by the commission to deal with process improvement. We have often observed that companies with an engineering background that are used to standards have much less problem transferring this approach to the software arena.

On the other hand, for example, young, but innovative software houses have much more difficulty!

Attendee: That's right. They are innovative, small, creative, but they have problems with the rigidity imposed on them by the more formal processes. Big companies grow into structure. To introduce a strict process, you have to go through difficult times to overcome resistance. But after, say, half a year, people start to understand that it is nice to be able to locate a software version archived some time ago.

Cronau: Configuration management and quality management are processes. You can improve acceptance if employees are involved in the development of the processes. Let people describe and document what they do, so they find themselves within the new system. But larger organisations already have thick structure, and people do not like to accept this without change.

But of course, formal processes are necessary for larger organisations. Small companies can live with more freedom. (Example: 6 employees working in one project in neighbouring offices, but already not effective if not supported by CM).

There is the aspect of being controlled as well. Project management is understood as controlling activity. For the most part, people don't like to be controlled.

CM may also cause additional effort that is perceived to be clerical rather than creative, which results in further resistance. If supported by efficient tools, acceptance is more easily obtained.

Attendee: There is a serious problem caused by management, products shouldn't cost much and they have to be ready yesterday. Under most circumstances, this means that employees cannot be involved in process or tool development, because they have their project-related work to do. Furthermore, this pressure from management means that developers resent the imposition of anything that slows them down. Developers need to see their own advantage in using a configuration management tool/process and management has to be prepared to accept the necessity as well.

Much of this discussion is a surprise to me, because my background is hardware development. If a software developer is going to leave a company, he feels the right to take his "brain" with him leaving behind only marginal documentation. In a hardware development environment, documentation has a much higher appreciation and acceptance.

Software people do not want to be controlled! If they don't do it, they intend not to do it. It is silly to say that CM might be too complicated for them, because they are solving much more complicated problems in their daily work!

Attendee: Configuration management has to be slim!

Cronau: Developers see the advantage if they are working together on the same files. They find out very quickly!

Attendee: Another problem is customer perception. Version numbers are not allowed to be high, because customers think that frequent changes mean poor quality. That's why management asks for low numbers!

Cronau: Easy solution: strip the version numbers at the end.

Tichy: that's ok, create a side branch and merge back at the delivery.

Attendee: Baseline.

Haug: co-operation with customer, co-development, no walls possible.

Cronau: The problem not solved. We have some software at public agencies, and we are required to generate three new versions per year. Once, a head crash occurred. We had to recreate the original version, because only upgrades had been delivered in the past! This means that a new baseline per upgrade is necessary.

Tichy: You should be able to afford a CD burner these days. Then you can archive the complete version.

Attendee: This example is unthinkable in mission critical environments! It's basic ABC, to make baselines archives and save a complete version including tools. Why would you do otherwise?

Haug: Tools included? Delta or full versions?

Tichy: There are no deltas anymore! Storage is too cheap to worry about a few megabytes. It is a good idea to save a complete version that will be released to the customer in such a way that nobody can destroy this version. Again, CD burners are cheap.

Haug: Military projects spend more on these activities. Dr Cronau, you wanted to include your customer into the problem reporting system, e.g. using a WEB page.

Cronau: It's a problem to let your customers into your operational system. Think about the security issues.

Attendee: That is an old rule: no access from outside to your operational systems Replicate to a stand-alone server. Other rules, other protocols!

Tichy: Barrier!

Attendee: But that's only part of the problem. If we allow the customer to enter error reports, we need someone to look at those reports!

Attendee: This means a co-ordination problem.

Attendee: Forms have an additional problem: Different users will use different words to describe the same problem.

Haug: But this is no different from the traditional paper error reports! It simply makes it more convenient for the user to send you the report. Of course, convenience may mean that more reports are received, which will require additional resources to evaluate. But the customer is happier and the developers have more data to work with in dealing with ongoing issues.

Attendee: Use multiple choice?

Attendee: Do you plan to share this information with the customer, including status? I'm not entirely sure that this is desirable.

Attendee: We need better integration of change process with configuration management. I do not know of a standard tool that can track changes into modules and backwards. Including word documents or other specifications. The change process should always control changes.

Tichy: Most tools allow for this, even SCCS had this already. MKS Source Integrity offers a coding interface to other tools for communication of change information.

Cronau: But you still have to control the programmers. Spot checks, at least, are still necessary. It might be nice to generate a history file including all texts entered by programmers.

Attendee: What for?

Attendee: It must be automatic!

Cronau: There has never been a tool supplier who offered a useful integration over the life cycle (configuration management, quality management, program management, and do on) and between tools. Never! Why is that? PVCS is a good example of how bad this is!

Haug: One thing that hasn't been mentioned is test data and the test environment.

Attendee: Just treat it like source code.

Attendee: I don't see a difference, either.

Haug: You have to version the test harness as well!

Attendee: That is a problem because of size and complexity. Think of planning for backup systems to be used, etc.

Cronau: What we need is this: test tools should have programming interfaces as well! ChangeFlow should trigger the test environment when programmer declares a module ready.

Attendee: Big problem. Where are the test specs? What are you going to test against? This needs to be clear before you can do it automatically.

Cronau: It is necessary to manage the flow of control between tools.

Haug: Unfortunately, our time is up and the weekend is beginning. Thank you all for coming.

7.3.6   Workshop Findings and Lessons Learned

The workshop lessons included the following:

- The most serious problems with configuration management are people issues. It is difficult to get software developers to accept the structure imposed upon them by a formal configuration management regime.
- It is important to involve people in the definition of the CM process so that they do not feel put upon by a new structure.
- Training in the tools and methods is necessary so that everyone understands not only how to do configuration management, but why it is important to do it.
- The cost of commercial configuration management tools is significant enough that small and medium size organisations have second thoughts. From their point of view, it makes no sense to bankrupt the company in order to keep historical records that may never be used.
- There remains a significant integration problem for virtually all configuration management tools. Most specification, development and testing environments do not integrate well at all with CM tools (with the possible exception of CM tools from the same supplier). This means that CM relies on people to be rigorous about CM activities and this introduces additional potential for error.
- It is important to consider CM for all aspects of the software process. In other words, requirements, specifications, tests and so on should be included, not just code. This improves the overall lifecycle traceability of a project.

7.4   Workshops Summary

The CM workshops provided an important opportunity for the software community to improve its awareness of state-of-the-art methods and technologies recently available on the market and to gain valuable experience (state-of-the-practice) from the developed best practice in Configuration Management.

Many of the projects presented in these workshops have been successful in adopting and testing configuration management methods and tools to improve the software development and maintenance process of small as well as large organisations in Europe.

Any organisation that develops software, or equipment based on software, usually has some difficulty to organise and track the functionality and installed base of the different software versions. Configuration Management, including Change Management, is not a "silver bullet" by itself, but as we have seen in the workshops, it has shown a high percentage of success in solving many of the problems.

The intrinsic importance of CM increases due to the fact that the spread of errors through the number of active versions of different products across a number of customers has a great impact on the organisation.

While larger companies with substantial resources have obtained some but not all of the benefits configuration management can offer them, smaller companies have a much lower rate of penetration of this technology.

Although many workshop attendees were able to present anecdotal evidence, it is difficult to quantify the savings that result from CM due to the lack of rigorous historical measurements. This makes it more difficult to justify up-front costs to management. An organisation must begin evaluating its current situation by measuring actual quality, efforts, customer satisfaction, number of errors and other parameters in order to compare differences once a configuration management process has been used for a period of time.

The lack of desire to acknowledge errors is another factor that does not help quantification.

Configuration Management is essential, directly and indirectly, to many organisational components. From the management of product requirements, to software development, to installation and maintenance, the implementation of processes guarantees a higher control and a reduction of errors.

In the beginning, resistance can be expected from a development team, due to the difficulties of demonstrating the advantages of the approach up front. Developers need to see the advantages of configuration management tools and processes, and management must be prepared to support it as well. When an organisation has taken the decision to introduce a new set of practices and tools, it needs to be firm with respect to its definition and implementation, involving the affected personnel as much as possible. When people start to see the benefits, they will accept the new practices as part of their routine. As with any change in an organisation, communication and training must be used to overcome resistance.

The checklists below present a synthesis of the experiences discussed at the workshops, as interpreted by the editors.

The following features make Configuration Management, based on a configuration tool, a must for most software organisations:

- Management of the outputs of the software development life-cycle phases and their completeness once they are used as baselines to other processes.
- Configuration control is important, above all, in the final phases such as construction, implementation and maintenance. (During initial development phases the change management is more informal.)
- It helps to define and organise the process for managing change requests to a delivered software version.
- Once a version is delivered and operational, a CM environment and related procedures are capable of ensuring full control while avoiding extra effort for software maintenance teams.

- The written communication between client, change implementation teams, project managers and other involved roles, makes it difficult to forget or lose a client request.
- Sometimes it is crucial to be able to locate a particular software version (together with its environment) that has not been used recently.

The following should be considered when defining a configuration management strategy:

- Size of the company, focus on resources needed, and tool's included licences.
- Number of projects and development environments, focus on the diversity and distribution of the configuration items and versions that need to be managed.
- Level of software complexity, focus on the level of interdependencies among configuration items, number of tests and changes before version releases. Complex software systems need a higher degree of CM throughout all software development phases.
- Organisation and localisation of the software production unit.
- New development and maintenance life cycle model.
- Analyse the company culture in order to choose and adapt a configuration management tool, and do not expect that a single tool by itself will solve all problems. An automatic solution will always be based on a mix of tools and written procedures.
- Responsibilities to carry out the configuration management roles have to be clear and explicitly assigned at the beginning of the process definition

The following business benefits derive from configuration management:

- Better communication between customers and developers
- Better alignment of technological and business objectives
- Increased quality of the product as a whole
- Increased customer visibility and satisfaction
- Reduction of development time
- Reduction of effort associated with changes deriving from specification problems
- Minimised change cycle time
- Improved reliability of estimates for change implementation and verification
- Increased software productivity
- Reduction in Time-To-Market
- Increased information and data transparency and communication
- Elimination of team frustration leads to an increase in motivation
- Increased efficiency of human teams
- Increased number of defined and repeatable processes
- Increased company know how and assets
- Increased quality service (improving competitive position).

Configuration management processes, including version control, change management and tool support, is essential to proper software project management. Its introduction in an organisation should carefully address the experience and needs of the people involved.

A well-established configuration management procedure will support the assertion that the software produced is more easily maintained, more independent of the original development team, and better organised and documented.

8   Significant Results

G. Cuevas, S. Rementeria
SOCINTEC, Bilbao

Most of the participants in ESSI projects dealt with configuration management purely in a practical manner, working with tools and procedures from various commercial vendors to solve their immediate problems. However, we believe that standards are an appropriate way to organise and define configuration management processes generally. To that end, it can be said that Software Configuration Management is a control discipline within the software project. Configuration Management should be used throughout a product's life cycle, in development as well as during the maintenance process until the product is withdrawn. Three objectives should be considered in Software Configuration Management:

- Establish and maintain the integrity of a software product during its life cycle.
- Control the evolution of a software product.
- Facilitate the visibility of a product.

8.1   The IEEE Software Configuration Management Standard

In order to meet these objectives, the IEEE Software Configuration Management standard includes the four activities shown in figure 8.1.

- *Configuration identification* identifies a product's structure and components in an unambiguous way.
- *Configuration control* manages the versions, deliveries and changes to a product during its life cycle.
- *Status report generation* provides details about a product's status and change requests; the basis for product statistics.
- *Configuration audit* validates a product's completeness and the consistency of its components.

It is evident that the need for rigorous Configuration Management is even greater when the simultaneous maintenance of multiple versions is necessary.

However, the reality is that, even now, most software development organisations carry out this process with minimum quality controls.

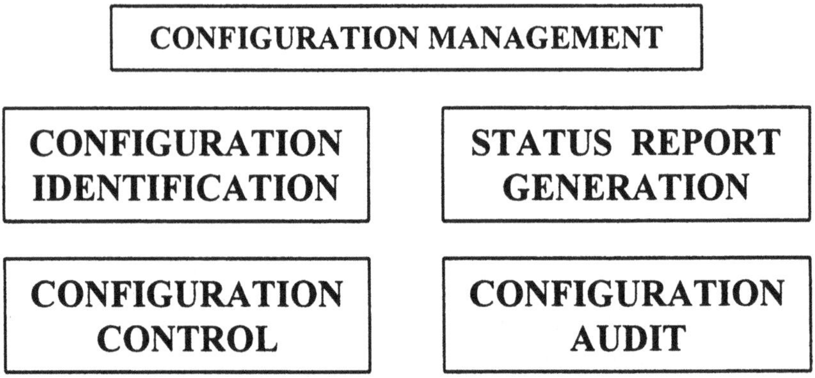

CONFIGURATION MANAGEMENT

CONFIGURATION IDENTIFICATION

STATUS REPORT GENERATION

CONFIGURATION CONTROL

CONFIGURATION AUDIT

Fig 8.1 Main Configuration Management Activities (IEEE)

The complexity of Configuration Management is marked fundamentally by two factors:

- Number of components to control.
- Changes in the product through its life cycle. As a project advances, more is known about the problem and how to solve it and business criteria evolve continuously as well. Change is necessary and cannot be avoided.

Configuration Management would be a lot easier if there was some way to describe the architecture of an application that permitted changes in the code, and to propagate its effects to the rest of the system in a simple way.

Likewise, Configuration Management is strongly related to software maintenance. Without good Configuration Management, product maintenance can be a nightmare.

Configuration Management also has an important influence on other aspects of software development, and its activities should be integrated with the development processes, environment and methodologies.

For every project, it must be decided which software configuration elements (SCE) will be used. A SCE should have characteristics and performance parameters that can be defined and controlled separately from other such elements. By this, we mean that an SCE should be a unit unto itself, which can be tested and used independently.

The size and complexity of a software component may require its break-up into several SCEs even though the component itself is an SCE within the larger framework of a complete application.

The baseline concept is a reference point in the software development process that is marked by the approval of formal technical revision(s) to one or more SCEs. It can also be defined as the point at which an element that has been checked and accepted and will serve as a base for other later developments, can only be changed further by a formal change control process.

The four basic Configuration Management activities are described further as follows.

8.1.1   Configuration Identification

The following tasks are often included in this activity:

- Establish a preliminary software product hierarchy (the first vision of the structure and elements of the complete system).
- Select configuration elements (it is important to publish the selection criteria).
- Define relationships within the configuration (to help understand where an element is placed within the hierarchy).
- Define an identification scheme (it is important to define the method used to define each SCE in an unambiguous way).
- Define and establish baselines (labelling each SCE and archiving them in a project library or publishing a configuration identification document).
- Define and establish the software libraries (a controlled collection of software and documentation).

8.1.2   Configuration Control Change

Two fundamental types of changes should be considered:

- Correction of a defect.
- System improvement.

At the same time, change control levels are established:

- Informal (before an SCE is part of a baseline).
- Semi-informal (once the SCE passes formal technical revision and is added to a baseline).
- Formal (once the product is commercialised and the SCEs are transferred to the software library).

While there is no standard for the control of informal or internal changes, there are some recommendations (IEEE 1024).

Concerning formal change control, the usual stages are:

- Change initiation.

- Change request registration and configuration.
- Initial approval or refusal of the change request.
- Evaluation of the change request, if it has been approved, to calculate the effort, possible secondary effects, global impact and estimated cost of the change.
- Change report to the Change Control Committee.
- Carrying out the change.
- Certificate for its correct integration.
- Notifying the change originator of the result.

8.1.3   Status Report Generation

The aim is to keep users, managers and developers informed about the various configuration stages and their evolution. This implies three basic tasks:

- Data capture.
- Data recording.
- Report generation.

Therefore, the products within this activity are fundamentally from two categories:

- Registers (changes, incidents, code modifications, database modifications, document modifications, releases, installations, minutes and configuration elements).
- Reports (change condition, configuration element inventory, incidents, modifications, and differences among versions).

This activity is important for:
- Maintaining the continuity of the project.
- Avoiding duplication of effort.
- Preventing the same mistake many times.
- Repeating what works.
- Helping to discover the causes of errors.

8.1.4   Configuration Audit

Configuration audits are used to ensure that the product under construction is indeed the one expected. The aim is to find problems. Two activities can be differentiated:

- Phase revisions at the end of each phase and
- Audits at the completion of software development to examine the whole of the product.

The revision task implies three types of functions:

- Verify that the actual software configuration corresponds to the previous phases.
- Validate that the actual software configuration satisfies the expected product function at each milestone of the development process.
- Evaluate whether a specific baseline is acceptable or not.

Two kinds of configuration audits can be distinguished:

- Functional auditing to check that a configuration element satisfies its requirements.
- Physical auditing to verify the suitability, completeness and accuracy of the documentation, which constitutes the design baseline.

8.2   The Configuration Management Plan

The main component of Configuration Management is the configuration management plan itself. It should be produced at the beginning of each project to define policies, standards and procedures to manage the configuration during the lifetime of the project.

A configuration management plan should contain the following sections:

- Introduction (Purpose of the plan, scope, definitions, acronyms and references).
- Management specifications (organisation, responsibilities, management policies and applicable procedures).
- Configuration management activities (identification, configuration control, configuration accounting statement, configuration auditing).

Configuration Management, as do all software engineering activities, needs resources. Unfortunately, resources are not always made available, or they may be drained away by activities perceived to be of greater importance. What happens, then, if the effort is not undertaken? Product quality will suffer and there will be less opportunity for reuse of the development products.

With regard to metrics, it is preferable that they are simple and direct. If complexity is introduced, there should be a clear advantage to the information provided and its ability to direct the project.

Among the potential metrics to be used, there are:

- Trend analysis of irregularities and change requests, or at least an account of them.
- Number of change request as a function of project complexity.
- Number of configuration elements by hierarchy levels.
- Change request implementation and overall response times.

Our discussions can also help to profile the people who implement configuration management:

- Software development experience.
- Technical environment and management knowledge.
- Communication ability.
- Meticulous, conscientious and organised.

Finally, it should be clear by now that, for Configuration Management to be successful, the entire organisation must be committed to its success.

Part III

Process Improvement Experiments

9 Table of PIEs

Table 9.1 below lists each of the PIEs considered as part of the EUREX taxonomy within the problem domain of Configuration and Change Management.

Table 9.1 Table of PIEs

Project No	Year of CfP	Acronym	Project Partners	Country
10965	1993	AERIDS	SAIT DEVLONICS	B
21766	1995	AIM	ABN AMRO BANK N.V.	NL
21511	1995	APPLY	VERILOG	F
23955	1996	ARRIBA	AEROSPATIALE	F
21820	1995	AUTO-DOC	DATACARE COMPUTERS Ltd	IRL
10564	1993	AUTOMA	DATAMAT INGEGNERIA DEI SISTEMI SPA	I
21682	1995	AVE	MUNICIPALITY OF KAVALA	GR
10334	1993	BRED	LLOYD'S REGISTER OF SHIPPING	UK
10358	1993	CEMP	ROBERT BOSCH GMBH	D
10358	1993	CEMP	SCHLUMBERGER INDUSTRIES S.S.	F
10358	1993	CEMP	DIGITAL EQUIPMENT SPA	I
21568	1995	CMEX	SYSDECO INNOVATIONS AS	N
23661	1996	CMOS	EUROELETTRA	I
24051	1996	COMANCHE	SOFTWARE UNO Srl	I
21830	1995	COMMITS	IT SOFTWARE	I
24362	1996	CONFITEST	TeSSA NV	B
23891	1996	CONFMANAG	VALMET AUTOMATION INC	SF
23697	1996	CREDIT	TRENDSOFT Ltd	IRL
23670	1996	CUSTOMIZE	TTS AUTOMATION AS	N
21593	1995	DIGIDOC	DIGIANSWER A/S	DK
23696	1996	DSP – ACTION	NOKIA MOBILE PHONES R&D	SF
10542	1993	EASIER	CMA SPA	I
10453	1993	ELSA	ENEL SPA CENTRO RICERCA DI AUTO-MATICA	I
23724	1996	ESTREMA	GRUPPO PRO	I
23794	1996	EURO2000	CONFEDERACION ESPANOLA DE CAJAS DE AHORROS (CECA)	E

Project No	Year of CfP	Acronym	Project Partners	Country
21532	1995	EXCUSES	SODALIA S.p.A.	I
10760	1993	FAME	FIRST INFORMATICS S.A.	GR
10603	1993	FOCUS	INSTRUMENTOINTI OY	SF
24189	1996	GEARS	MASMEC	I
21741	1995	HEMATITES	CRUZ ROJA ESPANOLA	E
24181	1996	HOSPUR	G.O.C.	E
24181	1996	HOSPUR	AITA MENNI	E
24181	1996	HOSPUR	B-KIN	E
21379	1995	ICONMAN	EVENT AS	N
23760	1996	IECS	JOANNEUM RESEARCH FORSCHUNGS-GESELLSCHAFT mbH	A
21628	1995	IMPACT	PRO DV SOFTWARE GmbH	D
24078	1996	IMPACTS2	DTK GESELLSCHAFT FÜR TECHNISCHE KOMMUNIKATION mbH	D
23780	1996	IMPOSE	MENTE SYSTEMUTVIKLING AS	N
21433	1995	IMPROVE-CM	SPACE SOFTWARE	I
21733	1995	INCOME	FINSIEL S.p.A.	I
10163	1993	IRMA	BRITISH AEROSPACE DEFENCE LTD	UK
21603	1995	ISOTOPO	IBERMATICA S.A.	E
21358	1995	ISUC	KNAPP LOGISTICS AUTOMATION	A
24155	1996	LANHOBEK	LANTIK S.A.	E
21473	1995	LARGECM	ALENIA un' AZIENDA FINMECCANIA	I
10549	1993	MARITA	ABB ROBOTICS PRODUCTS AB	S
10560	1993	MAUSE	01 – PLIROFORIKI S.A.	GR
21411	1995	MAZ PIE	MAZ HAMBURG GmbH	D
21244	1995	MIDAS	S.I.A. S.p.A.	I
21416	1995	MOODISC	MICROLOGICA COMPUTERSYSTEME GmbH	D
24196	1996	MPCM	TRANSACTION SOFTWARE GmbH	D
21547	1995	MSI-QBP	GEPIN ENGINEERING S.p.A.	I
10913	1993	OSEF	ALITALIA – LINEE AEREE ITALIANE SPA	I
24065	1996	PCS	CLOCKWORKS MULTIMEDIA	IRL
10438	1993	PET	BRÜEL & KJAER MEASUREMENTS A/S	DK
21531	1995	PITA	AMT-SYBEX (SOFTWARE) Ltd	IRL
21167	1995	PRIDE	BRÜEL & KJAER A/S	DK
21231	1995	PROCOM	PROTEC GmbH	D
24149	1996	PROMISED	CSTB	F
23845	1996	QARI	MAXWARE AS	N
21630	1995	Q-PRIME	PRODACTA GmbH	D
10497	1993	RECAP	ALENIA UN'AZIENDA FINMECCANICA	I
23893	1996	REJOICE	DERA	UK

Project No	Year of CfP	Acronym	Project Partners	Country
10714	1993	REQUITE	DATACEP	F
10714	1993	REQUITE	MARCONI RADAR AND CONTROL SYSTEMS LTD	UK
24257	1996	RMATN	ALCATEL TELECOM NORWAY AS	N
23673	1996	SCOUT	INFOSYS srl	I
10937	1993	SECU-DES	DALCOTECH A/S	DK
10824	1993	SIMTEST	DATASPAZIO TELESPAZIO E DATAMAT PER L'INGEGNERIA DEI SISTEMI SPA	I
10218	1993	SMETOSQA	INFOGEA SRL	I
21269	1995	SO.C.CO.MA	ISTISERVICE S.p.A.	I
23875	1996	SPECS	ITALTEL S.p.A.	I
10344	1993	SPIE	IBERIS LINEAS AEREAS	E
23750	1996	SPIP	ONYX TECHNOLOGIES	ISR
21799	1995	SPIRIT	BAAN COMPANY N.V.	NL
23947	1996	SYMQUAD	EROSKI SCOOP	E
21681	1995	TESOS	BIJO-DATA INFORMATIONSSYSTEME GmbH	D
23683	1996	TESTART	ISRAEL AIRCRAFT INDUSTRIES CORPORATE R&D (Dept 9100)	ISR
24091	1996	TOPSPIN	TEDOPRES INTERNATIONAL B.V.	NL
21336	1995	TPM	OY QUALITY & RESEARCH PRODUCTION Ltd (QPR)	SF
10798	1993	TRANSPEC	ADVANCED INFORMATION SYSTEMS N.V.	B
10798	1993	TRANSPEC	COMPETENCE CENTER INFORMATIK GmbH	D
10798	1993	TRANSPEC	CIM FABRIK HANNOVER GmbH	D
23754	1996	TRUST	AGUSTA UN'AZIENDA FINMECCANCIA S.p.a.	I
21434	1995	UFOSEP	AXIOMA INFORMATION SYSTEMS GmbH	A
21712	1995	VERDEST	TT TIETO OY	SF
23971	1996	VIGOROUS	RAMTEX ENGINEERING ApS	DK
10573	1993	WORKSHOP	CONSORCI HOSPITALARI DE CATALUNYA S.A.	E

10 Summaries of PIE Reports

10.1 AERDIS 10965

ESSI in Context of Rail Station Information Display System Software

The main interest, in ESSI action, for SAIT Devlonics is to introduce practically the concepts available in the quality manual. SAIT Devlonics wants to have a Quality System which automates certain procedures/methods. They are:

- to automate as much as possible the Software life cycle development;
- to execute a Configuration Management on the PC environment;
- to create a library of software components (reusability) and to incorporate its in the Configuration Management.

System in order to increase dramatically the efficiency of software development.

Application Experiment was performed on the Railway station Information Display System (AERIDS) software project. The RIDS is computing and dispatching information (train's departure time, train's destinations, etc...) to a set of display devices for the attention of the train's passengers.

The RIDS is a real time distributed system with a centralised data base and its software application is composed of several programs for an overall estimated size of 87000 lines of code.

The experiment was done on a part of the project (12000 lines of code) which has been easily isolated.

SAIT has carried out this pilot project to develop part of the RIDS using as set of CASE tools which have been integrated to work together and to automate the entire software development life cycle including analysis, design, implementation and maintenance phases.

A process group support has been put in place in the engineering department with two basic tasks:

- initiating and sustaining process change,
- supporting the projects as they use methods, standards, technology (normal operations).

This group serves as a consolidating force for the change that have already been made. Without such guidance, lasting process improvement is practically impossible.

At the end of this experiment, SAIT Devlonics has outlined the following key lessons learned:

- the introduction of an integrated tools support for the software lifecycle development are permitted to automate the procedures defined in the SAIT Quality System (SQS);
- the quality level was improved by a more involvement from the quality control (QC) and the existence of static and dynamic metrics. However, the lack of transparency between the host/target environment, the weakness of data set management and no functional testing must be still solved.
- the configuration management system is appropriate for documents management. Indeed, it offers much flexibility for adapting the configuration to the variety of projects developed by SAIT Devlonics. But the facilities availables for the configuration of sources code and executables (software components reusability) are insufficient.

To conclude, this experiment has contributed to the SAIT Devlonics efforts to pass the ISO 9001 certification.

The next actions will be carried to improve the software components reusability and to increase productivity in order to avoid to loos competitive power.

Sait Devlonics
Belgium

10.2   AIM 21766

An Experiment With an Automatic Repository Based Impact Analysis Mechanism

Business Motivation and Objectives

Demonstrate the improvement of the software development- and delivery process in a limited experiment directed towards solving the problem of conflicting components within complex information environments, using standard software packages. The expected result will be a significant improvement of the quality of implemented software thus reducing the number of errors occurring during delivery and during execution of software systems. Targets: reduce delivery-errors to zero, reduce errors related to impact by 50%, reduce capacity needed by 60%, Increase availability to 24 hours a day, 7 days a week.

Banks and other financial institutions in general use complex information environments (hardware, software). Changing software-components in these environments is an activity with a high risk, because of the (mostly not completely known) complexity of the relationships between the components under change.

Also other financial institutions are forced to change their information systems because of the year 2000 and the introduction of the Euro. ABN AMRO Bank as a major financial institute uses its experience with complex information environments to perform the experiment and wants to exchange the experience on a European level with other organisations.

The Experiment

The aim of the experiment is to demonstrate the improvement of the software-delivery process using a Repository-based fully automated impact-analysis mechanism.

After the repository has been populated with all components and all relationships between these components, a change to any component will signal the impacted components to their owners and will automatically regenerate the affected components.

To be able to control a large number of projects, often making changes to or affecting the same set of components, a release-control mechanism will be used to order the delivery of the changes.

This release-control mechanism will be included in the repository.

The project team will consist of 9 people during the building-phase.

The experiment will be performed on all projects which will deliver changes to ABN AMRO's MVS production environment during the period September-December 1996. The preliminary results will be used to further improve the system. Some of the projects will make significant changes to the administrative processes related to the most integrated administrations available, the financial and clients administration.

Expected Impact and Experience

We expect a major improvement of the time-to-market of our software products resulting in an improved time-to-market of banking products. Above that we will improve the control of the change process, the quality and stability of our information systems and our potential to make changes related to the year 2000 and the Euro.

Future improvement plans based on the results of the experiment will be extending the solution to other platforms thus improving our capabilities to make changes in client/server applications in a controlled manner. Because of the general approach taken, also changes in systems software and hardware can be implemented using the same system.

We plan to further develop the described system to obtain planning and actual information about projects executed, thus making it possible to constantly improve the development process.

To be able to start-up projects faster than today, we also plan to add resources with their skills and skills needed by projects, thus making it possible to help project teams in allocating the proper skills on the planned starting dates.

Abn Anro Bank N.V.
Netherlands

10.3   APPLY 21511

Amplified Process Performance Layout

VERILOG is a manufacturer of software and system engineering tools. VERILOG was looking for an improvement of its internal practices to deliver better products to its customers and for an increase of its experience to help external organisations to plan and implement its technologies.

The APPLY project is the experiment of the combined application of recommendations coming from a global Process Improvement Program initiated after a CMM self assessment. The main objective of APPLY was to implement the recommendations on a real size project in order to validate them and to obtain a quantitative project profile (cost break down and benefits) to facilitate internal and external replication.

The main achievement of APPLY are:

- Definition of a Project Control Panel capturing metrics on process performance, quality of the final product.
- Implementation of new practices supported by tools in the areas of:
  - Requirements Management.
  - Project Planning and Tracking.
  - Configuration Management.
  - Test and Validation.

APPLY results are:

- A better project control:
- Initial budget respected, delivery time managed within a 5% window (but the initial date is not respected).
- A higher reliability of the final product:
- Remaining bugs are divided by 2 for the same test effort
- Economical consequences have to be evaluated on market side rather than on the internal productivity benefits. For instance, VERILOG has had 40% product sales growth and an increase of maintenance contract renewal.

The description of this experiment could give to other organisations ideas and facts in order to replicate such improvement. This work has been financed by the European Commission as part of the ESSI program.

Verilog
France

10.4 ARRIBA 23955

Requirements Capture Improvement for Behavioural Simulators

ARRIBA addresses the necessity for rapid, efficient and economic capture of customers' requirements for the elaboration of complex C3I (Command Control Communications and Intelligence) systems. The experiment was based on the confrontation between a new Object Oriented approach using emerging hypermedia technologies and Java language and a baseline methodology using SES Workbench and Ilog Views. ARRIBA demonstrated the feasibility as well as the advantages and limitations of hypermedia behavioural simulators in Java language.

To avoid misunderstanding on the customer's needs and ensure customer satisfaction, the capture process uses behavioural simulators representing the future C3I system, providing an efficient way to describe functional requirements and to collect customer opinion about the architecture and expected behaviour of the future solution together with the integration of possible additional requirements.

The customer's requirements capture process has three basic steps, implemented in an iterative flow:

- the requirements capture itself
- the requirements analysis
- the requirements validation by the customer.

In this iterative process that requires typically from 4 to 8 cycles, the duration and the cost of each iteration need to be optimised. The Java technology has been selected for its unique assets in terms of the object orientation, client server architecture and independence from the platforms.

The comparison between the ARRIBA solution and the baseline shows a clear technical and business advantage for the ARRIBA solution, although the baseline approach allows, at this stage, faster performance and a larger scope of functionalities.

Applicability will expand with build-up of libraries, and consequent reuse strategy.

Benefits form the large scope of SES/Workbench, but is heavy to exploit for the implementation of the customer feed-functions back loop, and altogether less cost-effective than ARRIBA.

The results from ARRIBA are now being disseminated and promoted internally, to be implemented in a selection of activities, building progressively libraries of reusable components.

External promotion of ARRIBA achievements is being done via publications in international conferences, as well as through Fi System web site and the Aerospatiale intranet that reaches the whole Aerospatiale group.

Aerospatiale
France

10.5   AUTO-DOC 21820

The Introduction of an Automated Document Management System

The project has aptly been given the acronym "AUTO-DOC" as it is concerned with the introduction of an automated documentation system to automate recognised documentation practices in the software process. Documentation is defined as "a means to an end", that is, the end business goal of producing quality software. The project emphasis, although concentrating on "documentation", is not simply the production of "documentation", but rather, the successful production and control of software development, using and with the assistance of an automated document management system.

The two key areas of focus for the PIE are Configuration Management and the Software Life-cycle.

The PIE project has proved :

- a reduction in the risk identified at the outset of the project, that was, being unable to control or manage growth due to inadequate methods or processes in place.
- a reduction in the amount of time spent on Baseline and Release Management activities by 80% due to the introduction of adequate documented procedures, supporting tools and documentation
- the removal of total dependence on individual members of staff due to increased repeatability of work practices
- a cost saving to the company due to the presence of documented repeatable procedures.
- increase in awareness of quality issues among all members of staff as a result of training, awareness and feedback workshops and questionnaires on quality topics

- an improved service offered to clients due to a formal method for handling client requests as part of the Change Control process.
- increased visibility from 0% to 100% of Problem Reports and Change Requests from all sources.
- reduction in "Rework" occurring in the software life-cycle by at least 70%.
- interesting trends in the effectiveness of error/defect detection and correction earlier in the software development process.

The main interest groups for this project are companies who are involved in software development and wish to improve their configuration management and software life-cycle processes, using and with the assistance of an automated document management system.

The AUTO-DOC project began in January 1996 and completed on 30 th of June 1997. The project was 18 months in duration with 9 people involved in DATACARE and 7 people involved in VOCEAN. The project followed a plan of work packages which mapped the entire project from beginning to end. These work packages fitted into the overall framework of Assess, Improve and Measure allowing analysis of the outcome of the experiment and assessment of it's effectiveness in the organisations.

Members of the AUTO-DOC project wish to acknowledge the opportunity given to them to undertake this process improvement experiment by the ESSI Group at the European Commission. Without the financial assistance, such a project would not have been possible.

Datacare
Ireland

Vocean Ltd.
Ireland

10.6   AUTOMA 10564

Automated Corrective and Evolutionary Maintenance for Database Intensive Application Products

The AUTOMA experiment has concerned the improvement of

- maintenance activities for complex data management applications, through the formalisation and automation of
- requirements management
- configuration management
- regression testing

The project has selected the appropriate tools and technologies, and has used them to build two complementary experiment scenarios, based on the maintenance activities of two project groups (one for each partner).

The project has been fully successful in the experimentation of Configuration Management and Requirements management

In the first case, the whole maintenance line of a complex system has been put under fully automated control, developing (on top of the selected tool) a CM environment and related procedures capable of ensuring full control while avoiding any extra effort for the maintenance teams (actually contributing to improve the overall efficiency).

On the second aspect, the specifications of another system (in continuous evolution due to changing and increasing user requirements) have been formalised and are now under tool-supported control.

The results obtained on testing shows some problem; at the beginning, more resistance has been experienced on these aspects by the development teams, despite the reduced involvement requested (the preparation of test procedures was performed by dedicated resources), due to the difficulties of showing the advantages of the approach.

The preparation phase has been however successful, and allowed to derive interesting lessons on how to extract and formalise the functional knowledge required to prepare good, effective functional tests.

Once an initial set of automated test procedures has been prepared, its exploitation suffered problems related to the high level of changes that the two systems are still experiencing from one release to the other; this has prevented, till now, a real deployment of automated testing on one of the two systems, while a partial automated testing approach is currently operational for the other.

Despite these difficulties, however, the need to formalise test procedures has injected a radical organisational change in the two maintenance teams, that now handle testing-related activities in a quite better way. This is demonstrated by the comparison of the process assessments conducted before and after the experiment.

3F Datasyst
Italy

Datamat Ingenieria dei Sistemi Spa
Italy

10.7   CEMP 10358

Customized Establishment of Measurement Programs

The Goal/Question/Metric (GQM) approach to measurement of software processes and products has been used successfully in selected industrial environments.

This report summarises results and lessons learned from its application in three European companies:

Robert Bosch, Digital, and Schlumberger.

Project Goals

Main objectives of the CEMP ("Customized Establishment of Measurement Programs") project were (i) to introduce and perform measurement programs based on GQM related to quality aspects of reliability and reusability in all three companies, (ii) to compare and analyse their results and experiences, and (iii) to derive replicable cost/benefit data as well as guidelines and heuristics for widespread establishment of GQM-based measurement programs in European industries.

Work Done

To increase validity of results, the project was organised as a synchronised and co-ordinated parallel case study. All application experiments performed the following main steps:

- Characterisation of the application environment.
- Definition of GQM-plans for reliability and reusability.
- Planning of measurement programs.
- Realisation of measurement programs.
- Company-specific analysis and interpretation of collected data.
- Packaging of results.

Additionally, comparison of results across companies were done to analyse commonalties and differences. Dissemination of experiences gained in the project was organised.

Results Achieved Including Their Significance

Measurement programs for reliability and reusability were successfully introduced and realised in all three companies. Additional pilot measurement was included during the 22 months of CEMP project. After careful analysis of measurement results an improved understanding of software development with an increased awareness of strengths and weaknesses of products and processes was achieved. Based on established baselines for all topics under considerations, suggestions for improvement with high impact on quality of software development were derived. As an additional deliverable, tool support for performing goal-oriented measurement was developed by Digital.

Across the replicated pilot projects at the experimental sites a comparative analysis was done wrt. the introduction of GQM-based measurement programs. Commonalties and differences of all results and experiences were related to specific application domains and project characteristics to better enable transfer and application of the overall CEMP project results in other environments and organisations.

From the CEMP experiment it was shown that total effort for introducing GQM based measurement is about one person year. Project team effort devoted to GQM was proven to be less than 3% of total project effort. Taking into account achieved benefits, effort was considered to be an efficient investment even for the first measurement project. Reuse of experiences and results in the second pilot projects resulted in improved cost-benefit ratio. From a methodological point of view, CEMP-project experiences in performing goal-oriented measurement were summarised in a detailed process model which is accompanied by guidelines and heuristics for its implementation. This considerably facilitates the application of the approach by other organisations.

Next Proposed Actions

All three companies achieved a higher maturity in software measurement. They will introduce GQM for an increasing number of projects or even for all software projects as in the case of Schlumberger RPS. Results and experiences of CEMP-project initiated improvement programs for participating companies and will enable other companies to learn when starting with goal-oriented measurement.

DIGITAL EQUIPMENT SPA
Italy

ROBERT BOSCH GmbH
Germany

Schlumberger Industries S.A
Netherlands

10.8   CMEX 21568

Configuration Management Experiment

This experiment aims to improve the efficiency in a software development department by introducing a new and advanced configuration management system. The aim of the experiment is to reduce the number of error reports by 10% and the time-to-market by 5%.

The experiment was done in the development department of Sysdeco GIS AS in Norway, developing software for the mapping industry or GIS sector (Geographic Information Systems).

The experiment shows significant better results than originally aimed for. The errors have been reduced by 35,7% and the development effort has increased by

22%. The latter has contributed to bring the new products quicker to the market. The identified process improvement is not just a result of introducing a new system, but a result of many additional factors as general process improvement, product maturity and a focus on new development, to mention the most important.

Apart from the result above, the key lessons from the experiment have been:

- To introduce the new configuration tool, ClearCase, was more difficult than anticipated. Careful planning and experimenting took more time than planned and caused more problems for the developers than expected.
- Too little training using the new system made the introduction of the system difficult.
- Well-established routines for handling errors and a well-experienced development group significantly contributed the success of the experiment.
- Relevant background data to measure the improvement was harder to collect than anticipated. It took more time and required also more effort to analyse than expected.
- The management of the project has gained valuable experience in how to collect and analyse data regarding process improvement. New ideas for further improvements have been identified.

The success of the experiment makes it evident to continue to use the new system in our development and maintenance of our products. Further improvements can and will be done. We have also identified new areas for improvements and we plan to do a similar experiment introducing automatic testing tools.

This experiment is relevant for SMBs planning to introduce new tools in their development department, especially configuration management tools. The European Commission through the ESSI/PIE program with project 21568 has financially supported this project.

Sysdeco Innovation AS
Norway

10.9   CMOS 23661

Change Management of Software

Business Motivation and Objectives

The purpose of this PIE is to experiment a Software Change Management (SCM) process for managing new releases and many tailored versions of our software products for plant automation. These products typically are made up of a set of standard procedures which are tailored to the customer's production process. In this framework, this PIE aims at experimenting a SCM process which will a) allow visibility of product status and the tracing of its modifications; b) guarantee the alignment between the customer's version and the one on our file. Integration of the SCM process within our Quality Management System (QMS) will be ensured.

The relevance of this experiment to the business of the participant relies on the need to:

- maintain flexibility in the software maintenance though being able to guarantee quality and product reliability to safeguard both the operator's safety and the production level;
- achieve a greater efficiency in the maintenance process to reduce costs and release valuable resources for new projects;
- reduce the risks associated to unchecked changes to the product directly implemented on the plant by our customers' personnel.

The Experiment

The achievement of the project's objectives implies the realisation of the following activities:

- the analysis of the current practice and the set up of a remote monitoring environment; the definition of an improved SCM process;
- the creation of a common understanding of the SCM issues by providing training in the use of the tools;
- the experimentation of the new process on a baseline project and on another product with the same problems in order to make a comparison.

Expected Impact and Experience

The likely impact of the experiment will be:

- to minimise the risk connected with the customer's direct interventions and to reduce the number of free-of-charge interventions to repair the effects of modifications for which it is difficult to ascertain the author;
- to obtain a greater product quality: the controlled management of the modifications in fact allows to pay closer attention to the quality of the interventions and to carefully screen the custom-made modifications to be transferred into the standard product;
- to increase the maintenance efficiency and allow for a greater interchangeability of maintenance personnel working on installations;
- to improve the work conditions for the programmers formerly operating on the plant, thanks to the possibility of using an automated environment to remotely work on the installed product

Euroelettra
Italy

10.10 COMANCHE 24051

Experimental Introduction of Configuration Management in a Project Subjected to Changes Due to Different Users' Environments

Business Motivation and Objectives

The development of software according to a total quality model is becoming fundamental for the success of a software company. For this reason Softwareuno intends to obtain the ISO 9001 certification. A fundamental step towards reaching the required degree of quality is the application of a sound configuration management methodology. This is particularly true when visual programming techniques are adopted, since the structure of a system is less linear than in the traditional approach.

The introduction of a configuration management method will allow Softwareuno to achieve objectives like: decreased costs of the production, installation and maintenance of its products; a higher degree of safety and awareness in the process of change; a decreased number of errors due to a bad configuration of a software package; a greater degree of the customers' satisfaction; a greater control on the actual status of the product.

The Experiment

The achievement of the objectives above will be to obtain introducing a Configuration Management method with support of an existing tool (e.g. SourceSafe, ClearCase, CVS or Continuous).

A constant control and support of all the activities related to the use of the Configuration Management procedures will be granted to the developers in order to obtain a correct and effective use of the tool. A series of statistical data will be gathered.

The experiment is part of a greater software application called Ospiti, which consists in an integrated solution to the global management of old people's homes.

Softwareuno employs 20 people, 10 of them are involved in the Ospiti project.

Expected Impact and Experience

Greater speed in the updating of the products, costs saving due to less effort spent in Configuration Management activities, increased control on the status of a software package, increased safety when changing a product, are all expected results.

The creation of new professional roles (related to the activities of the maintenance of the releases and the configurations for different customers) and the raising of the quality culture inside the company are complementary goals.

Software1 s.r.l.
Italy

10.11   COMMITS 21830

Configuration Management at IT Software

Business Motivation and Objectives

IT software has evolved from a Consultancy company to a Software Vendor company producing custom software. This focus shift, together with the growing complexity and size of typical software projects/products, has led to the need to achieve a better control on the software development process and an effective management of a cross-project library of reusable components.

The objective of the experiment is to introduce and institutionalise sound Software Configuration Management practices. The main expected business benefits are: to achieve a better control of the relationship with customers, to be able to provide a more effective maintenance service so expanding the commercial opportunities, to grow a baseline of reusable components so reducing the internal development costs.

The Experiment

The experiment is developed in the context of two consecutive baseline projects in the area of financial trading. The selected baseline projects are representative of the typical projects carried out at IT Software: about 5 months of elapsed time with a project team of 4-5 people, they share the same platform and development tools (Windows NT, Visual C++, SQL Server, SNA Server, Power Builder), and involve a similar technology mix (Client/Server architecture, distributed and replicated Database, real-time data feed, secured WAN inter networking, real time data visualisation).

The experiment, that adopted as a guidance the SEI's CMM framework tailored to the needs of a SME, proceeds through the achievement of four major steps, as follows:

- Ensure the needed precondition: develop an SCM Handbook that defines the Organisational Policy and the Operational Instructions for SCM; provide adequate resources including tools and training on involved people.
- Experiment SCM practices: establish an SCM Repository and perform SCM activities.
- Monitor the process improvement: collect measurement data on predefined indicators and quantitatively measure the process improvement.
- Disseminate the results toward both an internal and an external audience through in-house workshops, public presentations and publishing of the lesson learned on a Web site.

Expected Impact and Experience

IT software expects to improve software process capabilities in the area of SCM as a first step toward incremental process improvement that should lead to reach within two year the Capability Maturity level 2 and the ISO 9000 certification. Also, the success of this experience will raise the awareness that quality issues must be extended from the single professional to the organisational process and will increase employee motivation due to the recognition of higher quality and productivity of their work. From the business point of view, IT Software expects a bottom line cost saving by improving software reuse and reducing the day-to-day effort spent dealing with software changes and configuration management activities without an effective SCM strategy.

IT Software
Italy

10.12 CONFITEST 24362

Creating a Solid Configuration- and Test-Management Infrastructure to Improve the Team Development of Critical Software Systems

The experiment could only be carried out with the financial support of the Commission, in the specific programme for research and technological development in the field of information technologies. TeSSA Software NV is a developer of critical software systems for different markets. The baseline project is a typical TeSSA Software NV product, situated in the market of paypoints.

The experiment, situated in the domain of configuration-and test-management, has contributed to the aim of being a software production house that delivers quality systems in time. Before considering the work done and the final results, a summary of the project goals: By implementing the software control management the project manager can optimise the development process, in concrete terms:

- Cost reduction (10-15 %)
- Elimination of errors in an early phase of the process (1 in stead of 10)
- Quality improvement of delivered programmes.
- Reliability increase of installed programmes.
- And last but not least, acceleration of the definite product delivery. (about 10%)

Reaching these goals indirectly results in a better work-atmosphere for programmers, analysts, project managers and management.

This experiment will also be part of the efforts, TeSSA Software NV is making to produce a quality manual and obtain ISO 9000 certification. (Specially ISO 12207) Work done.

A quality manager was indicated and an internal base-reference report is written, to situate problems and

costs. The global IT company strategy was defined and the specific requirements of this PIE are exactly defined to fit in this strategy. In the running of this PIE we had to change the global plan a few times. Looking for other existing models we found SPIRE (ESSI Project 21419) promoting CMM and BootCheck, 2 very interesting projects, giving a wider frame for the global plan.

The strategic choice between the different tools is part of this PIE and the choice has been made:

- Version control system and configuration management: PVCS
- Testtool: SQA Teamtest

One employee was trained in PVCS, another one in SQA Teamtest. Both products are installed, we got consultancy on both products and a global session on test-methods was given to everyone in the company. This was an important session to convince every one of the strategic choices. In both domains the first procedures were implemented.

Results

At the end of the experiment, every employee agrees that quality and reliability of the software development process is improved significantly. First figures give a global improvement of 5%. This is less then expected (7 à 10%), but we believe that the positive influence in productivity and reliability will become more and more visible in the next years. The confidence in this experiment certainly helps to get a better working atmosphere.

The responses of the customers prove the confidence in the strategy of our company, working hard on the improvement of our internal processes and they see the first results of the new working methods.

Future actions

Now the procedures are consolidated and standardised to support the development cycle internally on the same LAN, the next step will be to extend the procedures to also support external employees.

With the help of our internal organisation with Lotus Notes Applications, the proceedings and the procedures are nowadays continuously internally disseminated.

At this moment we're still looking for opportunities to disseminate our knowledge externally.

TeSSA Software NV
Belgium

10.13   CONFMANAG 23891

Enhancing Software Configuration Management for the Process Control System

Business Motivation and Objectives

The objective of this PIE is to introduce software configuration management practices and measurements for faster delivery of products and for faster customer responses, to give good support for parallel development, for geographically distributed teams and for multi-platform environment. The customers will be satisfied with the much better product support that can be given to the old releases of products. Other objective is to measure our maturity level by applying the ISO-SPICE which is being developed within the ISO framework. The quantitative target of the project objectives is to increase the efficiency of the software configuration methods by reducing the costs 30 %.

The Experiment

Achieving the objective above requires the improvement of software configuration management practices supported by tools as follows:

- Configuration management using ClearCase.
- Geographically distributed software development using ClearCase Multisite.

These tools make it possible to develop the product together with parallel projects. Projects' members can also be located in different regions. The product can be developed for different platforms.

The experiment will be performed around Damatic XD (Distributed Control System developed by Valmet Automation). Valmet Automation employs 1800 people.

The results will be measured comparing the new methods with the current methods.

Expected Impact and Experience

Valmet Automation expects to gain know-how in the efficient usage of ClearCase and Multisite in software configuration management. With this knowledge it is possible to raise the product quality and speed time to market for Valmet Automation's products.

Valmet Automation Inc
Finland

10.14   CREDIT 23697

Client Requirements Definition Improvement

Business Motivation and Objectives

To effectively meet the increase in demand for our products and services Trend-Soft has recognised the need to put in place the necessary underlying structures and processes. TrendSoft is currently implementing a Quality Management System and has identified the critical area of accurate Client functional requirements definition as being a fundamental aspect of our on-going Client management and thus future success. TrendSoft recognises that improvements in this area will yield a positive benefits down-the-line throughout the remainder of the development process.

This is a common concern to the software industry where the primary business objective is to meet the customers requirements in terms of product as required, within the agreed costs and timeframe.

The Experiment

The achievement of the above requires both the building of a "Stakeholder Partnership" between ourselves, as supplier, and the Client, and, through this partnership and supported by methods and tools, an improvement of the company's ability to gather, specify and manage Client functional requirements. An appropriate method will be tailored to suit our needs. The tools would include:

- Analyst Workbench e.g. System Architect. Used to manage and control the clients information.
- Data Modelling e.g. ERwin. Used to model data relationships and elements.
- Document Management. Used to manage document versions. MS Word may suffice.

Vision Express are a major chain of Optical Product retailers. TrendSoft is continuing to develop the product in line with their needs and will use the 5th Phase of this project as the baseline application.

TrendSoft employs 20 people, 13 of whom are involved in software development.

Expected Impact and Experience

The experiment is expected to yield higher productivity, shorter development time-scales, and reduced levels of change requests and problems. It is also expected to lead to improvements in the company's testing capability, to an enhanced product quality, to increased client satisfaction and to a strengthening of the company's client retention capability. It will also raise the skill and motivation levels of our staff and, in tandem with our quality programme will enhance the quality culture of the organisation.

Trendsoft ltd
Ireland

10.15 CUSTOMIZE 23670

Efficient Development and Maintenance of Similar, but not Identical Customised Software Products

Business Motivation and Objectives

TTS delivers turnkey robot production systems with customised software for the shipbuilding industry. The customised software products are very similar, e.g. they have approximately 90% common source code, but not identical. The customised software accounts for approx. 25% of the total source code of a typical TTS contract, while the life cycle costs related to customised software accounts for in the area of 50%. The project objective is to reduce the life-cycle cost of products in a series of similar, but not identical customised software. The life-cycle cost will be reduced by putting more effort into the development of the base software. Reusability of source code, documentation and maintenance are the main items which will be addressed. The primary goal is to reduce the life-cycle costs of customised software with 30% over a product series of four similar, but not identical products. The problem TTS faces with a large number of similar, but not identical customised software products is very common in the SME segment of the automation and production system industry.

The Experiment

The scope of the project is to create a framework, that is tools, techniques and training for handling series of similar, but not identical software products. The experiment will be carried out in three phases. Firstly, the tools and techniques for implementing such a framework are acquired and implemented at TTS. The second phase is the actual implementation of the experiment. Revision training and dissemination are carried out in the last phase. The baseline project will be the development of the new TTS PC based CAD-robot interface software starting in 1997. TTS' software developing unit consists of 9 people.

Expected Impact and Experience

It is a goal for TTS that the quality of the customised software shall approach the level of standard software. Further on, the resources involved with supporting and maintaining this type of software shall coincide with the size and complexity of the source code. Notice, the most important deliverable from this experiment is the organisation consisting of trained personnel and the knowledge of how to implement the techniques derived in this project.

TTS Automation AS
Norway

10.16   DIGIDOC 21593

Implementation of a Highly Integrated System for Documentation Configuration and Code Re-Use in a Heterogene Software Development Environment

Business Motivation and Objectives

The need for high product quality and traceability in the development process is a growing demand in the very competitive telecommunication market as is the need for short time-to-market development. To meet these demands the development process must be improved in project management, quality and efficiency. Because of this the objective is to implement and evaluate 1) an on-line software documentation system performing satisfactorily in a heterogeneous software development environment, 2) an on-line configuration management tool to keep track of versions and releases, with key words being high integration, easy usage and low administration costs.

The Experiment

The experiment will be based on what is known as the second generation Home Communications Centre(HCC), which combines several home office functions such as handsfree telephone, answering machine, telefax, modem and much more into one stand alone unit. The HCC project will be used for quality measurements of all project objectives. Time to market, software error reduction in the development phase as well as on final releases, unambiguous version and release control and documentation will be the basic yardsticks for quality measurements.

Digianswer A/S employs 20 people, approx. 10 people will be involved in the experiment.

Expected Impact and Experience

The expected results of the project are: improved control of project management, more effective design process, easier and more systematic training of new engineers and improved motivation for quality aspects during software development.

This will make Digianswer A/S a more professional business partner and a more competitive product development company.

DIGIANSWER A/S
Denmark

10.17 DSP-ACTION 23696

Improving DSP Software Documentation Process to Promote Reuse

The efforts invested in the development of digital signal processing software are increasing dramatically, especially in telecommunication applications. Design of optimised mathematical algorithms has dominated research and product development, but as the size of software has grown, a need for improved software development practices has emerged. DSP-ACTION is a joint-project of Nokia Mobile Phones (NMP) and Finnish Technical Research Centre/VTT Electronics.

The project was funded by the European Union under the ESSI program. The objective of this process improvement experiment was to improve DSP software development process in order to promote reuse of every level of design documentation. The experiment was piloted in a real product development project aiming at solving practical problems in everyday design and development work in industry. Effective review practice was introduced by defining elements of DSP software quality after analysing the customer needs of both forthcoming and current projects. Current revision management system was hierarchically restructured to intuitively reflect every domain of the pilot project's DSP software. Creation and collection of process documents into a single location founded a base for continuous process improvement. The expected impact of the experiment was faster cycles of high-quality product development with the use of collective base of design level experience. Quantitative measurements were used to guide current and future process development activities.

The experiment indicated that DSP software process can be improved using systematic approach and taking into consideration practical needs of the pilot project. Measurements also indicated significant reusability improvements in many aspects compared to the previous situation. We believe that efforts required for this kind of process improvement are biggest in the beginning, but after the organisation has gained experience on process improvement less effort is required to continue with next steps of process improvement. Our next steps will include continuation of the follow-up with most interesting metrics, gaining more experiences from project, and replicating proven best practices in other DSP software development projects.

Nokia Mobile Phones
Finland

10.18   EASIER 10542

Enhancing Application Software Implementation for Programmable Logic Controllers

The report is aimed at presenting the results achieved during the EASIER application experiment. It is the purpose of the experiment to ascertain effectiveness and ease of use of a model, and the relative methodology, conceived for supporting the initial phases of PLC software life-cycle, namely customer requirement specification, software design and disciplined coding.

PLC controlled systems are reactive, in that they maintain permanent interactions with the environment; they present high degrees of complexity, since they are made of many interacting components; they are real-time, being events involving them temporally related.

The model is object-oriented and its primitives are ontologically justified. Model effectiveness is proved with respect to relevant system representation problems: identification of independent control modules by applying a bedded encapsulation mechanism, representation of system dynamics by means of synchronised state diagrams, recognition and representation of both context-free and context-dependent behaviours of system components.

Taking into account the characteristics of the EASIER project, its technical details can be of some interest for different communities: in particular, enterprises producing automated systems controlled by PLCs, software houses developing embedded real-time software, consultants and researchers involved in activities related to this software engineering application field.

The work presented in this Final Report has been financially supported by the European Commission under ESSI, the European Systems and Software Initiative, as Application Experiment n. 10542 – EASIER.

Bonfanti
Italy

CMA Spa
Italy

Trascar
Italy

10.19   ESTREMA 23724

Estimation Improvement Based on Improved Requirements Management

Business Motivation and Objectives

Gruppo PRO's core business is information systems automation in medium and large industrial companies. We customise and install products developed by ourselves and we provide assistance to the start up of the automated systems. Our process suffers from the low accuracy of the initial estimate of the customisation task. Due to the incompleteness of the initial requirements and to unmanaged changes a considerable percentage of unanticipated work creeps in during the very last project stages. Our goal is to increase the reliability of our cost and schedule estimates and to reduce the percentage of unanticipated work by improving our requirements management capabilities, including control over the requirements changes.

The Experiment

The main actions in ESTREMA will focus on the following tasks:

- experimenting a methodical approach to the identification and representation of the user requirements. This method will involve the delivery of a feasibility study document serving as a basis for the initial cost and schedule estimate
- defining and experimenting a change control procedure to manage requirements modifications and their impact on the initial estimates
- experimenting with a project performance assessment practice to establish requirements fulfilment and estimation accuracy; to this aim the collection of project performance data should allow the creation of a historical baseline to be used for improving successive estimates.

In ESTREMA the experimentation will be carried out on a baseline project which consists of the adaptation and installation of our management information systems package PROJ in two companies belonging to sectors which are strategic for our business, and where the requirements are so different that our requirements and estimation process could be affected.

Expected Impact and Experience

We expect that we will achieve a smaller deviation from the costs and schedule anticipated initially. Also, a higher estimation accuracy should allow a better planning of our resources and avoid that delays in one project preclude the release of precious resources. Finally, thanks to the definition of company standards and procedures more people will be in a position to estimate projects reliably, whereas this responsibility is nowadays vested on few people with great experience.

Gruppo Pro
Italy

10.20   EURO2000 23794

Systematisation of Global Software Adaptation Efforts

Business Motivation and Objectives

The interest of CECA, as the Spanish Confederation of Savings Banks, in this PIE lies in the development of its business strategy: to act as the sponsor of technological development and test site for new technologies for its 50 associated Savings Banks.
The objective of the project is to implement an organisational structure and a method to handle global changes to a complete software portfolio.

At present, Savings Banks (as well as a large number of other organisations) are facing critical global changes to face the year 2000 problem and to make themselves capable of handling the Euro single currency.

We will use these critical global changes as the baseline project to test the method by using it to adapt the applications of the payments area, the resulting method will then be used to adapt CECA's complete software portfolio and will be disseminated to its 50 associated Savings Banks.

The Experiment

The PIE will consist of:

- The implementation of an organisational structure that will be based on: The Euro2000 Steering Committee, The Euro2000 team, The adaptation teams and the Users team.
- The implementation of a Method based on the following phases: 1) Applications Architecture Definition; 2) Planning and Prioritisation; 3) Change Management Set-up; 4) Detailed Situation Analysis and Solution Design; 5) Solution Implementation; 6) Test and Quality Analysis.

These organisational structure and method will be used to make the applications of the payments area capable of handling the Euro and be free of the year 2000 problem.

Expected Impact and Experience

The Spanish Confederation of Savings Banks, CECA, expects to obtain the following benefits from the process implemented trough this experiment:

- Ensure that all its portfolio of applications is prepared to handle the Euro currency and year 2000 dates by 1999
- Ensure that the best business sense and cost effective solution is taken for each application.
- Guarantee that the conversion process will not cause problems to the applications in production.
- Reduce risks of failure by ensuring that 98% of the required conversions are performed, tested and accepted by its business users.
- Increase the productivity form the present level of 2 programs of 2.5000 lines corrected per day to 8 programs of the same size corrected per day.
- Eliminate the person-application dependency which in-turn will increased the flexibility to use contracted programmers to speed up the work.
- Decrease cost by reducing the labour for detecting potentially troubled situations by 70%.
- Raise awareness and guarantee involvement from the senior management and business users in the resolution of this two critical problems.

Confederación española de Cajas de Ahorro
Spain

10.21 EXCUSES 21532

An Experiment for Use Case in Capturing User Expectations in Software Development Projects

EXCUSES – Esprit Project 21532 – is one of the projects of the European Systems and Software Initiative (ESSI) within the fourth Framework Programme as part of the Process Improvement Experiments (PIEs) category.

The objective of the experiment was the introduction, in Sodalia, of the Use Cases methodology for capturing the user expectations and the preliminary requirements and for tackling the definition of a high level architecture of a system in the specific context of the initial phases of an iterative development process which is object oriented and reuse oriented.

The experiment was structured on the following main steps:

- tailoring of Sodalia's "Guidelines for Use Case in User Expectations Gathering" to the specific needs of an internal baseline project;

- conduction of the experiment by the baseline project ensuring the necessary training by the methodologies area;
- assessment of the achieved results both on a qualitative level (by surveying the customers, the requirements team members, and the requirements users) and on a quantitative level (by measuring the productivity and quality achieved throughout the experiment).

Sodalia SpA
Italy

10.22 FAME 10760

Framework for Management and Design of Multimedia Applications in Education and Training

This report describes the FAME application experiment, an experiment which adapted and integrated state-of-the-art methodologies and tools in most phases of the development of an educational multimedia application in order to improve the software process. Specific goals of the experiment were to increase the product quality, reduce production duration and cost, apply more efficient monitoring and management processes, and improve quality assurance mechanisms. Furthermore, through several dissemination actions, the participants aimed at promoting their ability to exploit state-of-the-art software supports, enhance their credibility and improve the efficiency of respective software products and methodologies.

The experiment adapted and integrated these methodologies and tools during most phases of the development of a real application, the baseline experiment, emphasising requirement analysis and specification, design, quality assurance, metrics, review and evaluation. A small scale experiment adapted carefully selected parts of the application experiment to a different environment, a museum.

For dissemination and transferability the experiment also established a small special interest group, whose members included cultural and educational organisations and multimedia technology professionals. Among the participants? future plans are to extend the experiment to other phases of the life-cycle and to use the results and experience gained from the experiment to other projects in their organisations, aiming at continuously improving the software process.

This report describes the most significant results of the experiment, experience gained and important lessons learned, concluding that software process improvement should be a continuous goal in the organisations, and continuous evaluation and commitment to quality by all people involved in the development should be the main ways to achieve these goals. The report also presents some problems encountered, especially when measuring the results of the experiment. It therefore interests multimedia applications developers and multimedia project managers, providing them with experiences, good and bad, gained from introducing best practices in multimedia applications development. This report may also interest organisations or individuals involved with education and culture, since they will discover the benefits of using multimedia technology as a means for distributing knowledge. Finally, anyone with a special concern for best software engineering practices, either as a software engineer or project manager, will be interested in the report since it presents experiences gained from an experiment which tries to adapt and apply state-of-the-art methodologies and tools in the area of educational multimedia applications development.

This report relates to work carried out by First Informatics SA, Lambrakis Research Foundation and Benaki Museum, in the framework of the ESSI Programme, with a financial contribution by the European Commission.

Benaki Museum
Country: Greece

First Informática S.A
Greece

Lambrakis Research Foundation
Greece

10.23   FOCUS 10603

Formal and OO-Methods for Customer Driven Specifications

The FOCUS (Formal and OO-methods for Customer Driven Applications) application experiment was a project in the European Systems and Software Initiative (ESSI). The aim of the ESSI Application Experiment (AE) projects was to experiment with new technologies, in real life projects, to learn new ways to be more competitive and productive, and to disseminate the results to the wider community. FOCUS concentrated on improving the software development process with new formal and object-oriented methods in the software specification phase. One of our baseline projects was a large and complicated military system, and another was a small but critical embedded system. Instrumentointi was the prime user of the project and there were two different baseline projects. Tekla was the partner and it had a separate baseline project. The main technology vendors were the Tampere University of Technology and the Jyväskylä Institute of Technology. Instrumentointi and Tekla shared the same customer and it was also involved in the project.

This report describes the original objectives of the project, the work performed, the results, key lessons learned, and conclusions drawn. Even though our project had problems, we were still able to learn valuable lessons, some of them were good, some of them not so good. The main lesson was undoubtedly the fact that we should have needed a lot more resources – time and money – to actually change the way we produce software. All the developers in both companies were compeletely involved in the customer projects and they simply did not have time and enthusiasm to learn new ways to work while stressed by everyday routines.

The communities of interest most likely to be interested in the technical details of this report are software producers like us: SME companies developing customer software. The researchers of the formal methods may also be interested.

As this project was carried out in the framework of the ESSI programme, it was supported by the Commission of the European Communities. The financial contribution to support the completion of the work was made by the Technology Development Center of Finland.

Instrumentointi Oy
Finland

Tekla Oy
Finland

10.24 GEARS 24189

Gaining Efficiency and Quality in Real-time Control Software

Business Motivation and Objectives

MASMEC's software is an integral part of the machinery produced by the company; it is the discriminating element which determines the user's satisfaction as regards operating flexibility and reliability under heavy operating conditions.

The target objectives of this project will support the company's policy in trying to enter new market segments and reinforce its presence through its customers, and specifically:

To increase of the company turnover, within 6 months after the fulfilment of the PIE it is expected a growth by 15% of company turnover.

To increase the production efficiency and profitability of each new supplied product.

• Reduction of the cost for producing embedded software based on the company's standard components and templates.

- Reduction of the time to market of the overall machine, by diminishing the effort for software standardisation and customisation for new machines;
- Reduction of the unitary costs of production for a machine;

The Experiment

The PIE will be conducted on an already planned baseline project of strategic relevance for the company: the design and software implementation for stands performing test on assembled parts.

The goals of the experiment are:

- To better and formally structure the software system specification process, by easing the modelling of the real-time behaviour of the testing machines and its translation into software systems specifications.
- To improve the degree of reusability of the company's standard software components, by revising and re-engineering them in terms of granularity, flexibility of use and access methods.
- To improve user's interaction modalities through the introduction and formalisation of graphical layout standards
- To improve the management of quality throughout the overall software process, by introducing, also, a first set of essential process and product quality metrics.

MASMEC actually employs 33 people, 10 of them are involved in software development.

Expected Impact and Experience

MASMEC expects to enrich its know how on the system requirement specification, reducing the time necessary to produce its software, easing the software engineering process, and reducing the people effort.

Another important goal is to improve the management of quality through all the software process, introducing a first set of metrics regarding the product and the quality, and to assess a system of documents especially suitable for software development.

The expected results should also lead to a better acceptance of the system functionality and performance by the clients and to a more extensive reuse of base software components with reduced maintenance costs.

Masmec
Italy

10.25   HEMATITES 21741

Helping Humanity With Better Software

This document tries to report the activities performed during the HEMATITES experiment, and the main achievements up to date. The intention of the Cruz Roja Española with HEMATITES is to perform an experiment that establishes methods, techniques and tools to reduce development time and modification implementation time; to trace requests from local organisations, to provide installation and testing standards, and in summary, to acquire a situation to permit efficient IT systems development and exploitation.

The potential for replication is directly applicable to other Red Cross or social distributed organisations. It is very applicable to medium distributed organisations of other areas, ranging from small to medium companies, and those big organisations whose IT systems are based on databases and applications on top of them (most of Business Systems).

The following activities have been performed:
- A Software Plan has been defined and it is being applied to the whole software process.
- The Metric Model has been defined also, and a set of support applications have been developed in order to perform the data acquisition in an automatic way.
- The selection of the tool set to be used in HEMATITES has taken place (MS Exchange, MS Office, MS Project, and the 2000 CASE tools from ORACLE).
- People were trained, not only in the use of the above tools, but also on the software methods that are being applied (test methods, configuration control practices, and other standards).
- Two baseline applications were (re-)developed: the Human Resources application (an existing application that was redeveloped), and the Ambulance Transport application (a new one in the Spanish Red Cross).
- The baseline applications have been delivered. The HEMATITES database is being populated (more or less automatically) with the data that is the input to compound the selected metrics.

The results collected along the experiment have been studied and decisions were taken, in relation to the techniques and procedures applied in the software process for the Spanish Red Cross. Such results have been disseminated in other Red Cross Offices (not Spanish), and the final procedures and standards for the rest of the offices along the Spanish geography, have been implemented.

From here, our acknowledgement to the European Commission for its support in this ESSI PIE. Thanks to all the people who helped and work with us making careful suggestions and showing interest in HEMATITES, and particularly to Ms. Mechthild Rohen, for her comments and her valuable time spent with the Spanish Red Cross.

Cruz Roja Española
SPAIN

10.26   HOSPUR 24181

User Requirements and Reuse in Health Management Systems

Business Motivation and Objectives

The partners want to measure the potential for improvement in product quality and user acceptance derived from formal procedures in user-supplier communication, while compromising with a cost-reduction strategy of software reuse. The main objective of the project proposed is to measure the impact of User Requirements Management (URM) on two main features of the software developed: quality, by means of an improved user-supplier communication, and cost, by means of increased software reuse.

The Experiment

Establishing a cost-benefit analysis through a controlled experiment will allow us to validate the procedures, methods and tools defined to do URM in a baseline project. We will measure the effect of URM in the key features of quality and cost of the resulting software product. Quality will be measured in terms of the percentage of changes attributable to badly understood requirements. The current reference measure is 50%, which includes changes in software developed by G.O.C. and collaborators like B-kin Software. Cost will be measured indirectly in terms of reuse as the percentage of new code that is directly derived from previous developments. The current reference measure is 60%.

The baseline project selected is the development of a major revision of the Integrated Hospital Management system running in Aita Menni. The SGIH97 is a complex application covering all aspects in the daily work of a hospital: check-ins, check-outs, resource allocations, medical records, maintenance of facilities, invoicing, waiting list management, etc. The final user, Aita Menni, will define its user requirements and validate the delivered product. The consultant and application developer, G.O.C., will help to define requirements and develop software that responds to user's expectations. The systems engineer, B-kin Software, will design and put in place the system architecture needed to solve the needs of the complete solution.

Expected Impact and Experience

The partners often need to work very closely during the user requirements specification phase. All of them, from different perspectives, share the goal of better conformance to requirements of the product delivered and lower costs due to improved use of resources. The three companies recognise the fact, based on previous experience and expert counselling, that a formal procedure and method for

URM is needed in order to achieve their goal. They expect to set up the first URM system in each company and build up in their knowledge and awareness of software best practices.

G.O.C
Spain

10.27   ICONMAN 21379

Implementing Configuration Management in Very Small Enterprises

This report is based on work performed in the ICONMAN project during the 18 months (June 1996 – December 1997) of the process improvement experiment. The experiment was sponsored by the CEC under the ESSI Programme, project no. 21379.

The project's main goal was to implement configuration management in three small software companies and assess the effect of this effort. The main conclusion from the project is: Implementing configuration management is worthwhile in very small companies. This is based on both qualitative and quantitative measurements and observations.

The companies have with respect to their own judgement successfully implemented routines for configuration management. Even though the process has been more demanding than expected, the maturing of the system development process was a necessary step in developing the business processes in the companies as a whole.

The main lessons learned were:
- Configuration management is a complex activity with far reaching consequences for the business as a whole.
- Implementing configuration management is an iterative process, and requires continuous refinement.
- In very small companies the introduction of configuration management should be tested in a controlled, but real-life environment.
- It was difficult to identify quantitative data to measure process performance, but the defined simple metrics were essential for evaluation of the experiment.
- The existence of an operative configuration management system has shown to make a positive impact on customer relations.
- The existence of an operative change request database has proven to be valuable in planning product releases.
- The existence of an operative configuration item library has proven to simplify the process of reconstructing earlier releases, and led to a higher service level for the customer.

Event/TSC/Aktuar Systemer
Norway

10.28   IECS 23760

Improvement of Efficiency by Introduction of CCM and Software

Business Motivation and Objectives

The department of Industrial Image Analysis as part of the Institute of Digital Image Processing of JOANNEUM RESEARCH develops customer designed systems for industrial applications based on image processing techniques. The company was certified according to ISO 9001 standard 1995, but the guidelines for software development given in ISO 9000-3 are not fully applied. A couple of problems have been observed in the past and are still present in the software development process, which have to be corrected. An assessment of the current status showed big need but also big interest of the employees in more software quality management.

Main objectives of this PIE are:

- Shorter software development cycles
- Better code reusability
- Increase of reproducibility and readability of code
- More efficient Configuration and Change Management (CCM)
- Better documentation and problem tracking

The Experiment

In this PIE, the influence of the establishment of a CCM tool is measured. As a prerequisite for selection and usage of this tool, a complete software lifecycle model will be worked out, which will act as basis for the CCM procedures. Especially the influence on code quality, error frequency, customisation, maintainability and reuse will be investigated in detail. Measured parameters indicating this influence will be: code metrics, efficiency based on time statistics, error statistics and reuse statistics

Expected Impact and Experience

- Reduction of error frequency and time for solving errors
- More flexibility in planning of personal resources
- Better reuse of code
- Easier maintenance of code
- Higher confidence of customers
- Increase of motivation

Joanneum Research Forschungsgesellschaft mbH
Austria

10.29   IMPACT 21628

Improving Horizontal Activities in Project Execution: Project Management, Configuration Management and Change Management

The main (i.e., experimental) part of the experiment was finished by the end of December 1996. Remaining work packages essentially comprise termination, reporting and dissemination activities.

The process improvement experiment (PIE) provided us with an opportunity to experiment with and evaluate new methods, procedures and tools in a real life environment. To date the approach used proved itself to be extremely valuable.

By the experiment we aimed at sophisticated method and tool support to keep projects in line wrt effort, time and costs. Experience data collected in the project will be used for improved estimation and planning of future projects. Another objective was reliable and consistent managing of software documents and products of different versions. Furthermore, we aimed at reliable and fast handling of change requests. Finally, the motivation and skill of our employees to apply and continuously improve our quality management system should be developed.

In order to achieve these goals we established a project management method supported by the tools Microsoft Project and Excel. Furthermore, a configuration management system relying on the tool PVCS was applied to control the access to, and delivery of, all individual software documents belonging to a software product. Finally, a change management system was established for controlling and reporting change requests. This task is supported by the tool ChangeFlow.

From a technological point of view we learned that an appropriate and comprehensive project plan, with estimated project parameter values (effort, time, costs) and continuously collected actual values from all professionals involved in the project, is crucial for successful project management. Though it is necessary to apply tools, we had to notice that Microsoft Project 4.0 doesn't serve for sufficient and adequate support in project management. As a kind of work-around we used a combination of Project and Excel for this purpose.

From a business point of view it became obvious that transparency of the software development process towards the own company management and to the business client, by delivering project management documents and periodical status reports, significantly improves confidence of all parties in the software process and the resulting products. Nevertheless, the application of tools is not for free and thus it is crucial for the success of changing established ways of working that the people concerned are convinced that the additional work eventually imposed on them will be for their own benefit.

The results of our experiment are of main interest to software suppliers and consultants in the area of technical and business orientated systems.

PRO DV Software GmbH
Germany

10.30 IMPACTS2 24078

Improvement of Process Architecture Through Configuration and Change Management and Enhanced Test Strategies for a Knowledge-Based Test Path Generator

Business Motivation and Objectives

DTK is developing a knowledge-based test path generator for safety relevant analogous hardware components for the use in the railway environment. High transparency, high traceability up to the developer in the case of incidents and very high product quality is required. It will be demonstrated how the process architecture for this test path generator can be improved by applying configuration & change management methods as well as enhanced test strategies.

The Experiment

The development process shall be significantly improved by focusing on two key areas of SPI: testing and configuration & change management. Thus the PIE will deal with the following:

- Introducing configuration & change management techniques and tools,
- Introducing systematic testing methods and procedures, supported by suitable tools.

The PIE will concentrate on that part of the software that is already multiply reused under different configurations. This part would benefit most and has the most significance for the successful evaluation of techniques and tools. It will be referred to as the baseline project.

Expected Impact and Experience

DTK expects to gain know-how on optimising its software development process with respect to configuration & change management and testing. Improved effort, time and cost estimations and planning of future projects will be achieved through enhanced test strategies, reliable managing of software documents as well as fast handling of change requests.

DTK Gesellschaft für technische Kommunikation mbH
Germany

10.31   IMPOSE 23780

Improvement Object Oriented Methods in a Very Small Enterprise

Business Motivation and Objectives

The business idea of Mente Systemutvikling AS is to offer consultancy software development and software systems for the fishing industry. Projects getting out of control causing enormous internal costs in order to gain control has resulted in low profit from development projects.

Appropriate cost estimates based on better requirement specifications is expected to increase control and profitability. The project is expected to reduce overrun time by 30%.

Similar problems are common among software companies in Norway and Europe. The results and the lessons learned will be of relevance to all software companies coping with the same kind of problems.

The Experiment

The technical aim of the experiment is to improve the quality of the requirement specifications which the cost estimates are based upon. The method for cost estimation is also going to be improved. This will secure the business goal which is to make a profitable business on consultancy software development.

Existing routines will be evaluated, new routines will be developed before they will be implemented in the organisation. The new routines will be used in a baseline project to gain experience and to measure their effect. The baseline application is likely to be a project developing solutions for the alimentation industry.

The company has 6 employed software developers, in addition the general manager takes part in planning and preparation of the projects and also some of the project administration.

Expected Impact and Experience

The expected results are: 30% reduction of total overrun time and 20% reduction of financial loss caused by overrunning cost estimates and missing milestones. The experiment is expected to have a positive impact on the organisation and the software development cycle.

By successful completion of the PIE the next step will be continuous improvement of issues related to software development that are defined as critical. It is very likely that testing and verification will be the next area to put focus on.

No barriers or reluctances are seen within the organisation. Reluctances are only met among other software organisations unable to see what a very small enterprise can achieve by going trough a project like this.

Mente Systemutvikling AS
Norway

10.32 IMPROVE-CM 21433

Implementation of a Central Repository to Support Effective Configuration Management

This PIE experimented the effectiveness of the CM practices implemented using the Change Configuration Control (CCC)/ Harvest tool application [Ref. 1], to reduce the effort for S/W library management and to encourage the reusability of software modules for the Space Software Italia (SSI) projects. As expected, the enhancement mainly resulted in the improvement of the Change Control process for software and documentation that, thanks to this PIE, can now be made uniform and systematic for all projects. Furthermore, the analyses of achievements on the baseline project, encourage us to anticipate a major competitiveness due to costs reduction, with regard to Configuration Management activities, and an increased productivity in developing and maintaining software.

The baseline project for this PIE was the Assembly, Integration & Verification – Data Base Software (AIV-DB S/W) development project [Ref. 2]. It revealed to be a suitable pilot project for the purpose of this PIE: (1) its development schedule has satisfactorily overlapped the PIE timeframe; (2) its management plan was based on the parallel management of two different software versions (Maintenance of Release 1 and Development of Release 2), so demanding a more complex approach to Configuration Management.

AIV-DB is a database software product based on Oracle DB Management System; it is a flexible tool to control and manage the AIV activities during the development of systems of different size and complexity, such as Satellite, an high speed Train, or a Navy.

According to the PIE work plan and the proposed schedule, the following have been the main achievements:

- training activities have been performed on Assessment and Improvement methods and on the use of CCC/Harvest
- a formal qualification of the PIE, in terms of an assessment of the SSI CM process, has been satisfactorily achieved and an improvement plan, identifying measures and indicators to monitor the PIE, has been finalised
- a Software Life Cycle model, adequate for change control purposes, has been defined and set-up using CCC/Harvest, and its experimentation has been satisfactorily completed on the baseline project
- a Software Problem Management model, fully integrated with the Software Life Cycle model, has been defined and set-up using CCC/Harvest, and its experimentation has been satisfactorily completed on the baseline project
- metrics have been collected on the baseline project and their analysis has been performed for monitoring the actual CM process and provide corrective actions and evaluating the process improvement achievements

- a Documentation life-cycle model, fully integrated with the Software Life Cycle model, has been defined and set-up using CCC/Harvest, and its experimentation has been satisfactorily completed on the baseline project
- a common S/W repository, easily accessible from any SSI computer platform on the LAN, and even from authorised WAN nodes, has been established that will let all SSI employees to safely access and modify any S/W versions, without regard on which platform and where it was originally developed. We believe that this is a prerequisite for an easy and effective software reuse management and to increase productivity
- a final evaluation of the experiment has been performed with a formal assessment of the resulting status of the PIE

The use of a CM tool implementing advanced concepts (i.e., process modelling, parallel development) and a new approach (i.e., CCC/Harvest provides a unified framework supporting all the core functions in software development) has revealed beneficial for the baseline project, even if it has led to devote a particular effort in training people.

Space Software Italia
Italy

10.33   INCOME 21733

Increasing Capability Level with Opportune Metrics and Tools

Business Motivation and Objectives

The Finsiel Group is achieving ISO 9000 certification for most of its Business Units and continuous process improvement is one of its major management goal. The goal of the experiment is to demonstrate how the use of an assessment method such as the emerging SPICE standard and a goal-oriented measurement approach like ami along with specific tools can help a medium to large critical and complex software development project improve its development process in its weakest areas and achieve ISO 9001 compliance. The areas identified and selected for improvement are Project Management, Configuration Management and Testing. Indeed, matching deadlines and delivering successful software in terms of costs and quality are common problems in software industry.

The Experiment

The baseline project selected for the experiment is a CASE tool development project. A self-assessment has been carried out using SPICE, as well as a successful third-party ISO 9001 audit. A goals tree will be developed using ami and suitable metrics will be derived to monitor the achievement of the management goals. An improvement plan will be defined and commitments established with all project working groups involved. The plan will describe specifications for each improvement action in terms of what practices to implement according to what model (SPICE BPG or CMM).

The implementation of improvement actions in the baseline project will include the definition of improved standard processes, the installation of selected tools, training, and the collection of process effectiveness and efficiency data. Progress will be periodically monitored and improvements will be confirmed by carrying out a second SPICE assessment. The experiment will be accomplished by the Tecsiel Business Unit within the Finsiel company. Tecsiel employs 250 people.

Expected Impact and Experience

In case of success (i.e. achieving the SPICE target capability levels) the new processes and methods will be integrated in the Tecsiel Quality System first and then properly adjusted to be exported to the whole Finsiel Group. Furthermore the expertise gained and the lesson learned in the experiment concerning the SPICE procedures and the ami method can be capitalised for general internal process assessment and improvement. For a wider exploitation of the experiment results an ami case study will be produced at the end of the project in order to provide a good basis for replicability and feed-back will be provided to the SPICE project on the application of the current standard. An evaluation of the effectiveness of the CASE Tools will be produced as well.

10.34 ISOTOPO 21603

Integrated Software Management Through Process Improvement

The objective of the Process Improvement Experiment (PIE) ISOTOPO was to improve the competitive position of IBERMATICA in its market. Prior to the experiment it was established, by the strategic analysis performed in the ongoing long term project MIDAS, the key factor need to improve the competitive position, in short: better service, in providing improved products to the customers, and professionality with fulfilment of commitments.

Guided by the strategic plan, the experiment starts with a focused assessment of the software process in the areas related to the factors which control the competitive position. Following the assessment results, three parallel working groups were set up assigned to the three selected improvement areas:

• Requirement Management

- Software Project Planning, and projects tracking and oversight.
- Software Testing

Previously a model was selected to guide the assessment and the improvement, the model selected was the SEI's CMM. In order to obtain these objectives a number of preparative actions oriented to assure the success of the experiment were also carried out:

Training and promotion in the necessary techniques and methods in order to go ahead the improvement process; including training in effective team work.

- Assess the Area situation of the software production processes, against the selected reference model: CMM.
- Define the Unity strong and weak points and identify the priority improvement key areas.
- Investigate the state of the art in Software Integrated Process management.

The improved process definition has been carried out by the Working groups in participative and collaborative fashion, that is one of the key success factors. Work performed included:

- Carry out the improvement actions that meet the Area necessities, regarding mainly the client attention and the productivity improvement.
- Define the procedures that solve the key area of Requirements Management and Preparation for testing in pilot projects.
- Define the procedures for the Planning and tracking Area and oversight and tracking projects.
- Define the software procedure and testing techniques.
- Test the defined procedures in pilot projects.
- Procedures Optimising.
- To continue with the Procedures Institutionalisation Plan in the whole Organisation.

The analysis of the final results show that the main points of the objectives were reached and the effect in face of the customers involved in the pilots phase has been positive with a high level of satisfaction and excellent evaluations of the qualification and professionality of the staff and of the process defined.

As a conclusion we can state that our process improvement experiment was successfully.

Ibermatica
Spain

10.35   ISUC 21358

Improving Software Quality Using CASE Methods

The following document presents work performed during the ISUC ESSI-21358 project. It is mainly targeted to organisations which consider the introduction of object-oriented technology (OT) for their software development.

The work has been carried out thanks to a financial contribution of the European commission under the ESSI programme of the III framework of RTD in the field of Information technologies. KNAPP engages in introducing OT for the whole software department to handle further projects faster, more efficiently, with higher quality, and lower maintenance expenditure in the future.

The switch to OT does not only mean to use a new object oriented programming language like C++. Object oriented methods must be introduced. Defining an appropriate software process in parallel helps to handle OT as a new technology.

The experience gained from object-oriented methods, the experience made with an object-oriented CASE tool, the definition and refinement of the software process and determining heuristics for project estimation are of great relevance for a wider audience.

The goals of the experiment are to reduce maintenance costs, to improve software quality and to reuse software parts.

The first activity of the PIE was to select a suitable object oriented method for analysis and design. We chose Booch for designing and analysing. Additionally using use cases in the notation of Jacobsen, the analysis was extended.

The second step of the experiment was to evaluate and to introduce an OO-CASE tool supporting the selected methods. KNAPP decided to buy Rational Rose C++. The software process was defined in harmony with the CASE tool.

In the context of the experiment we have defined a metric suite with quality and design metrics. KNAPP searched for an appropriate metric tool to get parameters from the baseline project. We did not find any suitable tool for UNIX. So we decided to write a simple metric tool outside the ESSI project collecting the metric suite for C++ and Java in parallel. The parameters obtained from the tool are a result for this experiment.

On November 1996 the team members started to analyse and to design the objects for the underlying baseline project according to our defined software process.

The implementation of the baseline project was finished by the end of May, a test phase continued the activities during the end of the baseline project. The software of the baseline project is regarded as stable and KNAPP now starts the transition of the baseline project from a development project to a customer project.

Knapp Logistics Automation
Austria

10.36   LANHOBEK 24155

Client Relationships and Requirement Management Improvement

The objective of the experiment was to establish and institutionalise management and engineering practices in the area of Acquisition, Definition and Management of User Requirements, in order to proceed with more stable specification downwards.

A working group within the internal structure was created, with user participation and the assistance of an external consultancy company, with a primary focus on technology transfer to the organisation. Quality assurance activities and processes were defined in this experiment to the extent of the Requirement processes, including acceptance tests. Other QA activities will be established in the future.

New processes for Requirement Management and Requirement Definition were developed, tested and managed in the organisation within a pilot project. Some project objectives (increase in customer satisfaction, reduction of development time and maintenance costs) were nearly reached with significant advances and other (reduction of time-to-market, increase in software production, rise a level in SPICE processes related to requirements) were widely surpassed. The new processes are clearly useful in the organisation, helping to improve the service to the clients.

The organisation is working to institutionalise the new processes, following a plan that was developed in the last phase of the project.

This Process Improvement Experiment (PIE), named as LANHOBEK, was run by Lantik, S.A. as prime user without associated partners, and has been 100% funded by the European Commission, DG III, within the European Systems & Software Initiative (ESSI) in the Information Technologies programme (ESPRIT).

Lantik
Spain

10.37   LARGECM 21473

Configuration Management in the LARGE

This paper describes the ESSI-PIE "Configuration Management in the LARGE". The LARGECM experiment is related to research carried out by Alenia in the frame-work of the ESSI Community Program with financial contribution by the Commission.

The experiment concerns the improvement of the Configuration Management practice by moving from traditional version control of sources (SCCS like) to a comprehensive Configuration Management System.

The new Software Configuration Management activity cover all process arte-facts, on a large and varied set of hardware/software platforms, assuring data in-tegrity, inter-operability, improving security and automating main configuration management practices.

The Alenia's Needs for an advanced Configuration Management have been identified doing interviews to a selected pool of specialists and managers; the needs have been deduced from the perceived Configuration Management limita-tions. The needs to satisfy for the Configuration management system are reported in the document "Configuration Management NEEDS".

Analysis of CM available Commercial tools has been done to identify the right tool to use for the needs of the Alenia Radar System Division; that is reported in the document provides "CM Technology Selection". A CM Product Model has been defined as a collection of linked artefacts (resulting from the software devel-opment/maintenance process).

The main CM practices (Process Model) have been formalised, rigorously modelled and their enactment (execution) have to be supported by a process/work-flow engine.

Integration and consistency of the Process Model and the Product Model has been of primary concern. Conformance with ISO CM requirements (i.e. ISO 9004-7) has been the target. The experiment has had the purpose to identify the software configuration items and to carry out a systematic control of its changes, in order to maintain its integrity and traceability throughout all Life Cycle phases.

The new software CM system has been implemented by Alenia/DSR Software Unit, with the selected Technology, and then used on the baseline project evaluat-ing the benefits.

The baseline project has been the Reply Processor & Channel Management (RPCM) and the Operator Control Panel (OCP) Computer Software Configuration Items (CSCIs) of the SIR-S secondary radar. The management organisation and resources applied to this baseline project, procedures, methods, tools and facilities to implement Configuration Management activities during the software life cycle have been described in the Software Configuration Management Plan. Benefits for involved people result in enhancement the efficiency of the software maintenance and its reuse. These aspects all contribute to increase the overall competitiveness on the market. This experiment contribute at on going standardisation efforts, CM practice is intended to be institutionalised as part of company Quality System.

Alenia un Azienda Finmeccanica
Italy

10.38   MARITA 10549

Management of a Flexible and Distributed Software Production

This paper deals with the experience ABB Robotics Products AB have gained during the transition from a traditional functional project development to a continuous component-oriented process, i.e. to build products from components, a process which an increasing number of companies may be forced to adopt to remain competitive. This implies using object-oriented technologies to promote reuse.

The aim of a component-based development process is to shorten lead times to market, enabling developers to "snap together" generic components and customise them for local market requirements, or specific market segments, as these arise. Cycle time is shortened if "component development" and "product assembly" is done in parallel and if customisation can take place locally, implying the need for distributed support for component-oriented development.

The ESSI experiment, MARITA, had the goal to identify the configuration management processes needed to support component-oriented development and to automate as many of these processes as possible through the use of tools. It was found more difficult than anticipated to adopt existing tools on the market to the component-oriented process. During the experiment a number of project organisational changes had to be added. Even the development model had to be redefined. ROP does not claim the measures taken are the only possible or the best ways, there are still things to improve, but it has improved the maturity of ROP as a software supplier.

The MARITA experiment have been carried out within the framework of the ESSI Community Research Programme with a financial contribution by the Commission.

ABB Robotics Products AB
Sweden

10.39   MAUSE 10560

A Methodological Approach in the Use of Software Engineering

This paper describes the results of the MAUSE (ESSI-10560) project. This project was a Process Improvement Experiment (PIE) supported by the early phase of the ESSI programme. MAUSE was carried out by two Small to Medium Enterprises (SMEs) which aimed at assessing the benefits of adopting a methodical approach to S/W development. The approach taken was to adopt a methodology framework for analysis-design and project management assisted by design and development tools. MAUSE was based on the integration of the following components:

- A formal requirements and analysis and design process (SSADM).
- A solid management framework (PRINCE).
- CASE support to improve the productivity of the Analysis and Design (Systems Architect).
- GUPTA development environment to support windows user interface development including prototyping to provide portability, scalability and operation in Client-Server mode.
- The measurement basis of the experiment was set up according to DESMET (a methodology for determining an appropriate evaluation method for new methods/tools, funded by UK Dept. of Trade & Industry), and MERMAID E-2046 for software cost estimation.

Although the metrics taken do not show dramatic improvements in productivity the overall quality of the software has significant raised. The main benefits in MAUSE which are the dramatic improvement of maintainability of software and product quality, come from the adoption of the methodological framework. In addition, the SSADM framework encouraged a formal and professional interaction with the clients. The use of CASE within this project was mainly to facilitate documentation. The adoption of the development platform has given a number of benefits mainly in the area of prototyping. Observable improvements were taken in the following areas:

The SSADM methodology ensured that requirements, design and implementation documentation was produced in a standard, generally accepted format, therefore, the communication between the software development team members has been enhanced.

The availability of prototypes allowed the customer early visibility of the "look-feel" of the product and, again, led to the identification of defects prior to implementation. For the products developed in MAUSE, no support has been required and no defects reported in the first 3 months after their release.

- Reuse of screens/forms was enabled.
- The amount of code produced was substantially decreased.
- The data collected during the experiment has provided an effort estimation model that can be used to assist the costing of future products.

This experiment should be of interest to Small companies producing bespoke or packaged commercial data processing software, who currently use informal software production methods. Both companies participating in the experiment regard the project approach as proven and are adopting it throughout their organisations.

Pliroforiki   Sunsoft
Greece   Greece

10.40   MAZ PIE 21411

Software Development Process Improvement Experiment

This report describes the results of ESSI Project No 21411, MAZ PIE. The project has been completed after two extensions in time at the end of November 1997. The work done in this project has been supported by the European Commission. The Commission owns the copyright of this report. The report is public and may be disseminated freely.

The project is concerned with the introduction of methods and tools to improve software development with respect to object-oriented analysis & design (OOA/OOD) as well as configuration management (CM).

This report is primarily written for software developers and software development managers. It is consequently addressing software houses as well as all companies with at-least a medium-sized software development department (e.g. 5–15 employees).

This PIE has been submitted as a direct consequence of a formal BOOT STRAP assessment, which ranked the software processing unit involved at 1.25, among other reasons due to the lack of a formal quality system, replicable software design processes, and configuration management. A quality system in accordance with ISO 9001 has meanwhile been installed through efforts outside this PIE.

The PIE is designed to address some of the remaining shortcomings. In the course of the experiment appropriate tools have been selected and are subsequently applied to a baseline project. The PIE includes training on methods and tools for the staff involved. The PIE has three primary goals:

- Improvement of software development by object-oriented analysis & design and configuration management
- Incorporation of these methods and tools into the quality management system in which the software engineering sub-model of the V-Model has been adapted to the organisation's needs to describe the software process.

This must be extended to include regulations for object-orientation and reuse. and in the consequence

- Increase of BOOTSTRAP ranking to 2.5–3.0
  Here are some of the more general key lessons:

- Acceptance in the company is high because management is dedicated to quality improvement and developers are young (usually graduates from university) and eager to learn new things.
- Selection of appropriate tools is a complex task that must not be underestimated. In order to minimise efforts use evaluation reports, experience reports, and strong filter criteria to reduce the number of tools to look at.

- Even if properly selected, introduction and application of new tools and methods will not be smooth and much time will be spent to cope with unanticipated difficulties.
- With OOA/OOD, consistency between analysis, design, and implementation is high for the static architecture of a program, it is however not supported for its dynamic architecture.
- With CM, build times for release builds have been reduced by up to 80%

A final BOOTSTRAP assessment resulted in a ranking of 2.25 for the entire software processing unit, and 2.5 for the PIE's base-line project. Aspects related most closely to the PIE objectives where rated at up to 3.0.

10.41 MIDAS 21244

Measurable Improvement of Development Deployment and Operation of Interbank Automation Software

The MIDAS project aims at a measurable improvement in the reliability and availability of interbank services offered by SIA, the organisation in charge of running, developing, and maintaining the National Inter-bank Network of Italy. Such improvement is achieved by establishing an effective CM process, i.e. to define CM procedures and policies, to select and customise automated tools supporting CM activities and to experiment the new CM process in a baseline project. A suitable measurement program was defined – using the Goal/Question/Metrics (GQM) technique – and executed in order to objectively assess the effectiveness of the new CM practice.

This document describes the achievements of the MIDAS project. The document is addressed to both managers and technical people. In fact both organisational and business-oriented issues, as well as technical information (mainly excerpts from the deliverables) are reported, in order to provide a picture of the project as comprehensive as possible, and to allow readers to be informed about all relevant issues concerning the establishment of CM and measurement processes.

CM policies and tools: this is the core activity of the project, since CM is the main innovation introduced in SIA with the experiment [1]. The following steps were performed:

- Definition of the CM process for the pilot project development environment. The pilot project is the NRO project. NRO will provide a full range of services for the management and operation of the SIA network. It also provides APIs and interfaces to allow SIA customers to interface their own applications with SIA services.. It is one of the most strategic product that SIA will deliver in the next five years.
- Selection and customisation of a supporting tool (CCC/Harvest).

- Deployment of the CM system for the NRO software, training of NRO project people, establishment of an on-line support service (help desk).
- Optimisation of the CM system, according to the results of measurements, monitoring, problem reports and spontaneous feed-back.
- Definition of the GQM plan and the measurement plan to assess the effectiveness of introducing CM in SIA.
- Execution of the GQM measurement program: results are reported in [3,13] and briefly outlined in section 4.1 of this document
- External dissemination: the MIDAS project, its objectives and results have been presented in several conferences and meetings.
- Internal dissemination: MIDAS objectives and technical and managerial implications were discussed in SIA, involving both people from the pilot project, people from other projects and departments, and also some suppliers.

Lessons learned in the project and reported in this document concern the establishment of CM in a controlled way (with a special reference to the integration of process modelling, improvement and measurement), optimisations of the process (specially as far as data collection, process monitoring, support and enforcing are concerned), tool selection and customisation, management and cost issues.

SIA
Italy

10.42   MOODISC 21416

Methods for Object Oriented Design and Implementation Supporting Changes

The implementation of this project and the results of this project are of interest for SMEs with development and maintenance of large and complex software systems, which want to improve their configuration and change management and/or their development processes.

The companies Micrologica GmbH and Phoenix Contact GmbH & Co have worked together in this project to improve their software processes and to gain experiences for other companies in similar situations. Both companies have since some years quality management systems, which are certified according to ISO 9001, but they have been awaked further to improve their processes. Each partner has had experiences on the field that was of interest for the other and could exchange it to the other partner. Between both partners there is no competition in business fields.

Micrologica's objectives have been to improve the Configuration and Change Management (CCM) for development, customising and maintenance of its software products in order to save time in these process phases and to consolidate the base for a stable quality.

Phoenix Contact's objectives have been to introduce Object Oriented Analysis and Design methods (OOA/OOD), to improve the reusability of software elements by this means and to shorten the time to market for its products.

To detect the gained benefits the basic idea of this PIE has been: Assessments of the SW-processes before and after all improvements in both companies will show the improvements of the processes. At the beginning of the PIE assessments of SW-processes have been carried out in both companies to get Bootstrap like process-profiles as a base for the comparison after the PIE. These profiles have shown that Micrologica has been rather weak in CCM-methods and –tools and that Phoenix Contact has been rather weak in the methodology for analysis and design.

In the preparation phase of the project all members of the involved staff have been trained for the usage of suitable CCM-methods and -tools respectively for proven OOA/OOD-methods. In the experimental phase these techniques have been established and used in the baseline projects of both companies successfully.

Micrologica has worked out detailed user guides and special labour instructions for handling of projects and files for different groups of development problems, customisation and maintenance. The selected CCM-Tool is suitable very well for development problems with a great number of files and a high rate of multi-used files in different projects. It has enough flexibility for customisation and maintenance processes also. In this way the developments under CCM save time and have higher reliability. Measurements during the PIE have delivered characteristic dates of all CCM-actions:

To hold older versions and configurations with their history in an efficient way gives more flexibility and also more safety for development, customisation and maintenance of large software systems.

About a third of all modules are reused now by sharing from other projects. This gives a high reliability and saves development time and costs.

Although the number of installed systems for customers has quadruplicated throughout the PIE and despite a new software version was introduced at the last one third of the PIE, the number of all errors found in these systems has only triplicated in this time. The average error rate at the end of the PIE is about one error per installed system per quarter of a year and is decreasing more rapidly.

The effort for debugging of the errors of all installed systems decreases about 25 per cent in a quarter. For Micrologica the assessments after the PIE have shown, that the total score for all attributes of the Configuration and Change Management has been doubled against that at the start of the PIE.

Phoenix Contact has chosen and adopted the OO methodology, which was used for some years at Micrologica and which was developed by the STC (Software Technique Center of the University of Hamburg) originally for banking applications.

User guide lines and labour instructions for the OOA/OOD methods have been worked out and this OOA/OOD-methods were applied for the development of new functions in the baseline project of Phoenix Contact. To support the OO methods furthermore a new evolutionary development life cycle model was explored in this experiment which supports the OO methods much better than the traditional waterfall model used before this experiment.

The chosen OO methods could be applied successful. The development in the experimental phase was performed without tool support to get used to the new methods. We found that manually maintenance of development documents is rather cumbersome without tool support. Therefore we've checked whether a CASE tool could be applied for design and maintenance and found out, that this is possible and that this reduces the effort for complex designs.

This PIE has increased the skill of the developers and the awareness of the importance of software process in general and especially of usefulness of measurements. There are clear indications, that the improved software architecture reduces development time for changes and additions, but this could not be proven within this experiment because there was no redesign phase.

The process improvement gained by the experiment at Phoenix Contact was measured by assessments after the PIE. The total score for requirements engineering, design and implementation has been doubled against that at the start of the PIE.

This project has been carried out in the Specific RTD Programme of ESSI and was supported financially by the European Commission. The partners wish to acknowledge the European Commission for their subsidy and also for their organisational assistance to accomplish this project.

Micrologica GmbH
Germany

Phoenix Contact GmbH
Germany

10.43 MPCM 24196

Multi-Platform Configuration Management, Process Improvement Experiment

Business Motivation and Objectives

TransAction is a database technology company founded in 1987. The products of TransAction are: (i) the relational database system TransBase and (ii) custom database application development on behalf of our customers. The primary product, named TransBase, is a relational database system available on a variety of different system platforms ranging from Apple Macintosh to main frame VMS. Users expect identical quality, performance and programming interfaces on all those platforms.

One of the most important requirements is to assure quality in a multi-version, multi-platform environment. The importance of improving processes to ensure and increase quality in software development is not only recognised inside our company, but also expected by our customers who rely heavily on the quality of our software once it is released. Because the software is a basic part of their customer deliverables software quality of TransBase is very critical for our company and our customers.

This PIE project has the following goals:

Increase our software quality by improving the software development process. In our case, this means establishing programming conventions, improving source code control, and establishing effective multi-platform validation procedures.

Reduce manpower costs for platform-specific overhead.

The Experiment

Establish design and programming conventions that are obligatory for each programmer and system designer. Try to eliminate platform-specific problems as early as possible.

Improve configuration management. Replace or extend the current source code administration system by a more powerful system suited to handle multi-platform aspects and capable of handling code-related documentation and/or platform-specific test results.

Improve the testability and comparability of the developed software; in particular, develop test suites which are platform-independent and can be run on all supported platforms to guarantee identical behaviour of the software.

Expected Impact and Experience

We expect: to improve and stabilise our development process by establishing standards, to reduce manpower costs for platform specific overhead from around 50% to 30% or less, leading to more available capacity for product development, Reduce reaction time to customer maintenance requests while reducing maintenance charges

Transaction Software GmbH
Germany

10.44   MSI-QBP 21547

Maritime Safety Information Using Quality Best Practice

By means of this PIE Gepin Engineering Spa aimed to set up a centralised Software Quality Management (SQM) function with the role of driving and assuring the quality of both software processes and products developed and maintained in the company. The present PIE represented a substantial step towards such a goal, focusing, in particular, the improvement effort on the most critical supporting processes (for the company), that are Configuration and Change Management (CCM) and Documentation Development Management (DDM). The PIE was managed on top of a baseline project, relevant for the company, concerned with the treatment of Maritime Safety Information. The topics of the baseline project together with the subject of the software Quality Best Practices gave the title to the PIE.

The results concern:

- Well experimented and wide company accepted procedures and templates for managing Documentation Development and System Configuration/Change processes
- Customised support tools for the PIE focused processes: Lotus Notes for the Documentation Development Management process; CCC/Harvest for the Configuration and Change Management process
- Well experimented and wide company accepted Software Process Improvement (SPI) and measurement schemes, managed respectively by the SPICE [2] and the AMI [4] frameworks.

Key lessons learned

- About SPI
- SPI strictly depends on top management commitment and involvement
- SPICE and AMI can be complementary frameworks for SPI strategies
- About DDM and CCM processes

They positively influences improvement of both SLC Engineering and management processes because are the basis for:

- SLC documents produced according to well-established workflow models, to well defined documentation requirements, to well experimented documentation templates
- SLC work products under configuration and change control during the whole project lifetime
- effective project measurement and control
- About the selected technologies (Lotus Notes and CCC/Harvest)
- The Notes application (customisation of Lotus Notes environment) currently:
- drives every user to follow the planned document life cycle

- tracks all steps in the document life cycle
- allows full-text search in documents, improving document usability and reuse
- allows easy verification of planned life cycle compliance In the future, the Notes application will also allow:
- to get statistics on document management process
- to verify the project documents' progress
- CCC/Harvest is:
- a distributed environment for configuration management, accessible to all team people
- an environment easy to learn and to use

In the future CCC/Harvest environment will be more flexible and will allow an easy tailoring to suit the configuration management environment to several project needs.

Relevance and applicability of the results to the wider community

The potential users interested in the results of the MSI_QBP experiment are the many European SMEs working in Information Technology, because of the worry of competition and quality costs. The reference to well recognised international software engineering and quality standards, in the implementation of the SQM procedural and template framework, as well as the adoption of commercially available support tools allow the project results to constitute a well founded and repeatable framework for European software SMEs that would start an SQM program.

Also the approach followed by Gepin could be of interest of the wider community. It was based on the assumption that the improvement on a software process does not depend on the sophistication degree of technology. This one provides technicalities to manage base practices of a process, but does not provide features to institutionalise a process in a company. This require a well recognised improvement scheme which offers the way to reach a step by step process management capability spreading on the range of the process planning, measurement & tracking, documentation, standardisation, etc. practices.

Gepin Engineering S.p.a
ITALY

10.45 OSEF 10913

Object Oriented Software Engineering Flow

The OSEF project, an acronym for Object-oriented Software Engineering Flow, aims to set up a development environment, by assembling market available tools supporting all the phase of the software development cycle, according to the object oriented methodology.

The project's key lesson is the Alitalia and Siemens Nixdorf Informatica evaluation of the costs and of the benefits related to the use of the methodology on a real case of project development.

The topics this report deals with would be interesting for all the organisations that plan to introduce object oriented technology in their environment, or are already using it. They will find here a discussion and references on some of existing tools that support object oriented analysis (OOA), object oriented design (OOD), object oriented algorithmic and visual programming (OOP), object oriented data base management systems (OODBMS).

The project has been carried out thanks to a financial contribution of the European commission under the ESSI programme of the III framework of RTD in the field of Information Technologies.

Having in mind the main goal of our action, that is the introduction of object orientation in the companies' software development process, most of the work performed was devoted to the training of the project staff, to the internal dissemination and sharing of the experience made. Today both Alitalia and Siemens Nixdorf have an experience and a software infrastructure that is going to be reused.

Alitalia Linee Aeree Italiane S.p.a
Italy

10.46   PCS 24065

Project Management and Engineering Global Control System

This PIE (Process Improvement Experiment) was concerned with improving the software configuration management and version control systems used by Clockworks. The immediate objective and expected result was to reduce the incidence of configuration errors and the work involved in correcting these errors.

Part of the experiment involved looking for suitable software configuration management tools for use in localisation projects. However, our experience to date has been that there is no single tool that could be used to manage the thousands of separate items, the great number of versions, and the diversity of applications that a localisation project requires. Instead our solution uses a semi-automated system consisting of a Lotus Notes database, some file management tools (i.e. FileSync), a new directory structure, and naming convention and new procedures, and it relies on people to follow these procedures.

The localisation of "Oil Change", a product from Cybermedia Corporation, was selected to be the baseline project where the new procedures and technology were tested and metrics were collected. In the project very significant improvements in the configuration failure rate and repeat failure rate were experienced when the new system and procedures were introduced.

Due to the success of this experiment, Clockworks plans to use a generalised version of the new system and procedures in all its projects.

From the technological point of view the next stage is to publish the Notes data to the Web so that the customer and contractors that are involved in a localisation project have direct access to information about it. Also we plan to increase the functionality of the current Lotus Notes system.

The experience gained in this PIE is useful for many European localisation specialists, since they confront the same problems as Clockworks in managing their localisation work. Other localisation companies will be able to adopt similar approaches to those demonstrated in this PIE, and will have access to the same technical and commercial benefits.

Clockworks International
Ireland

10.47 PET 10438

The Prevention of Errors Through Experience-Driven Test Efforts

Through a rigorous analysis of problem reports from previous projects the companies behind the PET project have achieved a step change in the testing process of embedded real-time software. The measurable objectives have been to reduce the number of bugs reported after release by 50%, and reduce the hours of test effort per bug found by 40%. Both of these goals have been met. The actual numbers achieved were 75% less bugs reported, and a 46% improvement in test efficiency.

The problem reports have been analysed and bugs in them categorised according to Boris Beizer's categorisation scheme [BB]. We have found that bugs in embedded real-time software follow the same pattern as other types of software reported by Boris Beizer.

We have also found that the major cause of bugs reported (36%) are directly related to requirements, or can be derived from problems with requirements. Improved tracking of requirements through the development process has been achieved through the introduction of a life-cycle management CASE tool. Unfortunately the customisation of the life-cycle management tool took longer than expected, so no actual numbers on the positive effect of the tool are available at present, but it is expected that the integration and system testing phases can be combined, resulting in a major reduction of testing effort.

The second largest cause of bugs (22%) stems from lack of systematic unit testing, allegedly because of the lack of tools for an embedded environment. We have found that tools do exist to assist this activity, but their application requires some customisation. We have introduced a unit testing environment based on EPROM emulators enabling the use of symbolic debuggers and test coverage tools for systematic unit testing. The unit testing methods employed were: Static and dynamic analysis.

We have demonstrated that the number of bugs that can be found by static and dynamic analysis is quite large, even in code that has been released. The results we have found are applicable to the software community in general, not only to embedded real-time software, because the methods and tools are generally available. Finally a cost/benefit analysis of our results with static and dynamic analysis indicates that there could be an immediate payback on tools and training already on the first project.

The efficiency of static analysis to find bugs was very high (only 1.6 hours/bug). Dynamic analysis was found to be less efficient (9.2 hours/bug), but still represented a significant improvement over finding bugs after release (14 hours/bug). We achieved a test coverage (branch coverage) for all units in the product of 85%, which is considered best-practice for most software, e.g. non safety critical software.

The PET project has been funded by the Commission of the European Communities (CEC) as an Application Experiment under the ESSI programme: European System and Software Initiative.

BRueEL & Kjaer Measurements A/S
Denmark

10.48   PITA 21531

Process Improvement Through Automation

AMT-Sybex (Software) Ltd. conducted the PITA (Process Improvement Through Automation) project to improve the efficiency and effectiveness of the existing Quality Management System for Software Development, as well as gain control of software under development through the implementation of Configuration Management tools.

The present QMS is paper-based and has a significant amount of manual activity associated with it Refinements to the current system have taken place during its four year life and it has now reached a high level of maturity. The QMS was automated using Document Management and Workflow software. All document handling processes have been automated and placed under more secure access control. The routing of tasks through QMS processes has also been automated to provide better project control, reduce cycle time and increase individual awareness of deadlines and time-scales.

Key Results and Observations:

- The Configuration Management software (PVCS) has provided excellent version control for software under development and eliminated re-work due to over-writing development versions. The software has provided an environment which is conducive to simultaneous development. The key users of the PVCS have reacted very positively to its introduction.
- Experiment results were inconclusive in proving that the PITA software actually reduced project cycle time. However, the Project Manager of the projects used in the experiment strongly believes that PITA saves time and improves efficiency.
- PITA has been well received by staff members. Many staff have found it difficult to give up paper documents and this represents the biggest hurdle to acceptance.

Providing a facility for draft or single-use paper copies has facilitated the transition to electronic documents. Staff are pleased with the easy access to documents provided by PITA document management. They report that documents are always available and never "out-of-file."

- The introduction of the PITA project accelerated a planned programme of desktop hardware and software upgrades. As a result, all staff are now skilled in the use of Windows 95, Workflow, Image manipulation and Document Management.
- While it is possible to select "off-the-shelf" software tools for many applications, there is no "off-the-shelf" or pre-existing application solution for ISO 9001 Software Development. Business Processes and document management needs vary from organisation to organisation and therefore the Workflow which automates these processes must be created from "scratch" with the software tools provided. Therefore, the level of effort required to build a solution was more significant than expected.
- We were surprised to discover that the documentation and process flow diagrams which supported our ISO 9001 accredited QMS processes was not sufficient to create Workflow process maps. A significant amount of effort was required to produce process maps which could be translated by the developers into the Workflow software.
- During the development of the process maps it was discovered that underlying the paper-based QMS system was in fact a "Customer/Projects" database. Before automation of the processes could proceed an electronic database to store customer and project related data had to be developed.

The PITA project has been viewed as successful within the organisation and we will continue to expand its scope. However, we underestimated the amount of effort that would be required to develop a solution and did not plan resources appropriately. The overall acceptance of the automated processes has been very high. We have identified a series of future actions and continued growth for PITA and expect the software to form an integral part of our Quality Management System.

Amt-Sybex (Software Ltd)
Ireland

10.49 PRIDE 21167

A Methodology for Preventing Requirements Issues from Becoming Defects

Through a rigorous analysis of problem reports from previous projects Brüel & Kjær has achieved a major change in the requirements engineering process. We have developed and validated an experience based requirements engineering methodology, which has proven to give quantitative as well as qualitative improvements to our products and business.

Through our analysis of error reports in a previous process improvement experiment aimed at improving the efficiency of our testing process, we have found that requirements related bugs are the major cause of bugs. We also found that the vast majority of these problems (85%) were due to missing or changed requirements; and misunderstood requirements by developers and testers.

In both experiments we have categorised bugs according to a taxonomy described by Boris Beizer. For the current PRIDE experiment, however, we have limited the study to those bugs which can be related to requirements issues. We found that requirements related bugs represented 51% of all the bugs analysed.

Furthermore we have found that requirements issues are not what is expected from the literature. Usability issues dominate (64%). Problems with understanding and co-operating with 3rd party software packages and circumventing their errors are also very frequent (28%). Functionality issues that we (and others) originally thought were the major requirements problems only represent a smaller part (22%). Other issues account for 13%. The sum of these figures adds up to more than 100% because one bug may involve more than one issue.

A closer study of the bugs suggested a number of techniques that could prevent a significant number of requirements related bugs.

Since usability issues dominate, the corner stone of the new requirements engineering methodology was to introduce usability tests on very early prototypes. These were aimed at validating the development team's understanding of common use situations (scenarios) for the new product. Focused readings and specific actions to verify the resulting requirements specification were also introduced.

The validation techniques of the methodology were introduced on a real-life development project. On this project we achieved an almost 3 times increase in developer productivity on the user interface, and usability issues per new screen were reduced by 72%. The total number of error reports was reduced by 27%.

More important, however, the introduction of use situations (scenarios) and usability tests resulted in a totally revised user interface, which is regarded as a major breakthrough in understanding and supporting the users' tasks. And the product was released in time for shipments before the end of the financial year.

The PRIDE project has been funded by the Commission of the European Communities (CEC) as a Process Improvement Experiment under the ESSI programme: European System and Software Initiative.

BRueEL & Kjaer Measurements A/S
Denmark

10.50 PROCOM 21231

Process Improvement Trough Configuration Management

Business Motivation and Objectives

ProTec has to deliver software according to user requirements that frequently change due to the nature of the clients' business. This makes it increasingly difficult to keep control of critical project parameters like effort, cost and time. Additional challenges for a higher efficiency are the necessary cultural change towards a team oriented development process and the re-use of common software modules.

This is a common business concern and the main focus of the experiment whose objectives are more reliable commitments to our customers and improved product quality and maintenance. These are all key factors for better customer satisfaction which again is our strongest and most important directive for future business improvement.

The Experiment

The achievement of the objective above requires the following steps:

- Introduction to configuration management practices, identification and installation of an appropriate tool.
- Building up the configuration tree of existing software from the baseline project, re-usable modules and development lines from customer requests.
- Monitor the development of customer specific modules according to the fulfilment of the above objective.

The experiment will be performed around the development of a simulation system enabling companies to elaborate waste management concepts and waste balances according to national and international law regulating waste disposal.

ProTec GmbH employs 12 people, 3 of them are involved in the project team.

Expected Impact and Experience

ProTec expects to gain know-how on managing development projects for custom-ised software systems and on maintaining these systems in line with changing user requirements. The anticipated benefits will be an efficient, team-oriented devel-opment process, leading to better product quality and enabling ProTec to make reliable commitments to customer requests.

10.51 PROMISED 24149

Process Improvement in Intelligent Simulation Environment Development

Business Motivation and Objectives and the Experiment

The PROMISED experiment aims to increase the level of maturity of CSTB's development process from it's current status where procedures are performed on the basis of individual knowledge to a higher level of maturity (SPICE Level 3 – Well defined) where processes are described in a formal way and therefore can be repeated by new contributors.

The SPICE assessment of CSTB's current software process revealed the limits of this process and possible ways of improvements. The experiment will focus on the following improvements:

- process modelling including user-defined metrics
- traceability management
- configuration management.

The tool chosen for the experiment is Concerto/SKIPPER of SEMA Group (F). The baseline project (ISE v3) developed by the SDSC (Software Development and Software Certification) team aims to develop an Intelligent Simulation Environment in order to allow encapsulation, at a reasonable cost, of various simulation tools in a homogeneous and user-friendly application. CSTB employs 560 people, 13 of them are members of the SDSC team.

Expected Impact and Experience

The expected results of the experiment are improvements of CSTB's development process. These improvements will be measured in order to quantify the impact of the tested solutions in relation with their costs. This information will then be used as an input for a decision making process aiming to define relevant milestones for a total quality approach applied to the software development activities of the organisation.

CSTB
France

10.52 QARI 23845

Improving Software Development Processes by Applying Object-Oriented Methods and Techniques, Focusing on Better Specification of Functional

The objective of the QARI project was to test if MaXware could increase its margins by applying object-oriented methods for system documentation during the specification and design phases of projects. Such methods may result in reduced development time and costs, lower maintenance costs, higher product quality, more satisfied customers, and higher sales. All these factors may contribute to better margins.

The implementation of the projects Okeanos (baseline I) and Debis (baseline III), run without object-oriented analysis and design (hereafter called OOAD), was compared with the implementation of the projects, Athene (baseline II) and MXNIPS (baseline IV), which introduced and measured the effect of using the object-oriented methods. All baseline projects are finished, the analysis and comparison have been completed, and some conclusions have been drawn. There are different kind of conclusions, referring to the original goals, models for analysis, and registration of data from the baseline projects. Concerning the original goals, the analysis cannot make any conclusions about reduced development time and costs. The projects came out with very much the same productivity, regardless of whether OOAD were used or not. MaXware has, however, introduced OOAD in the organisation without any extra costs and time for the projects. That may indicate that in the future, when a sufficient number of developers master the methods, development will be cheaper. There are also indications that quality may be higher in projects using OOAD. There is not sufficient evidence to say anything about customer satisfaction and influence on sales.

The baseline projects differed substantially in size and complexity. As it is well known that productivity decreases as project size and complexity increase, the projects could not be compared without some kind of compensation for size and complexity. Estimating methods express such dependencies mathematically. Based on a widely used estimating model, we believe it is possible to compare software development projects in a reasonably objective way. Very much depends on the quality of collected data. We experienced that without very close follow-up, people tend to "forget" to register data during a running project. Also, projects does not always develop as planned, and may therefore be unable to provide data as presupposed. The advice and financial contribution given by the European Commission made it possible for MaXware AS to complete the work.

10.53 Q-PRIME 21630

Quality Oriented Software Process Management in Small Enterprises

This document contains the Final Report of the ESSI Process Improvement Experiment "Quality-Oriented Software Process Management In Small Enterprises" (Q-PRIME). This experiment was carried out by Prodacta GmbH within the ESSI (European Software and Systems Initiative) Programme and was funded by the European Commission. ESSI is part of the Specific Programme for Research and Technological Development in the field of Information Technology under the Fourth Framework Programme of the European Community.

The Q-PRIME experiment implemented software process improvement by introducing a business process-oriented approach for small and medium enterprises. The maturity of the software development process was to be raised to level 2 according to the CMM scale to ensure better quality and higher productivity within the Software Development Department at Prodacta GmbH. The main focus for improvement areas was on project management, requirements management and quality management.

The method employed in order to ensure the success of the experiment was to develop appropriate process models using a process modelling tool and introduce and evaluate them within the experiment. Organisational and technical process management was enhanced by introducing tools for configuration and documentation management, as well as for workflow management. Staff training sessions for organisational, technical and quality issues was provided and was followed by coaching activities to support the implementation of new or re-defined procedures.

Before defining process models the existing processes and procedures were analysed. Optimised process models were developed by customising the V-Model and the models defined within the Microsoft Solutions Framework (MSF). They were completed by the description of an adequate software life cycle model and a team-based model for project organisation which could be tailored according to the size of the software project.

To ensure systematic and useful project and product documentation a documentation concept was developed. It defined the documents which must be produced within the project and offers templates and guidelines for writing the documents. Another focus was the generation of documentation from available data to minimise the effort necessary to produce the documents. One major goal for the configuration management process was to implement the software life cycle model by documenting the development state of the product supported by the configuration management tool. This not only helped improve configuration management but also project planning and tracking.

In addition to the activities related to technical and process modelling issues, another major focus of the experiment was on achieving permanent support from the people effected by the changes. Their motivation is a key factor for process improvement, because they are the ones who perform the process improvement and use the new tools. Guidelines for people issues and organisational means for getting permanent feedback and improvement suggestions from the developers helped to increase acceptance of the experiment and achieve full support for the process improvement actions.

A major benefit of the experiment came from implementing a more structured and systematic way of working on all the activities of a software project. This translated into higher productivity and better process and product quality and a measurable improvement of the maturity level for Prodacta GmbH. The (re-) designing of different processes and putting them to use using a step by step approach (plan – do – evaluate) results in successful way of sustainable process improvement.

This report is of interest for anyone who is involved in software development (within small soft-ware development enterprises) and will be starting improvement activities from an initial maturity level.

Prodacta
Germany

10.54   RECAP 10497

Requirement Capturing Through Animation and MMI Prototyping

This experiment is of interest for people working in the fields of Electronic Engineering and in the development of complex computer embedded systems; providing information to the software engineers on the acceptance of a formal specification technique.

The ReCap experiment aims to increase the current software process via introducing technology (methods and tools) to support capturing and validation of user requirements, through animation of system requirements, and rapid prototyping of Man Machine Interface aspects. The experiment adds a process to the existing software development waterfall life cycle for the clear identification of user requirements in the very early phases of a system development project.

The work undertaken as part of this ESSI experiment has been :

- select a MMI prototyping technology toolset and then produce the graphic human-computer interaction aspects of the system and the related C-code.
- make use of the chosen Petri Net toolset (PACE) for the support of requirement animation model of the system.

The experiment measures the benefits of the new introduced technology on the stability of requirements and assesses the software development process improvement. The quantitative evaluation of the results has be done comparing the Application Experiment data with the Alenia's historical data collected from other similar projects.

The code generated by the tool used to produce the MMI prototype has been analysed using McCabe Toolset. The code evaluation checked its visibility and comprehensibility, verifying that no unneeded overhead has been added to the application, in terms of performance and of code size.

The most satisfactory results from this experiment, in terms of requirements capturing, are the use of the model for performance evaluation; in terms of MMI prototyping, are the creation of a customised system interface, obtaining a preview final result and generate portable C-code.

This experiment is related to research carried out by Alenia in the framework of the Community Research Programme with a financial contribution by the Commission.

Alenia Un'azienda Finmeccanica
Italy

10.55 REJOICE 23893

Requirements Engineering Through Joint, Object- Oriented, Interactive Consultation Experiment

Business Motivation and Objectives

Proper understanding of a customer's requirements for a system are crucial if problems such as cost/time overruns and re-work are to be avoided, and customer satisfaction is to be ensured. Unclear, incomplete and changing requirements must be enhanced and managed for a project to be successful, for both the customer and supplier.

The aim is to establish an improved technique which will assist customer and supplier to gain a better understanding of initial and changing requirements so that systems are delivered on time, to cost, and actually meeting the customer's real need.

The Experiment

The experiment defines a new requirements approach based on synergy between three strands:

- human interaction skills
- RAD and JAD
- formalised requirements management

This approach will be used on a representative project, typically the simulation of a sensor or a moving body. The experiences on this project will be compared with that of a similar project using existing requirements techniques.

DERA employs about 12,000 scientists from many disciplines. Its Software Engineering Centre, which will carry out this project, employs about 200 staff, all involved in software development to industry standards. Typical projects have a team of about 6 or 8 people, but can be much larger.

Expected Impact and Experience

The new technique is expected to be adopted as standard within the SEC, providing improved performance and customer satisfaction. The SEC has a role to promote best practice throughout DERA and more widely and will actively disseminate the project results.

DERA
UK

10.56   REQUITE 10714

Requite

The REQUITE Application Experiment succeeded in achieving its primary objective of improving the process of Requirements Analysis and Specification. It focused on the use of executable specifications for system modelling and functional prototyping. The partners evaluated the tools Foresight, Statemate, and OMT CoDe with ILOG Solver / Schedule, for building executable specifications. The experimental work was conducted within a semi-formal framework for process improvement.

The major achievement of both partners has been the evolution of an improved method for analysis and design which increases the developers' understanding of the requirements and promotes better communication not only among the development team members but also between supplier and customer. The opportunity for proving the improved process through an extended period of experimentation in each partner's business domain has given confidence that the process is both practical and sustainable. The improvements will therefore be carried forward into future projects.

The technical content of this report is most likely to be of interest to those concerned with the development of medium to large software systems having a real-time element, especially where the organisation has a generic system solution which typically needs to be configured quite extensively to meet the needs of specific customers.

The Application Experiment described here was financially supported by the European Commission under the auspices of the Pilot Phase of ESSI, Software Systems and Software Best Practice.

Datacep
France

Marconi radar and control systems ltd.
United Kingdom

10.57   RMATN 24257

Requirements Management in Alcatel Telecom Norway Defence Communications Division

Business Motivation and Objectives

Due to the increasing complexity of software projects, keeping track of requirements and ensuring that the end product satisfies all requirements is becoming increasingly difficult and time consuming. This may result in rework and error corrections causing projects to exceed deadlines and budgets, leading to increased time to market, reduced customer satisfaction and commercial losses.

This is a common business concern and is the main driving force for this experiment whose objective is to ensure that all customer requirements are fulfilled and that products are delivered on schedule. More efficient requirements management will significantly reduce cost and shorten time to market.

The Experiment

The achievement of the objective above requires the introduction of new procedures, methods and tool support, enabling the capturing and storing of requirements together with the rationale they are based on, in the early stages of a development project. New improved routines adjusted for the chosen tool support, for managing requirements throughout the project, will be introduced.

Alcatel Telecom Norway Defence Communications Division employs 270 people, of which 30 are expected to be involved in the process improvement experiment.

Expected Impact and Experience

Alcatel Telecom Norway expects to gain knowledge in requirements management and to increase staff awareness of the importance of proper requirements management. The experiment is expected to lead to a 70 % reduction in errors due to incomplete management of requirements. In addition, it should be possible to produce a complete list of the status for each requirement, within two hours, in connection with monthly project progress reports.

Upon successful implementation of the experiment, the new procedures will be adjusted, based on experience gathered during the experiment, before the results are disseminated in the organisation and implemented in all projects.

Alcatel Telecom Norway
Norway

10.58 SCOUT 23673

Software Configuration Usuable Techniques

Business Motivation and Objectives

The potential of maintenance cost savings, release time reduction, better reuse of software artefacts, enhanced development productivity has motivated Infosys in proposing SCOUT experiment.

Through the experiment, the proposer intends to verify how software configuration management best practices can help in pursuing company objectives such as: software maintenance costs reduction, better control of the software development process, establishment of a measurement system, help in reusing software artefacts, diffusion throughout the company of a formalised way of working.

The Experiment

The experiment named SCOUT intends to define a Configuration Management process suitable to the proposer's software development organisation. Then, by means of a selected CM tool, the process will be applied and experimented into a baseline project aimed to reengineer an off-the-shelf software package supporting civil engineers in CAD drawing and computations. The introduction of a measurement system will help in obtaining feedback on the achieved improvements as well as will establish a company metrics database.

Expected Impact and Experience

Final product assembly and delivery will occur faster, thus allowing proposer software development organisation to lessen the gap between change request (bugs or new functionalities) and its implementation. Software maintenance will also be improved since a formalised control of each artefact (code, test case, design specification etc.) concurring to final product.

The major internal impact resulting by this PIE is expected to be the set-up of the Configuration Management process, supported by a suitable Configuration Management Environment, where the defined procedures, standards and templates have been experimented and validated during the PIE, and so, can be adopted in all the other company software development projects.

Infosys s.r.l
Italy

10.59   SECU-DES 10937

Improved Methodology for the Design of Communication Protocols in Security Systems

SECU-DES was carried out in the framework of the Community Research Programme. It was supported financially by the Commission of the European Communities. The main message is that it is possible for a small company to successfully introduce advanced software design methods. It is also possible to improve the software development process substantially within a short time frame.

We selected and applied the Coloured Petri-Net (CPN) software design method. The results from this are of interest to communities searching for powerful software design methods for real-time systems.

We made procedures and instructions for software development. The results from this are of interest to communities working for software process improvement through use of a quality management.

DALCOTECH A/S's objective was to improve the level of software engineering through introduction of a formal software design method and establishment of a set of company procedures for software development.

We received intensive training in the use of CPN method and tools. The method and tools were then applied in the software design for the base-line project (a new generation of our security system). A set of company procedures and instructions were made for software development. These were also applied to the base-line project.

The application of CPN method and tools was successful, and will be employed in most future software developments. The application of the new company procedures to the base-line project improved several phases of the development process – especially in the requirements specification and design phases. The procedures and instructions will be applied in all future developments, and they will be further enhanced in the future.

The result of the project is thus that the objectives we set up at the start were all met!.

Dalcotech A/S
Denmark

10.60 SIMTEST 10824

Automated Testing for the Man Machine Interface of a Training Simulator

The project is funded by the EEC in the frame of the ESSI project; the goal of ESSI is to promote improvements in the software development process industry, to achieve greater efficiency, higher quality and greater economy.

This initiative required to select a baseline project (i.e. an existing development activity) upon which a new approach on some part of the life cycle could bring significant results in the above mentioned areas.

Dataspazio has successfully proposed SIMTEST, the evaluation of automated testing (i.e. the testing supported by a software tool) of the real time simulator of the SAX satellite (SAXSIM).

The experiment is meant to evaluate the differences between a "traditional" approach to testing (i.e. manual execution of test procedures coded by the developer) against the automated approach (i.e. automatic execution of test procedures where part of the code is automatically obtained by describing the expected behaviour of the test).

The automation of integration and test has shown important results :

- less expensive testing
- more reliable procedures
- test repeatability.

Mainly, lessons learned that have been derived from this experiment can be so summarised:

- it is better to take into account the use of these tools at a very early stage of system design as they could require architectural and/or implementation peculiarities;
- automatic test procedures can be more exhaustive and can produce a better coverage w.r.t. the traditional approach. This is paid with an extra effort in their preparation, although capture and playback features can ease the MMI test coding. An economical return is mainly possible for systems which undergo many

changes during their operational life and for which non-regression testing is a significant cost;

- the quality and the robustness of the software to be produced is better assured, as more deep and intensive tests can be easily implemented and run with a low cost;
- the repeatability of the tests is really granted using an automated tool, as there are no way to misunderstand or not fully perform a test step, as during manual test execution;
- if properly planned, the testing tool can do much more than just test for the system: it can effectively be used to encapsulate the application under development, reproducing the context environment and facilitating the integration.

As a result of the experiment, our Company is carrying out an evaluation of the use of the same approach for a new development in a similar application; the quantitative data collected during the experiment are being the basis for this decision.

Dataspazio S.P.A.
Italy

10.61   SMETOSQA 10218

Preparing SME Software Houses to SQA Implementation

A was aimed to select, install, and evaluate Software Engineering (SE) practices in a software development process for industrial control systems in a small enterprise (SME). SMEtoSQA covered the following areas:

- Requirements management;
- Modelling of the systems development life cycle;
- Co-ordination and communication with non-software groups involved in system design;
- Planning and tracking of the project.

A measurement mechanism was set up to assess the impact of the new practices on productivity and product quality.

SMEtoSQA focused on organisation, methodology and supporting technology.

Two partners were involved: the prime user Infogea S.r.l. a SME producing weight control systems, and the prime user's most relevant customer MG2 S.p.A. a producer of automated dosing machines for the pharmaceutical benefit from industry. MG2 has no direct involvement in the production of software but can significantly software process improvement initiative since software is rapidly becoming a core component of its product.

Our initial problem can be summarised as follows: we had to achieve compliance with the requirements of ISO 9001 because of the regulations concerning the validation of computerised systems in our main area of activity: process control in the pharmaceutical industry. However, given the initial state of our systems development process, the practices connected with Software Quality Assurance (SQA) were not immediately applicable. For this reason we applied for an experiment which covered the installation and evaluation of the founding SE practices enabling SQA implementation. Two formal audits to assess compliance to ISO 9001 were performed, one at the beginning and one at the end of the AE.

Third party assistance on SE and software quality was provided to Infogea by GEMINI, a not-for-profit consortium of software producers; further external support was acquired to carry out our internal training programme.

The AE followed a phased workplan which consisted of:

- An initial assessment, followed by the analysis of its findings which produced an improvement plan focused on process and people.
- Definition of a systems development life cycle based on the V-model, key SE practices were selected and applied to fully support the life cycle.
- Training on SE and SE practices.
- Tools selection, customisation and experimentation.
- Definition and implementation of a data collection and analysis process to assess the results achieved by applying the new practices
- Evaluation of the experimentation and review of the SE practices to achieve better applicability, ending with formalisation of the new practices by documented procedures.
- Design of the global structure of a Quality Management System having SQA at its core.
- Final audit to assess progress in the achievement of ISO 9001.
- Dissemination of the results at European and local events.

Overall our conclusions are:

- The AE has given a fundamental contribution to the definition of our software process and no significant activity related to our process has been left out
- The V-model, enhanced to better fit our needs, has proved usable and particularly adequate to our needs
- The definition of the process has considerably enhanced our capabilities in project estimation and project management
- The data collection process is a lasting and successful one and it allows us to analyse in a quantitative way the following aspects: product quality, process effectiveness, project estimation effectiveness and efficacy in the usage of the resources
- The final audit confirmed that we advanced considerably toward ISO 90001 compliance, which now can be considered a short term achievement

- All software engineers involved in this experiment achieved the culture and the understanding necessary to apply the new practices and to continuously pursue improvement
- The further external dissemination actions that we carried out locally confirmed that our experiment was replicable in many other SMEs
- The full commitment of our industrial partner remains hard to achieve and some better results on requirements management and inter-group co-ordination could have been expected if MG2 had more actively contributed to this experiment.

This AE should interest to:

- Those in the software development community who are involved in implementing SQA and Quality Management, with a specific focus on SMEs
- Those who are in the process of choosing SE methods and tools to support their process
- Those who are concerned by the issue of involving and motivating technical people in a process improvement initiative.

Infogea S.R.L
Italy

10.62   SO.C.CO.MA 21269

Software Change and Configuration Management

The PIE has been focused on the Software Change and the Configuration Management system (SO.C.CO.MA). Since the improvement of the change management process is considered significant for all data processing centers, SO.C.CO.MA project was felt a mandatory step to achieve that objective.

Methods and tools have been fully defined and implemented during the project to carry out the management of application software changes and to allow the centralisation of the management process. This report begins with a brief description of the company background focusing on goals of the PIE. Then the experiment is described following its evolution steps and giving in detail roles involved, procedural steps and work products, pointing out the tools used during the project (Endevor, JCR, Lotus Notes).

In conclusion, the report describes the results achieved under a qualitative and quantitative point of view, then the main lessons learned: both outline the importance of a Configuration System Management in organisations handling a combination of internally and externally developed software. Furthermore, the SO.C.CO.MA development process and its application have been contributory to the consolidation of a new and strong quality oriented culture inside the company.

Istiservice S.p.a
ITALY

10.63 SPECS 23875

Specifications Enhancement Through CASE and SDL

Objectives

The SPECS Project aims at introducing SDL based CASE tools as a support to the analysis/ design/ coding activities of Italtel BURM (Business Unit Reti Mobili), a Europe's leading full-line manufacturers in the telecommunications field.

The PIE falls within the scope of a large Process Improvement Program running at Italtel BURM after a process assessment performed in June 1995. In this context, the baseline project will be a major release of a Network Element of a GSM system.

Actions

The objectives will be achieved through the adoption of SDL (Specification and Description Language), a formal specifications language particularly suited for specifying and describing real-time systems (and thus for telecommunications software development projects).

The adoption of SDL will be supported by the adoption of the SDT CASE tool-kit.

The distinguishing characteristics of the PIE can be identified as follows:

- tool selection, in order to procure the tools that better adhere to the specific needs;
- customisation for the specific environment, in order to adhere to the peculiarities of the proprietary operating system;
- pilot application, to run the experiment;
- analysis of results, to evaluate the success of the initiative;
- preparation for deployment and widespread adoption, if the analysis activities bring to positive results.

Expected Impact and Experience

The PIE is expected to have a direct impact on several quantitative indicators such as Timeliness, Fault rate in analysis/design, Productivity. In particular, the main goals of the PIE are represented by the increase of the software productivity in development and the availability of better documentation both for internal usage and for customers; those aspects indeed have a direct influence on the costs and quality of the delivered products and hence on the company competitiveness.

Italtel s.p.a
Italy

10.64   SPIE 10344

Software Process Improvement Experimentation

Project Goals and Work Performed

The project's summary of main objectives and tasks performed is as follows:

- To transfer technology related with Software Process Improvement methods.
- To evaluate IBERIA's real software process capability according to recognised methods.
- To develop an improvement plan based on the assessment result.
- To set up an organisational structure fully dedicated to the improvement.
- To develop, based on the action plan, the guidelines, standards, metrics and training required to support the improvement process.
- To apply the new processes to the pilot projects.
- To evaluate the pilot projects results and to set up an institutionalisation plan.
- To disseminate activities throughout the project to promote awareness and to change personnel attitude toward the change initiative.

Achieved Results and their Significance

This experience brings up many technical benefits, but the main lesson that can be learned is that the assessment is only the first step, probably the easiest one, of a long path toward improvement. The improvement itself requires some fundamental aspects to succeed management commitment, a well defined organisational structure, prone to Personnel improvement, a team of persons with the appropriate attitudes and skills, an adequate pace and, last but not least, enough time.

Next Proposed Actions

Future actions can be summarised as follows:

- To set up an institutionalisation plan in order to be able to replicate the achieved results on other projects.
- To improve new areas, not covered by the present project,
- To replicate the improvement initiative on other company areas (different from software).

Dissemination Actions

IBERIA has spent many time and effort in the dissemination activities, both internal and external. These internal actions are very important, since they can change not directly involved management and personnel's culture and attitude toward the change program. External activities are particularly very useful to promote and share this kind of initiative with companies throughout the European Community.

Iberia Airlines
Spain

10.65 SPIP 23750

Software Projects Improvement Process

Business Motivation and Objectives

Due to ever growing user needs, software development complexity has reached a level where automated tools and methodologies have to be used. Our software development process needs reinforcement especially in the areas of testing and configuration management.

The PIE objectives are part of a larger program of improving our software development processes and practices. The software improvement process, although is a goal by itself, it is initiated by a wider, more important organisational and business goal, of positioning us as a provider of high quality software products.

The Experiment

The experiment will include selecting tools and methodologies for configuration management and testing. The tools and methodologies will be used by the baseline project for 9 months. During this time data will be gathered and the results of the experiment will be evaluated according to this data. Based on the evaluation, changes will be introduced (if necessary) and a plan for assimilation will be developed.

The experiment will be performed at our office on a client/server project of about 15 man years. Onyx Technologies employs 90 full time employees, 70 of them involved in software engineering. 6 as part of the baseline project.

Expected Impact and Experience

The expected impact includes: increase in customer satisfaction, reduction in the number of defects in the developed products, reduction in human resources needed for maintenance and increase in productivity.

Onyx Technologies
Israel

10.66   SPIRIT 21799

Software Process Improvement: Recondition Information Technology

SPIRIT is a subproject of the software process improvement project of Baan Development. Baan's business can be characterised as provider of enterprise resource planning (ERP) software-packages (standard software). These products come under the names TRITON (old) and BAAN (new).

Business Motivations

- Baan Development was assessed at CMM-level 1 (1994).
- The global release of a complex product requires improved reliability: TIME & QUALITY.
- Major customers appreciate commitment to Process Improvement.
- Approach of SPIRIT was a comparison between:
- The old Software Development Process (SDP) as used for the development of the Manufacturing package in the TRITON 3 release, and
- The improved SDP as used for the development of that package for the BAAN V release.
- Aims of SPIRIT were:
- Uncontrolled delay: 18 % to < 5%
- Bad fixes per 100 calls: 4 to 2
- Postrelease defects per Kloc: 2 to < 1

The enormous growth of Baan had some impact on SPIRIT: extension of the duration (from 18 till 24 months) appeared necessary due to a rescheduling of the baseline project and the second aim (bad fixes) had to be adapted because of a reorganisation of Baan Development. Moreover the approach of SPIRIT required adaptation because insufficient reliable data on TRITON 3 was available.

This document describes the four topics highlighted below:

Project Goals

SPIRIT aims to demonstrate that improvement of the Software Development Process (SDP) results in predictable SW-delivery and quality.

Work Done

SPIRIT incorporates assessment, development and implementation of software development process (SDP) practices following the CMM approach for development of BAAN V Manufacturing.

Results Achieved

SPIRIT reveals that we have currently the capabilities for CMM-level 2 and are approaching CMM-level 3.

Significance:

SPIRIT enables organisations to benefit from our key lessons:

- How to structure an SDP to enable controlled development in parallel with further process improvements.
- How to make an SDP description accessible to facilitate its application in daily practice.
- How to measure the kind of objectives as defined for SPIRIT and immediately feedback the measured results to all persons involved so that they are enabled and motivated to adjust timely.

The Commission of the European Community (CEC), funded SPIRIT as a process improvement experiment (PIE), under European Systems and Software Initiative (ESSI) project number 21799.

Baan Company N.V
Netherlands

10.67 TESOS 21681

Testing of Structured Object-Orientated Software Development, Orientated to Improving Software Quality

Objective of PIE was to test some new software development methods with a basic software project Already manufactured. PIE should test object-orientated programming, use of standard database Engine and integration in 32-bit operating systems. At the end of the project, the redesigned software should be multilingual and structured, using standard case- and database-tools. The expected results of the project were increasing of software quality and the introduction of a configuration and testing management system.

The company is producing and distributing special material for safety provisions for workers in Germany. The medium of published works is normally a book or a software application, produced with own software developing methods. No special testing and configuration management system was introduced in the company. The expected impact of this PIE to the software development process in the company was a better management during the whole developing process. The main motivation of doing this was the general problem with graphic development in DOS environment and the high costs in developing programmes for all needed European languages.

The nature of the work to be performed was the reconstruction and the redesign of some selected parts of the in-house software library with use of methods of software best practice. This means introducing a complete system of version control in addition of a configuration management system and an effective testing management system. The software has been redeveloped in a modern 32-bit operating system environment.

The selected subcontractor has developed some necessary drivers of the fundamental system library we need for our special equipment like special frame video cards we normally use together with our software.

BIJO-DATA Informationssysteme GmbH
Germany

10.68 TESTART 23683

Improvement of Software Testing Phase, Especially with Respect to Requirements Management and Change Control

Business Motivation and Objectives

Israel Aircraft Industries (IAI) develops, manufactures and maintains embedded systems for the aerospace and large electronics systems market. Software is an essential part of all IAI's advanced products. We are interested to enhance the efficiency and effectiveness of the software testing phase, a major quality factor and cost driver in complex mission critical systems, especially with respect to automation of requirements coverage and change control.

The objective of this experiment is to reduce the time and effort required for testing activities without reducing product quality, thus reducing the cost of development to improve our competitiveness and shortening time to market while improving customer satisfaction.

The Experiment

The aim of the proposed Process Improvement Experiment (PIE) is to improve the software testing phase at the component and at the integration level. The experiment especially focuses on the relation between testing and requirements coverage which is central to achieving satisfaction of our customers needs. This experiment will refer to following aspects of the development process:

- Software testing during various software testing phases to obtain satisfactory coverage within project time and budget constrains using the Logiscope tool (or similar).

- Management of system requirements allocated to software using RTM tool (or similar).
- Management of requirements changes using a data base application developed at IAI (RCR). This will be used to control requirements changes : description of desired change, cost estimation of the change, impact and risk assessment of the change and recording of resolution. The output of this change control process will drive the changes to the base line requirements data base in RTM.

The baseline project is an advanced avionics system enhancement including hardware modifications as well as extensive software development of its main five components. The development effort is presently estimated at over 20 man years. This baseline project is typical for IAI and reflects the commercial market trend of our products which demands high quality, increasingly complex functionality and short development time.

Expected Impact and Experience

IAI expects to increase test coverage of requirements, increase the percentage of code exercised in testing and reduce integration testing cycle time. Consequently we expect to reduce software development costs while increasing product quality, especially in mission critical systems.

In the PIE we want to demonstrate the following Measurable Objectives:

- Increase test coverage of requirements by 15%;
- Reduce integration testing cycle time by 5%
- Reduce software testing costs by 10%;
- Increase percentage of code exercised in testing by 15%.

Israel Aircraft Industries
Israel

10.69 TOPSPIN 24091

TOPSPIN Tedopres Project for Software Process Improvement

Business Motivation and Objectives

The company's main product, technical documentation, is undergoing a fundamental change from paper-based systems to electronically based systems. There is a need to develop client specific, high quality database systems. Technical and software expertise for this purpose is well-developed, but project management lacks behind. In order to meet timely completion very often extra effort has to be put in, resulting in exceeded budgets and therefore commercial losses on projects. The objective of the project is to counterbalance this situation by concentrating on improving some of the management aspects of new development project and bring them to a normal level of profitability.

The Experiment

The experiment will be performed in the course of a major development project for interactive electronic technical manuals combined with an interactive electronic parts catalogue for a company in forestry machinery. Improvements will be implemented in the following fields of project management:: analysis of requirements, systematising functional specifications, project planning and budgeting efficiency improvements relating to the process of development (administrative and technical) and project monitoring by generating new information on essential parameters. A better understanding of the customer's demands and wishes is an essential input for good project planning and project execution.

Tedopres B.V. employs 70 people, of which 12 will be involved in the project which will concentrate on the work in the Interactive Electronic Documentation Department.

Expected Impact and Experience

Through the project Tedopres will gain knowledge and experience to better prepare and plan projects on the basis of customer's requirements and to keep the projects in well-defined limits of costs and time, creating a positive margin on the projects.

Tedopres International B.V.
The Netherlands

10.70   TPM 21336

Towards Total Product Management in Tecnopolis

The results of the Total Product Management (TPM) process improvement project should be of interest to managers and R&D personnel. The target audience is especially the in rapidly growing small and medium sized software companies specialising in with packaged software products. The objectives of the project were to improve the maturity of the software product management (SPM) processes of the participating three companies. The maturity assessments carried out in the beginning and in the end of the project show that This objective was also reached in the project..

The improvements in the SPM processes of the companies have created facilities forced to increased the efficiency of production, saved valuable development time and improved overall along with these to increased customer satisfaction. It is very apparent that as a software company grows and the number of customers increases, the SPM processes must improve. If improvement is neglected, the company will lose its competitiveness. The practical level achievements of the companies are listed below:

* reduced time spent for solving product management related problems
* faster response times to customer service requests
* higher customer satisfaction gained by improved product
* support system
* improved quality of the products
* improved efficiency in the production
* faster building and re-building times of different product versions

One of the lessons we have learned is that collecting metrics is very demanding, but the results have proven to be very useful in securing management commitment and for convincing the developers of the usefulness of process improvement. We also found that an initial assessment together with final assessment are essential in the process improvement activity. It pinpointed the areas most in need of improvement and finally also the areas where some improvement had taken place. The need for continuous process improvement is also one of the key lessons of this project.

The PIE was divided into five main phases:

* maturity assessment of the companies in the beginning of the project,
* definition and implementation of the version control process and tools,
* definition and implementation of the configuration management process and tools,
* definition and implementation of the product management process and tools, and maturity assessment of the companies at the end of the project.

As a result of the project, product management processes have been specified and implemented in the context of baseline projects. The dissemination activities have been carried out successfully and the results of the PIE have been presented to a wide audience.

Modera Point OY
Finland

Oy Quality &Research LTD
Finland

Prosoft OY
Finland

10.71   TRUST 23754

Improvement of the Testing Process Exploiting Requirements Traceability

Business Motivation and Objectives

In the Aerospace Industry product costs and time-to-market are today 2 key competitive levers. Helicopter is a very software intensive product, in which the avionics software contributes to the product costs by more than 30% and to the overall time-to-market by 40%. The software Testing and Validation activities significantly contribute to the above mentioned high avionics software costs (50%) and lead-time (40%).

The overall objective of the TRUST PIE is to improve the Testing and Validation Process, in order to reduce the related costs by at least 15% and to cut the avionics software development time by at least 10%. The emphasis is on improving the process, rather than on just automating some of the testing/validation activities.

The Experiment

In order to achieve this objective, requirements traceability will be exploited, as the mean to directly and un-ambiguously relate subsets of testing and validation sequences to specific subsets of requirements. The goal is to keep track of what and how should be tested when requirements change or when amendments to faults in a product Release/Variant have to be propagated to all the other relevant active Releases/Variants.

Expected Impact and Experience

In the context above the expected impacts are:

* reduction of the development costs of new version/variant
* improvement of the testing effectiveness and consistent reduction of testing effort
* improvement of the global software life cycle efficiency due to better traceability support

Participants:

* Agusta – Un'Azienda Finmeccanica SpA: Helicopter manufacturer, having in charge the development of both mechanical and avionics
* TXT Ingegneria Informatica: software house with large experience in software engineering practice and products development involved as external assistance provider.

Agusta un'azienda Finmeccanica S.p.a
Italy

10.72 UFOSEP 21434

User Focused Object-Oriented Software Engineering Process

Axioma is an European software house with offices in Linz and Vienna both located in Austria. Founded 1990 we are currently employing 30 people and are providing "Solutions for Success" for the financial industry (securities) as well as for public services (marketing). The growing complexity of business and its impact on software engineering makes it necessary to gather requirements more accurately and to transform them to software (business objects) in a traceable way. Otherwise projects easily run out of time and budget or fail to deliver the requested product.

With UFOSEP (User Focused Object-oriented Software Engineering Process) we are currently introducing a new process model which allows us to register/implement user requests more efficiently. The customers get higher quality products in a shorter period of time. Development is done in iterations to allow the controlled reworking of parts of systems. We are able to correct mistakes or make improvements based on user feed-back as early as possible.

The new process model is applicable for the development of business software in all sectors (e.g. banking, insurance, financial services and public administrations) and is supported by rough tailored tools which will support our work more accurately in future.

The main achievements of the PIE were:

- the definition and introduction of the new process model UFOSEP
- supported by the Upper CASE tool Select Enterprise Modeler and
- by the object-oriented repository Softlab Enabler, with a
- bridge to our Lower CASE tool Axioma XCase

We verified our former visions within three experiments. The results are promising. We were able to significantly

- increase our overall productivity (16%),
- reduce change requests after the first installation (56%) and had a
- gain in the area of effort for Configuration and Version Management (28%).

The PIE which was executed between January 1996 and October 1997 was possible through the support of ESSI – a programme of the European Commission.

Axioma Information Systems GmbH
Austria

10.73   VERDEST 21712

Software Version Control, Documentation and Test Management

Project Goals

The objective of PIE is to purchase and implement version control, document management and automated software testing tools to improve and develop software design and development process itself in our company and in our associated partner organisations.

Work Performed and Results

Project gained its functional goals at the scheduled time. The expected technical, business, organisational and skill goals were mostly achieved. The actual cost was about 70 % of the estimated total cost

The experiment project was divided to three phases.

The first phase of the experiment project focused on the analyses and definitions of our traditional and the objective ways to manage the practices and methods. We also defined specifications of the tools to be used. After this we made a choice of the software tools to be used in the experiment project. We installed also the selected tools to our use. The result of the first phase was the summary documentation of defined practices and tools

The second phase of the experiment project focused on the implementation activities. This included more detailed definitions of the workflow management and how these definitions should be brought into use in the daily operations and routines in the baseline project. This phase included also user training activities. We also got preliminary results of the project concerning testing and version management.

The third and last phase of the experiment project included document management based on Intranet-solution including user training activities. The result measurement as well as the result comparisons to other projects was also included to this project phase.

TT Tiete Oy
Finland

10.74 VIGOROUS 23971

Version Management With Software Reuse Across Multiple Platforms And Projects

Business Motivation and Objectives

To reduce the time and cost overhead associated with collection, documentation and maintenance of reusable software modules.

A base of reusable software source modules and drivers creates a software foundation, which significantly reduces the total development time for a software project and time-to-market for new projects. Such a software base contributes significantly to the competitive power of a company.

Normally reusable software modules will be extracted from on-going software development projects, and adapted and documented for reuse in future projects, and as time evolve the most popular software modules usually exist in multiple versions for different embedded processor types and platforms.

The goal with this PIE is to be able to increase the birth-rate of reusable software modules and to prolong the operational lifetime of existing reusable modules, with a minimum effort in hours of work.

The focus will be on achieving better management and design methods with respect to potential reuse, so the amount of software modules, which afterwards can be extracted from the existing designs and incorporated in the base of reusable software source modules, are increased. An important underlying part of this reuse management improvement is better capability to keep track on current version and revision state of the reusable software modules during the continuously on-going extraction and updating process.

The Experiment

The experiment will be carried out over 2 software development projects (customer development orders) where reuse characteristics for the projects are measured. During the preparation phase of the PIE new CASE tools are taken in use, and new strategies are introduced. The first customer order acts as a reference and the reuse improvements are measured after the following customer project.

Expected Impact and Experience

The expected result from the PIE experiment is better capability to create and maintain a larger number of high quality and portable SW modules at a lower cost. To ensure the long-term effect of the PIE result RAMTEX Engineering expect to end up with a practical set of general project management and software design guidelines. These guidelines ("How to create and maintain reusable and portable software modules with minimum time and cost overhead") will be available via our WWW home page for use by programmers and managers of software development projects.

RAMTEX Engineering ApS
Denmark

Index

Druck: Strauss Offsetdruck, Mörlenbach
Verarbeitung: Schäffer, Grünstadt